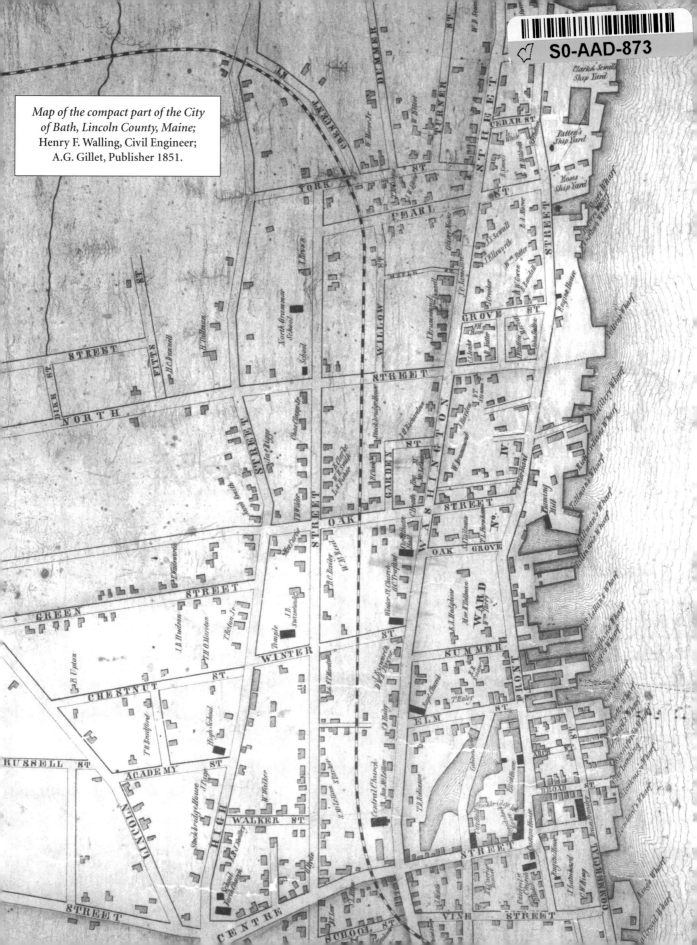

Map of the compact part of the City of Bath, Lincoln County, Maine; Henry F. Walling, Civil Engineer; A.G. Gillet, Publisher 1851.

THE PATTENS OF BATH

A SEAGOING DYNASTY

THE PATTENS OF BATH

A SEAGOING DYNASTY

KENNETH R. MARTIN

RALPH LINWOOD SNOW

MAINE MARITIME MUSEUM AND PATTEN FREE LIBRARY

BATH, MAINE

First Edition
Manufactured in the United States of America

Project coordination: Wordsworth Editorial Services,
    Spruce Head, Maine
Design: Sherry Streeter Design, Brooklin, Maine
Printing: The J.S. McCarthy Company, Augusta, Maine

ON THE COVER: John Patten & Son's *Moravia* off Alicante, Spain, sometime in the 1860s, as depicted by the Spanish pierhead artist Jose Piñeda. The *Moravia's* first captain was Charles E. Patten, whose British wife, Jessie, often sailed with him. In this watercolor, both Pattens can be seen on the *Moravia's* afterdeck. *Courtesy Maine Maritime Museum, Bath.*

Library of Congress Cataloging-in-Publication Data
Martin, Kenneth R., 1938–
        The Pattens of Bath : a seagoing dynasty / Kenneth R. Martin,
Ralph Linwood Snow.
        p.   cm.
        Includes bibliographical references (p.) and index.
        ISBN 0-937410-15-2 (pbk.)
        1. Bath (Me.)—Biography. 2. Patton family. I. Snow, Ralph
Linwood, 1934–   . II. Title.
F29.B4M38   1996
920.0741'85--dc20   96-19324 CIP

Contents

Acknowledgments

The writing, editing, and publication of *The Pattens of Bath* was made possible by contributions from the following Patten descendants and current and former occupants of Patten homes:

Frances Kendall Moon
Ross M. Patten
Gregory G. Gensheimer, M.D.
Richard G. Kendall
Charles E. Burden, M.D.
Daniel R. Donovan
John A. Ross
Mrs. Joseph Davis
Mr. and Mrs. Joseph A. Valdastri
Phyllis Schlomovitz Sorensen
as well as
The George Patten Davenport Trust
First Federal Savings of Bath

Preface

Keeping in mind the ancient Chinese curse, "May you live in interesting times," the authors affirm that writing *The Pattens of Bath* was an interesting assignment. When the book was first proposed, all parties assumed that, because of the importance of the subject, a scholarly search would uncover a hefty supply of documentary material. Maritime archives are replete with primary collections that provide rich profiles of nineteenth-century shipping enterprises. For example, the Maine Maritime Museum's Sewall family collection comprises 450,000 documents — a researcher's dream. Inasmuch as the Pattens, in their day, enjoyed a commensurate measure of success and prominence, it was reasonable to expect that a rich cache of documentary evidence on Patten enterprise lay somewhere close at hand. Alas, the opposite proved to be the case. The Sewalls may have saved everything, but the Pattens seem to have thrown everything away. Reconstructing the Patten story thus became a hectic search for countless needles in countless haystacks. Interesting.

Rudely awakened, and remembering the metaphor of the monkeys and the typewriters, we knew that a fine book could be written if we had an infinite amount of time to search those infinite haystacks. No such luck. Once accepted by its sponsors, the Patten project ran to a tight schedule: about fifteen months from commencement of research to delivery of completed typescript. Which needles? Which haystacks? Interesting!

As in earlier projects, we found that collaboration can compress the bookmaking process and take the sting out of tight deadlines. In this case, two heads were many times better than one. Accordingly, although there may be a few more haystacks out there, we are satisfied with the result. The nineteenth century's wide paper trail permitted us to piece together a selective, accurate history of the Patten maritime dynasty. Because of the repetitive nature of the clan's enterprise, we were able to draw general conclusions from selective evidence.

The Patten story is one of accumulated know-how and good timing, not a series of lucky breaks. Moreover, it is a relentlessly upbeat tale of a family that pulled itself from survival to success and, recycling its acquired knowledge, achieved spectacular success. Another positive element of the story is the theme of social conscience. In an era of untrammeled individualism and self-interest, the Pattens did not overreach. To be sure, they made a great deal of money as shipmasters, agents, and merchants. All the while, however, they were true to their shared view of personal responsibility. With one possible exception, amassing wealth was not their chief purpose in life. Furthermore, they believed in redirecting wealth toward the public good, and, for three generations at least, acted on that belief, producing dramatic results in Bath.

Note that we have described this history as selective. Circumstances selected many of the key players in the story while consigning others to obscurity. The brothers George and John Patten, central characters, were celebrated enough in their day to provide posterity with well-rounded portraits. But what of brother James, their investment partner and a successful captain to boot? Because of sparse documentary evidence, James appears as a peripheral personality, which is surely at odds with events in his own time. And what a pity it is that we know the sisters Kate and Hannah Patten only through letters that range in emotion from breathless joy to cold fury, whetting our appetite for more. A novel could be built around such letters, but the rules of history prohibit such latitude. Or take the brothers Jarvis and Bardwell Patten. The former — a shipmaster, author, and man of connections — is easy to know, thanks to his journals, publications, and press notices. But brother Bardwell, also a successful captain and a writer-poet, has been eclipsed by unfair posterity. A few years ago, Bardwell's journals, considered worthless, were thrown away, taking with them the details of a career that certainly would have graced this book.

What remains, however, is a coherent story that spans a century of enterprise, detailing the ways and means of shipbuilding and shipmastering in the age of sail. Needless to say, the story is interesting — and not in the Chinese sense of the word.

The authors gratefully acknowledge the work of Ruth C. Briggs of Hallowell, Maine, author of the unpublished monograph "Ship Ventures of Old Bath" (1987). This work was the first organized attempt to present the Patten clan's enterprise in coherent form. Briggs mastered the labyrinthine complexity of Patten kinship, successfully relating it to the history of the Kennebec region. In short, "Ship Ventures of Old Bath" was a pioneering study by a devoted, diligent Patten in-law. We have found its guidance immensely valuable in preparing this book.

Ruth Briggs's work was assisted by the groundbreaking research of Charles E. Burden, M.D. A one-time resident of John Patten's house and a longtime devotee of local history, Charlie amassed a detailed file on Patten ships and seafarers and dreamed for years of a book about his favorite maritime family. Tireless, determined to involve people and institutions that dream, undaunted by occasional indifference, and unable to take no for an answer, he bootstrapped this project into possibility and then into fruition.

Also important to the success of the project was journalist Mark Hennessy, who, over a generation, gathered and recorded in lively style a comprehensive collection of historical notes that are now part of the Maine Maritime Museum archives. More than thirty-five years after his death, Hennessy's notes yielded many anecdotes and insights that enrich this book.

We also gratefully acknowledge the interest and assistance of William D. Barry (Maine Historical Society), Nathan Lipfert and Elizabeth Maule (Maine Maritime Museum), Gary Mason (Patten Free Library), Earle Shettleworth, Jr. (Maine Historic Preservation Commission), Bill Bunting of North Whitefield, Maine, and Reg Ferrell of Arlington, Texas. These individuals pointed us to some of the best haystacks and generously aided our search.

Perhaps this book's appearance will unearth additional information on the Patten clan, providing future research opportunities. May those future researchers live in interesting times.

Ken Martin
Ralph Linwood Snow
Woolwich, Maine
January 1996

1

"A Good Many Schooners and Sloops"

Anyone who has traveled the twelve miles of Kennebec River between Bath and the open sea can't help but be struck by the powerful, ever-changing play of current, tide, and wind. Nonetheless, no outward-bound vessel has ever come to grief there — a fact of great significance in a region preoccupied with building, sailing, and managing ships. For incoming vessels, however, the story is quite different.

On 4 September 1834, the ship *New Orleans,* inbound to Bath with Portuguese salt, rounded Pond Island at the mouth of the Kennebec. Light winds and pleasant weather prompted Captain David Patten to enter the river "with all canvass spread." Suddenly the wind shifted and a squall blew up, forcing the *New Orleans* onto the Outer Sugarloaf ledge. There she stayed.[1] The crew got off safely, but the *New Orleans* appeared to be a total loss, so her principal owners, brothers George and John Patten of Bath, promptly sold the wreck for salvage. Wreckers eventually dislodged the vessel and, once repaired, she continued her career under Boston owners. The crew's good luck and the owners' prudent insurance kept the *New Orleans* scrape from becoming a disaster. But the incident was a stern, eyewitness lesson for all.

George A. Rogers, master of the Houghton-owned ship *Hanover,* may have been thinking of the *New Orleans* episode when, fifteen years later, he guided his ship with its cargo of salt toward the mouth of the Kennebec. A violent storm was raging, and for some reason Rogers selected an unorthodox approach to the river. At noon on 12 November 1849, the Pond Island lightkeeper's son watched in dismay as the *Hanover* hit bottom, swung, and was capsized by massive broadside seas. She quickly went to pieces and disappeared. All hands perished.[2] The unidentified, battered bodies that washed ashore were buried in a mass grave close to the disaster site. Even to people inured to maritime hardship and danger, the *Hanover* incident was a profound shock.

The loss of the *Hanover* was the Kennebec's worst disaster but by no means its last. On 19 November 1853, the ship *Maine,* under Captain William Freeman, was wrecked on Pond Island Bar, not far from where the *Hanover* struck. Loaded with salt and English iron, the *Maine* bilged, rolled onto her beam ends, and filled, but her officers and crew escaped unharmed. The Bath steamer *Seguin* and several small craft were dispatched

The ship *Maine,* built by G.F. & J. Patten in 1844, shown approaching Liverpool under Captain Abner Wade. In 1853, commanded by William Freeman, the *Maine* was wrecked on Pond Island Bar, at the mouth of the Kennebec River. All hands survived. *Courtesy Peabody Essex Museum, Salem, MA.*

downriver in hopes of salvaging part of her cargo, but not much was left.[3] Fortunately for owners George and John Patten, insurance covered part of the cargo's value and about two-thirds of the *Maine*'s.

In hindsight, those destroyed men, ships, and cargo — all of which went down just miles from home — would appear to be a severe blow, perhaps a warning that there were less risky and easier ways to make a living. But hindsight is misleading. In the early nineteenth century, Bath was a boomtown, and its citizens were more than ready to assume the financial and physical risks of maritime enterprise. First among those citizens were George and John Patten, brothers who had grown rich and influential by building, owning, and managing merchant vessels. At the time of the *New Orleans* loss, George was forty-seven; John, forty-three. Throughout their lives, the two were said to be as close as peas in a pod. And, a few years after the *Maine* disaster, they also were said to control the nation's largest private fleet of merchant vessels. Men like that could manage a setback or two.

Despite the occasional setbacks, the firm of G.F. & J. Patten enjoyed decades of success. Unlike many entrepreneurs who got rich quick during boom times in U.S. shipping, the Pattens diversified and multiplied their financial power over the years. Thereby hangs an interesting story. Business aside, the owners and their descendants proved to be public-minded citizens whose community service and philanthropy shaped the unique character of Bath. More than a century later, that influence is powerful and still literally visible in the City of Ships. Being high-profile civic leaders, the Pattens also set the pace for the self-conscious social life of the city. That, too, makes interesting reading.

This base of wealth and power rested on a family maritime tradition that began back in colonial times.

In the 1720s, four Scotch-Irish brothers named Patten emigrated from Derry, Ireland, to the New World, landing in Boston. In the early 1730s, the eldest brother, Matthew, moved downeast to the Saco region of Maine, where land was plentiful and cheap. A few years later, about 1738, Matthew's brothers Actor and Robert joined him in Saco. William remained in Boston, where he achieved some success as a merchant.[4]

In the early eighteenth century, the district of Maine, then part of Massachusetts, was a true frontier, a zone between aggressive British empire builders and the defensive, reactive French. Native American inhabitants of the area, caught between these two superpowers, took sides as best they could to minimize the threat to their survival. Maine settlers such as the Patten brothers and their families lived in perpetual fear of attack and dispossession. Not until Britain defeated France and her Indian allies in 1763 was the region considered secure. When, in 1775, the American Revolution erupted, Maine settlers faced more hard times, because the Boston government and the Continental Congress were too weak to defend the frontier adequately.

Why, then, did European settlers stay? Many did not; others didn't live to see their pioneering efforts bear fruit. But despite its drawbacks, the Maine wilderness offered opportunity to anyone prepared to seize it. For most immigrants, a few years of dedicated, resourceful work could provide a standard of living higher than that of the Old Country. Such a prospect was irresistible to people like the Pattens. With few resources besides courage, gumption, and sweat, these settlers laid the foundation for Maine's spectacular success in the maritime world. From that clutch of early pioneers flowed a substantial group of prosperous farmers, merchants, shipbuilders, shipmasters, mariners, and civic leaders.

Farming was the chief occupation of Maine settlers, but it wasn't long before the newcomers were exploiting the region's rich timber resources and tidal streams, building small sailing vessels and taking lumber and firewood to Boston or other coastwise points. One of Matthew Patten's sons, John, captained homebuilt vessels and died in a shipwreck in 1783. Matthew's son Robert, described as a mariner and shipbuilder, continued to live in the Saco area until his death in 1819. At least one of Robert's sons was likewise a mariner, dying at sea in 1828. That branch of the family continued to practice shipbuilding and seafaring for at least another generation.

Actor Patten, meanwhile, had moved to Surry, east of Penobscot Bay, with a group of Saco residents who found the pressures of encroaching civilization too restrictive. He died during the American Revolution, when that area was effectively under British control.

The true progenitor of the Patten maritime clan was Actor's son John. Born in Ireland, John had accompanied his parents to North America at the age of ten, later moving with them to Saco. In 1749, John moved to the Topsham/Bowdoinham area, where he had purchased rights to 661 acres on Cathance Point near Merrymeeting Bay, a broad tidal bay formed by the confluence of the Androscoggin, Cathance, Muddy, Abagadasset, Eastern, and Kennebec Rivers. He cleared the land with the help of his brother William and his wife Mary's brother, Thomas Means. They planned to stay and raise a family. They succeeded on both counts: John and Mary eventually produced fourteen children.

Cathance Point was an ideal location for farming and assorted commercial ventures, because the various connecting rivers provided highways into the heavily forested interior. Below Merrymeeting Bay, the Kennebec resumes its course to the sea. The river narrows at The Chops — two jutting points on either bank — then, a short distance downstream, forms a broad, straight, three-mile stretch called Long Reach, a perfect site for shipbuilding. There, twelve miles from the sea, the city of Bath would grow and prosper. At a time when land communication was little more than a few paths in the wilderness, waterborne commerce gave every settler a lifeline to trade and, possibly, prosperity.

At Cathance Point, John and his brother William, plus brother-in-law Thomas Means and cousin Actor (son of Robert), literally began to chop a fortune out of the wilderness. By 1764, John and William were among the group of settlers who successfully petitioned Massachusetts Bay Colony to incorporate the town of Topsham.

In their monumental *History of Brunswick, Topsham, and Harpswell, Maine* (1878),

Patten Point, a bend in the Cathance River, looking south toward Merrymeeting Bay. Once densely forested, the point's combination of raw materials and riverside convenience fostered a generation of Patten shipbuilding. *Courtesy Ralph L. Snow.*

George and Henry Wheeler describe pioneer John Patten as "a farmer, [who] had also the trade of a blacksmith.... He was also engaged in the lumber business..., and was a proprietor in the Cathance Mill...and of one-sixteenth of the sawmill and stream. He was somewhat engaged, also, in ship-building and navigation, and he, with John Fulton, Adam Hunter, and William Patten, built the first vessel ever launched above the 'Chops' and the second built upon the Kennebec, above Bath."[5]

That first vessel, finished about 1768, was the 90-ton coasting sloop *Merry Meeting*. Her completion, of course, was big news in the Cathance backwater, and everyone who could do so attended her launching. It is likely that many if not most of John Patten's adult male neighbors were engaged in the vessel's construction, so the launching undoubtedly was an extended-family affair. The Pattens provided dinner for all. William Patten, the *Merry Meeting*'s skipper, loaded her with firewood, which he sold in Boston on favorable terms. On subsequent voyages, the *Merry Meeting* also carried timber.[6]

How John, William, and their associates acquired the skills to build a coasting sloop is not clear; most likely, they had gained some shipbuilding experience in Saco. They probably also recruited nearby settlers who possessed similar skills and enough free time in summer to lend a hand. Customarily, those who helped or provided construction materials would be compensated with shares in the vessel.[7] One thing is certain: The *Merry Meeting* made money.

Another sloop, *Defiance*, followed, and in 1772, John Patten and his partners launched the schooner *Industry*, the region's first vessel designed for the West Indies trade. John Patten's partners in this venture included his son Robert and son-in-law Robert Fulton. Another son-in-law, James Maxwell, would be captain. With the *Industry*, the Patten clan took a momentous step, graduating from coastwise vessels and voyages that had served mainly to get their agricultural products to market. Entering into Caribbean commerce was a commitment to maritime enterprise that, after the Revolution, would eclipse farming as the mainstay of Patten prosperity.

The *Industry* was loaded with locally sawn boards, shingles, and masts — items that could fetch huge prices in the Caribbean — and made two voyages before the American Revolution throttled trade. Her return cargoes undoubtedly were rum, molasses, and sugar — all in great demand along the Kennebec.

Captain James Maxwell, who had lately married John Patten's daughter Peggy, typified the farmer-mariners of colonial times. Family tradition has it that the newlyweds were living with the John Pattens until they could afford a farm of their own. They planned to recycle James's earnings from the *Industry* in that direction and take up farming as soon as they could swing it financially.

During Maxwell's second voyage, a patch of rye he had planted in a clearing on Bowdoinham Neck, six miles away, was ready for harvest. Peggy, busy with an infant daughter, had been instructed to hire someone to cut the rye, but she found that everyone was fully occupied with other harvesting chores. The story goes that Peggy, with her baby, rowed from the Cathance River across Merrymeeting Bay and upstream on the Kennebec, hiked through a mile of woods, harvested the rye, and returned home in a day.

When James returned, he and Peggy settled into their own place, and both lived to ripe old ages.[8] James's later success as a farmer was aided in part by his maritime connections, which made it easy to turn a profit on farming surpluses. By the time of the Revolution, the people of Topsham, Bowdoinham, and the burgeoning shipbuilding town of Bath enjoyed increasingly comfortable lives, thanks in large part to the new opportunities of the West Indies trade.

Those lives changed dramatically when the Revolution broke out. Local sympathy with the Continental Congress was strong. In 1775, Topsham raised a body of militia under Robert Patten, one of John's sons. Robert's brother Actor saw action with that unit in 1779, during the "Penobscot Expedition" fiasco, a poorly executed American attempt to drive the British out of Castine, farther downeast.[9]

Economically speaking, the American Revolution was disastrous to the Kennebec region. Trade dried up. Money and basic goods were in critically short supply. For years, the Royal Navy and British sympathizers harassed the Maine coast and, wherever possible, hassled citizens — the Pattens, for example.

In August 1775, a party of Cathance farmers, including John Patten's sons John and William, and son-in-law Robert Fulton, set off on a haying expedition. Tradition has it that this unfortunate venture was along the Kennebec, but it is more likely that the group had traveled east via the Sasanoa River to the Sheepscot River. An enemy raiding party nabbed them and took them to British territory (probably Nova Scotia), where they were imprisoned and William Patten and Robert Fulton died. The rest eventually returned, but young John died in 1780, shortly after his homecoming. Those purposeless, untimely deaths were a crushing blow to the small, close-knit clan.

Meanwhile, the schooner *Industry*, which had generated so much prewar wealth, became a wartime white elephant. Her owners sold her off for $3,200 in Continental paper money, theoretically a small fortune at face value. Reportedly, Captain Robert's $400 share was only enough for him to buy a horse and saddle.[10]

Trade revived and prosperity returned to the Pattens in the postwar years. The patriarch John died in 1795 after falling from a horse, at age seventy-seven. He was reliably described as "a man of good appearance, tall and well proportioned, of commanding presence, active and quick in his movements, kind and affectionate to his family, and to all within the circle of his acquaintance."[11] Given those attributes, it is hardly surprising that he was also a community leader and a pillar of the Topsham Congregational Church. By the time of his death, he had amassed a substantial estate.

John's brother, Captain William, continued to follow the sea. In 1793, his son, Charles, drowned during a voyage home from the West Indies. A cousin, Captain John Patten (son of Matthew), was lost in the wreck of the sloop *Judith* off Marshfield, Massachusetts, in 1783.

Like his father and partner, Captain Robert Patten was well off by the time of his death in 1841, despite losing two homes to fire and six ships (in which he'd invested) to maritime disasters. Following the Revolution, he constructed at least ten vessels for local partnerships: the sloops *Industry* (93 tons, 1783), *Friendship* (81 tons, 1785), and *Susannah* (94 tons, 1799); the brig *Minerva* (128 tons, 1797); and the schooners *Peggy* (119 tons, 1795), *Orange* (120 tons, 1796), *Lark* (108 tons, 1800), *Topsham* (99 tons, 1800), *Mercury* (105 tons, 1802), and *Venus* (106 tons, 1804).[12] The brothers Wheeler assure us that Robert "was a person of remarkable health. He was never confined a day by sickness for nearly or quite ninety years, never took any medicine during that long period, and retained all his teeth, fair and sound until within a short time of his death, in his ninety-eighth year."[13]

Meanwhile, the focal point of local shipbuilding was moving from Merrymeeting's brackish streams to Long Reach. To anyone interested in shipbuilding, life at Long Reach was an attractive proposition, thanks to the available timber, a gently sloping bank, and the wide expanse of unobstructed river. But because of recurring colonial warfare and Indian hostility, settling anywhere in the area had been downright hazardous. Accordingly, only a few families tried to put down roots along Long Reach.

There was, however, some shipbuilding. Apparently, Jonathan Philbrook and his two sons built the sloop *Dolphin* and at least one other vessel between 1741 and 1755, work-

ing at what is now the site of Bath's Customs House, near the Carlton Bridge.[14] The Philbrooks were one of about eight families in the immediate area. By 1746, Indian hostilities had driven out four of the families. The rest, including the Philbrooks, built a fortified blockhouse for security and stayed on. Jonathan Philbrook apparently used the *Dolphin* to carry lumber cargoes to Boston, along with pelts from his own trapping forays. Proceeds from this activity paid for a farm and, considering the rough-and-ready character of those times, a comfortable standard of living.[15]

It was a beginning. About the time John Patten was getting started on the sloop *Merry Meeting* over on Cathance Neck, Joshua Raynes built the 140-ton sloop *Unity* (or, possibly, *Union)* on Long Reach for six local investors. The *Unity* engaged in the West Indies trade until the outbreak of the Revolution.

During the 1760s, William Swanton operated a shipyard near the site of the Philbrook enterprise. Tradition has it that Swanton built the area's first full-rigged ship, *Earl of Bute*, for Scottish interests. He subsequently built several other ship-rigged vessels and is credited with the celebrated, Salem-based Revolutionary War privateer *Black Prince.*[16]

In 1781, the settlers of Long Reach, who until then had constituted the second parish of the island territory of Georgetown to the east, withdrew and incorporated the town of Bath. At the time, most of the citizens were farmers, although presumably these families provided the occasional labor necessary for shipbuilding. It took a lot of imagination to see any connection between newly incorporated Bath and the chic, urban English masterpiece that was its namesake. As Henry Owen puts it in his 1936 history, "There

James Maxwell of Bowdoinham, skipper of the schooner *Industry* (ca. 1772), one of the Patten clan's earliest vessels, active in Caribbean trade before the American Revolution. A Patten in-law and a landsman at heart, James used his earnings at sea to buy a farm. His son, Noble, would enjoy remarkable success and wealth as a Patten shipmaster and investor. *Courtesy Maine Maritime Museum, Bath.*

were no streets except the town road, now High St., and the road, now Western Ave., leading to the meeting house.... The [Congregational] church was the only public building. Schools were kept in private houses. The center of trade for the region was still at ancient Georgetown village."[17]

Jonathan Hyde, who visited Bath in 1792, remembered it as a bucolic spot: "[Downriver] there were but few houses; they were scattered along the banks of the river in little green openings; could see a good many single deck schooners and sloops passing up and down, deeply loaded with lumber; all which, on coming in from sea, had a very romantic appearance. Bath did not appear much like a village; a few stores and a very few houses were near the river, and a few houses were scattered along on the country road which is now High St.; there were no roads, streets, or buildings between that road and the river; it was chiefly pasture...considerably covered with trees and bushes."[18] The population of the area was probably under a thousand.

Hyde remembered only three wharves in Bath in 1792, and the town may have looked to him like a one-cow parish, but what stands out in his description is the sense of considerable maritime activity. Vessel construction was picking up, not just on the banks of the Kennebec but also along a freshwater creek (later filled in) that emptied into Long Reach. The chief spur to this enterprise was the revival of West Indies trade following the American Revolution (although Britain closed her West Indies possessions to U.S. vessels until 1794). Maine wood products and fish had a ready market and fetched very high prices in the islands. Caribbean sugar and rum were always in demand at home. With good timing, a schooner or brig could complete two Caribbean round trips in a year without interfering with local planting and harvesting schedules. Another opportunity arose with the outbreak of European war in the wake of the French Revolution. With Britain and France attacking each other's colonial trade, neutral Americans stood to make a killing. Inevitably, larger, more costly vessels were in demand.

Wharves and shipyards financed by local businessmen grew up along Bath's waterfront.[19] Shipbuilding capital came not so much from self-propelled, mutually supporting clans like the Pattens as from successful merchants eager to get in on maritime trade. Construction was seasonal, constrained by weather and the agricultural distractions of the available workforce. Jobs proceeded under the direction of a master carpenter whose experience made up for the lack of plans and drawings. The work was inherently noisy, probably made noisier by the regular ration of hard liquor to all hands. To a landlubber, Bath's yards would have presented a disordered appearance, cluttered as they were with stacked lumber and wooden structural components. Depending on the season, they could be very muddy or very dusty places. But the sight of even a small vessel being framed up was always an exciting picture. It still is.

Between 1789 and 1808, more than forty Bath-based businessmen built at least one vessel. In the years 1789-1800, at least seventy-four vessels were launched in Bath — representing a total of more than 10,300 tons.[20] Resources were pooled and risk was spread through the device of multiple shares. Seldom did a large vessel have a single owner.

At the beginning of the nineteenth century, Bath had a population of about 1,225 and was taking on the look of a permanent town with a distinctly maritime character. Just back of the docks and yards ran Front Street, which paralleled the river and bridged the creek. The shipbuilding industry had attracted ancillary businesses such as rope and block makers. The town's money was beginning to show, thanks largely to profits from the West Indies trade. Long Reach was a magnet for investment capital and shipbuilding skills. Perhaps it was just a matter of time before a few enterprising Pattens moved from Topsham to what was now literally the mainstream of regional shipbuilding.

Notwithstanding the visible growth in ship tonnage and local wealth, American vessels were running into trouble with the European powers. With the onset of the wars of the French Revolution, U.S. sympathies were sharply divided between a wish to exploit reestablished trade with a former enemy and a desire to keep on the good side of a fellow revolutionary (and, technically speaking, allied) republic. Britain, of course, took a dim view of Americans' trading with France or her overseas possessions. Enjoying naval superiority, the British could and did harass American commerce. Vessels of the Royal Navy and privateers under British colors boarded, searched, and seized vessels and individuals — all in all, a severe blow to U.S. trade in the Caribbean.

Americans found these acts against a neutral nation intolerable, but the British were not inclined to be conciliatory. In 1794, after American public opinion had been thoroughly aroused, the British agreed to abandon their most extreme acts against U.S. commerce and, in the bargain, open the British West Indies to U.S. vessels. That came as a great relief, but America's trade problems were far from over. France now chose to interpret the 1794 rapprochement with Britain as a hostile act by the United States, whereupon American vessels fell prey to French warships and privateers. Soon, French spoliation rivaled that of Britain, and insurance on American vessels went sky-high. These seizures, which were partly an attempt to manipulate U.S. public opinion, became political dynamite in America. Attempts to negotiate a settlement plummeted, and, by 1797, the United States and France were engaged in an undeclared sea war. Congress authorized a major buildup of the U.S. Navy.

The undeclared war made Maine mariners cautious, but it did not halt the boom in overseas trade. People like the Pattens clearly believed that the rewards were worth the risks. Those risks may have seemed remote when viewed from Cathance Point or Long Reach. Once again, the Pattens, despite their frontier existence, were face-to-face with The World Situation.

In Topsham, Captain Robert Patten had continued the family tradition of shipbuilding. In 1796, at age fifty-three, he completed a 120-ton schooner, *Orange*, intended for the West Indies trade. One of Robert's three partners was his younger brother Thomas.

In October 1798, the *Orange* fell victim to the undeclared Franco-American war. The previous month, under John Holman's command, she had cleared Bath for Curaçao in the Dutch Caribbean with a load of lumber. En route, running short of water, she headed for the British island of Barbados, where she sold her cargo and loaded rum and sugar for the homeward voyage. For safety's sake, the *Orange* left Barbados in convoy with some Liverpool-bound ships, but she was soon on her own and in range of privateers from the French Caribbean. Captain Holman's worst fears were realized when a distant sail bore down upon him. His pursuer was *La Resolve*, under Captain Antoine Triol, flying the French Tricolor.

As Holman later reported to the owners, "I try'd every method to get clear but it was in vain, for in the course of 2 or 3 hours they boarded me. She proved to be a French Pirate of 14 guns, full of men, mostly negroes, they took all my crew out & told me they meant to send me to Guadalupe, and put on board 9 men. I begged them not to plunder my people. The Capt who was a white man promised they should not loose [lose] a single thing. As for myself after I went on board the Orange they strip[p]ed me down to my shirt."[21] The privateer sailed with the *Orange*'s crew for Guadeloupe; the schooner was taken to Saint Martin, where she and her cargo were sold at auction. French authorities turned a deaf ear to Holman's protestations.

Ragged and penniless, Holman somehow managed to escape and make his way to St. Barthélemy (St. Barts) in a small boat. There, he hopped an American brig, the *Betsy*, ready to sail for New York. Holman entered a formal protest in New York, then set off for home as best he could. "You may expect to see me in Topsham soon," he wrote to Robert Patten from Salem. "Give my respects to all you[r] familys & altho I've been unfortunate, I hope it has not lessened the friendship of you all."[22]

Dozens of cases like the *Orange*'s occurred during the undeclared war. In 1800, after a series of naval engagements persuaded France that the Yankees would enforce their neutrality, French depredations against American commerce ceased. As part of the settlement, the U.S. government assumed responsibility for settling American spoliation claims.

Having entered such claims, the owners of scores of lost vessels could only hope for the best and wait for governmental procedures to run their course. And wait. And wait. Robert Patten, however, was luckier than some. He had insured the *Orange* before her fateful voyage. In June 1799, his Boston agent paid him and his partners $3,000.[23] That didn't begin to cover the total loss, however, so after the 1800 agreement with France, Patten and associates had reason to expect additional compensation once the wheels of the federal bureaucracy ceased grinding. Alas, the grinding continued for *one hundred years* before Patten's heirs received a final payment.[24]

In 1800, after the French and American governments pulled back from their undeclared naval war, the future began to brighten for merchants and shipbuilders in the Kennebec region. In 1802, when peace broke out in Europe, the future looked rosy and U.S. commerce looked safe. Although Britain and France went back to war after little more than a year, Americans felt free to trade as neutrals with all parties. To circumvent belligerents' strictures against imports of enemy products via neutral vessels, the Americans revived the practice of the "broken voyage," which they had perfected in the 1790s. Yankee vessels would land goods loaded in a foreign port — Port au Prince, say — in the United States. Once U.S. duty was paid, those goods were technically American and therefore "neutral." Such cargoes could be reloaded and shipped to another foreign port (Liverpool, for example), where wartime shortages guaranteed high prices. The duties paid in the United States were conveniently rebated.

In 1805, however, Britain declared the broken voyage to be an unacceptable wartime loophole, and the Royal Navy began searching U.S. ships suspected of exploiting that device. Seizures followed, and suspected British subjects often were removed from American vessels and forced into service aboard British warships. By 1807, worsening conditions on the high seas precipitated a naval incident when the HMS *Leopard* took the USS *Chesapeake* under fire and seized several *Chesapeake* sailors. Was another undeclared war in the making?

Tensions escalated further when Napoleon declared a paper blockade of British ports, decreeing in effect that any neutral vessel trading with the enemy was in violation of a military blockade and therefore subject to seizure. The British quickly retaliated with a similar decree against the ports of France and her continental allies. In December 1807, unable and unwilling to defend American commercial rights, Congress passed the Embargo Act, a ban on U.S. trade with any of the warring powers. Suddenly, the bottom dropped out of Maine's prosperity. Except for a few enterprising souls who defied the act, Maine's maritime community fell on very hard times indeed. In 1808, the citizens of Bath built a poorhouse.[25]

The Embargo Act was a political disaster for Thomas Jefferson's administration. When it was repealed in 1809, President James Madison replaced it with the less restrictive but still draconian Non-Intercourse Act, which blocked U.S. trade with Britain and France. Meanwhile, the federal government sought in vain a negotiated solution to the international impasse.

The silk purse of U.S. maritime trade had become a sow's ear. Some investors, refusing to believe the lockup would last, continued to commission new vessels even as older ones idled at the town wharves. Eventually, though, the Kennebec River's once-booming shipyards fell silent, and once-venturesome merchants watched their fortunes go sour. Bankruptcies became common.

Worse things, of course, could have happened — war, for example. In 1812, with New England's economy on the rocks and anti-British sentiment raging in Washington, the war came.

One of Robert Patten's seagoing brothers was Thomas, co-owner and sometime skipper of the sloop *Industry* and partner in the ill-fated *Orange*. Thomas and his wife Katherine Fulton had eleven children, eight of whom lived to adulthood. True to family traditions, two of his progeny, John and James F. Patten, followed the sea and became captains. A

Indestructible John Patten. Although no youthful view of Captain John has survived, this photograph captures his vitality, which served him in good stead almost until the day he died at age 97. It does not, alas, do justice to Captain John's unflaggingly upbeat spirit. *Courtesy Maine Maritime Museum.*

third son, George F., stayed ashore but went into partnership with brother John and became one of the region's most prominent shipbuilders and managers.

When the War of 1812 began, George F. was twenty-five and John twenty-three. George, who never went to sea, earned a landsman's captaincy in the local militia. John, who had been a mariner for three years, was at sea when hostilities broke out. He later recalled that before Britain and the United States had gone to war, he found himself "before the mast in the ship *North Star* of Bath, sailing along the English channel.[26] It was in the time of the famous paper blockade. By his decree..., Napoleon had declared one whole side of Europe in a state of blockade. A French man-of-war came along side of our ship and took possession of us. The mate and captain were taken out of the ship and carried to France. We sailors were fastened down in the forecastle.

"The next morning it begun to blow very heavy and our captors let us sailors up to take in sail. We got her reefed down snug, and on the other tack and then they fastened us down again. But we didn't stay long.

"An Englishman came up with us and took us away from the French. (This was before war had been declared between England and this country, remember.) The Englishman carried us to Portsmouth, where we were soon joined by our mate and captain who had escaped in a fishing smack.

"From Portsmouth, the *North Star* went to Londonderry, and there we took a load of emigrants for America. Off Newfoundland, we were stopped by an English man-of-war. Her crew boarded us, well armed. From this, we thought war had been declared, but they did not tell us. We bore well to the north to keep clear of cruisers. As we made Mt. Desert [Island, Maine], we were boarded by a privateer from Portland, and then we learned for a fact that there was a war. We sailed down the coast and got into Bath all right.

"I next went out of Portland as mate of a brig, bound for the West Indies. The third day out, an English man-of-war took us and carried us to Bermuda. They did not harm our men."[27]

Somehow, John Patten got back to Bath. There, despite his recent harrowing experiences, he elected to join in a voyage of trade with the enemy: "I kept up my courage and went out of Bath as the mate of a schooner. We got to Bermuda all right and sold our cargo. While there, a new brig from Portland was brought in as a prize and sold. I got a chance to go in her as mate to Trinidad, where we took in rum and molasses and went back to Bermuda." With U.S. commerce being disrupted by the British, Patten evidently had decided that patriotism made no sense: "From there we went to Halifax. It was a captured vessel and we were under the English flag, mind. On the way to Halifax, we were taken by an American privateer and brought into Portland.

"In 1813, during the embargo days, two or three of us made our way down[east] to St. John [New Brunswick] in a small boat, and I got a chance to go as mate of an English schooner to Newfoundland. We had discharged cargo and were on our way back to St. John in ballast, when I again fell into the hands of an American privateer.

"In the early spring of 1814, I joined a privateer in Portland, and [in 1815] we were cutting her out of the ice and getting ready to start when the news came that peace had been declared."[28]

Captain Patten, who possessed the family genes for longevity and lucid recall, related this precise tale to a respectful newspaper reporter in 1887, at the age of ninety-seven. For the journalist, the War of 1812 was ancient history and the storyteller a living fossil. John's story is of course interesting because of its picaresque nature: He was captured six times by warring vessels of three nations. On two of these occasions, his captors were Americans. A record, perhaps?

What is especially interesting about John Patten's early nautical career is his casual attitude about sailing on enemy vessels in wartime. The War of 1812 was, to put it mildly, obnoxious to Mainers — so much so that separating New England from the Union and adding it to Maritime Canada was a British wartime strategy. Which probably explains why John Patten, a downeaster, found it easy to move in and out of British territory almost at will. Like countless others, Patten had seen his family's fortunes eroded by the Embargo and Non-Intercourse Acts. War was simply the ill-advised but inevitable outcome of such policy. Enough, perhaps, was enough.

Patten's apparently cavalier attitude was by no means unusual. It may even have reflected the majority sentiment among Maine's mariners and businessmen. Bath's enterprising merchants had found bureaucratic loopholes through which they continued to trade with the British even as the enemy blockade tightened around Maine. For example, William King, Bath's leading merchant and banker, who was also a wartime general of militia and, after statehood, Maine's first governor, dispatched Bath vessels to British ports under neutral Sweden's flag of convenience. Bath merchant Peleg Tallman sold such dispensations in his wartime capacity as Swedish vice-consul. King, and possibly others, also operated under specially purchased British licenses that exempted the bearing vessels from British search and seizure, regardless of nationality.[29] In his altogether casual attitude about working with and for the enemy, John Patten was in good company.

At war's end, John Patten was back home safe and sound but, like people at all levels of society, broke. Although the wartime fear that the British would penetrate the Kennebec defenses and raid Bath had not materialized, the local economy was in paralysis. But the general peace of 1815 held promise that fortunes might be recovered, so people along the Kennebec tried to scrape together the wherewithal to give ships and shipbuilding another go.

What else could they do? For one thing, they could endure a bit more hardship. Topsham had suffered a spring flood that severely damaged the area's saw- and gristmills and wrecked the looms of the Androscoggin River's textile mills. The long-range impact of that disaster was compounded by the severely cold weather of 1816-17, caused when volcanic eruptions in East Asia deposited dust in the earth's upper atmosphere. Crops in the Kennebec region failed, food prices skyrocketed, and business again stood still.

In the midst of this economic and natural disaster, John and his brother George F. decided to build a brig. John would be captain, George would be master builder.

George F. Patten, born in 1787, was the eldest son of Captain Thomas and Katherine. He never went to sea. He did, however, find a career as a shipbuilder at the Cathance Point (now called Patten Point) shipyard run by his uncle Robert. George had grown up here among the stacks of timber destined to become the *Peggy*, *Orange*, *Minerva*, and *Susannah*. When the Patten Point yard fell idle, there were other work opportunities at nearby shipbuilding sites along Cathance Neck or Cathance Landing (Bowdoinham). Refinement of those arcane skills would be the foundation of a substantial personal fortune.

George's first independent venture was the construction of a small schooner, *Una*, which he sold in Bath. In 1815, he began investing in vessels, his first venture being a share of the Topsham-built schooner *Sarah*.

In 1816, brothers George and John formed a partnership to build a 153-ton brig, *Ann Maria*. Their father took shares in the vessel, but where the two found the rest of the resources to build the brig is not known. With John in command, the *Ann Maria* engaged in West Indies and coastwise trade. The brothers' second vessel was the brig

Statira, named for their youngest sister. Another sibling, Captain James F., had shares in this venture.

The *Ann Maria* and *Statira* undoubtedly made handsome profits for their owners, for the relatively safe postwar years saw a dramatic surge in trade, notably to the British West Indies. In the words of Bath historian Parker Reed, postwar Bath "became a mart for wholesale trade in West India goods. There was a DISTILLERY in town, and this consumed large quantities of the imported molasses, especially of the inferior grades.

"Besides long lumber, shooks, headings, and hoop poles for cooperage, these vessels carried out dried fish, pork, beef, and among the return cargoes were raisins, oranges, lemons, and fruits of West India growth and salt. Vessels were constantly going out and coming into the river, and employment was given men and youths who chose the sea for a vocation. Sailors of foreign birth were rare. So lively was commercial business that vessels were at times compelled to anchor in the stream for weeks waiting to procure berths at the wharves."[30]

Meanwhile, a new source of opportunity had emerged: the cotton trade. The Patten partners sometimes employed the *Ann Maria* as a coastwise cotton freighter, but it was

Fire in his belly? An early portrait of George F. Patten, on his way to wealth and influence. As a youngster, George learned shipbuilding in the Patten Point yard of his uncle Robert, then moved his skills to Bath in 1820, a case of perfect timing. *Courtesy Patten Free Library, Bath.*

increasingly obvious that the big money lay in taking large cargoes of American cotton to industrial Europe. Every year, demand for cotton increased. Obviously, whoever could build large cotton freighters — full-rigged ships — and manage them prudently stood to make a fortune. Or two fortunes. But that task could not be accomplished in the Cathance backwater.

The family holdings at Patten Point were being increasingly subdivided by successive generations of Pattens. The abundant timber that once cloaked the land was now cut over heavily. And, if larger ships were the wave of the future, getting them in and out of the narrow, sometimes shallow, rock-and-mudbank-strewn channels of Merrymeeting, with their ferocious currents, would be an endless headache. A larger, better situated shipyard would have to be found. The obvious site was Bath.

Accordingly, George and John Patten moved their enterprise to Long Reach, where, at the north end of Bath, they built a shipyard and office in 1820. Although in their early thirties, they came equipped with years of onshore and offshore expertise and were comfortable with command decisions. Moreover, in keeping with Patten tribal tradition, they were mutually cooperative and inured to hardship.

George and John Patten, in other words, were now in the right place at the right time, and they began taking full advantage of the opportunity that lay before them.

NOTES

1. Logbook of ship *New Orleans* of Bath, 1833-34 (Peabody Essex Museum, Salem MA), quoted in Ruth Briggs, "Ship Ventures of Old Bath" (typescript), Maine Maritime Museum, Bath, Maine (hereafter cited as MMM), chapter III, p. 4.

2. William Avery Baker, *A Maritime History of Bath, Maine and the Kennebec River Region* (2 vols., Bath, ME: Marine Research Society of Bath, 1973), p. 547. The disaster inspired a memorable, three-view painting of the wreck and a cenotaph made from *Hanover* flotsam, both of which are part of the Maine Maritime Museum's collection.

3. *Bath Weekly Mirror,* 25 November 1853; Mark Hennessy, comp., Historical Files on Bath Ships and Shipping (MMM).

4. Throughout this book, Patten genealogical information is drawn from vital records of Bath, Bowdoinham, and Topsham, ME; Cemetery Records (Bath, ME); Captains' File (MMM); Charles E. Burden, comp., Patten Genealogical Records (MMM); Walter Goodwin Davis, *The Ancestors of James Patten, 1747?-1817* (Portland, ME: Southworth-Anthoensen Press, 1941); and various Bath newspapers of the period.

5. George Augustus Wheeler and Henry Warren Wheeler, *History of Brunswick, Topsham, and Harpswell, Maine* (1878; reprint Somersworth, NH: New Hampshire Publishing Company, 1974), pp. 781-82.

6. Ibid., p. 331.

7. Erminie S. Reynolds and Kenneth R. Martin, *"A Singleness of Purpose": The Skolfields and Their Ships* (Bath, ME: Maine Maritime Museum, 1987), pp. 5-6.

8. Briggs, chapter I, pp. 13-14.

9. Wheeler and Wheeler, p. 685.

10. Ibid., p. 331.

11. Ibid., p. 782.

12. Briggs, chapter I, p. 8.

13. Wheeler and Wheeler, p. 783.

14. Baker, p. 67.

15. Parker McCobb Reed, _History of Bath and Environs..., 1607-1894_ (Portland, ME: Lakeside Press, 1894), pp. 302-4.

16. Baker, pp. 101, 116.

17. Henry Wilson Owen, _The Edward Clarence Plummer History of Bath, Maine_ (1936; reprint Bath, ME: Bath Area Bicentennial Committee, 1976), p. 130. See also Levi P. Lemont, _1400 Historical Dates of the Town and City of Bath, and Town of Georgetown, from 1604 to 1874_ (Bath, ME: By the Author, 1874), p. 40.

18. Jonathan Hyde, quoted in Owen, p. 131, and Baker, p. 158.

19. Baker, pp. 160-61.

20. Ibid., p. 167.

21. Captain John Holman to Robert Patten et al., Salem, December 1798 (Patten Papers, MMM).

22. Ibid.

23. Robert Patten to Peter Chardon Brooks, Topsham, 21 June 1799 (French Spoliation case file FS 137, Records of the United States Court of Claims [Record Group 123], National Archives and Records Administration, Washington, DC), quoted in Briggs, chapter I, p. 11.

24. Briggs, chapter I, p. 11.

25. Owen, p. 145.

26. The 293-ton _North Star,_ under Captain Levi Peterson, was built in Bath in 1810 (Baker, p. 210).

27. Captain John Patten, quoted in _Bath Daily Times,_ 26 February 1887.

28. Ibid.

29. Marion Jaques Smith, _General William King: Merchant, Shipbuilder, and Maine's First Governor_ (Camden, ME: Down East Books, 1980), pp. 48, 51.

30. Reed, p. 150.

2

"Pride and Interest"

The Pattens were not the only ones to see opportunity in Bath's infrastructure and changing patterns of world trade. The year before George and John Patten moved to Bath, the Houghton family built its first vessel on the Kennebec River. Two years after the Pattens arrived, in 1823, William D. Sewall launched his first ship. These modest operations would evolve into shipbuilding dynasties that were a major source of Bath's nineteenth-century wealth.

As they prospered, the Pattens, Houghtons, and Sewalls proved to be venturesome in spotting new opportunities but conservative in managing their operations. That proved a prudent strategy for the long run, but, in their early years, matters beyond their control got G.F. & J. Patten off to a slow start.

It turned out that peacetime did not completely clear the way for American merchant ships. As before (and for years afterward), American commerce caught cold every time Britain sneezed. Meanwhile, growing American sectionalism divided the country into special-interest groups. Southern cotton producers, growing fat on exports, favored free trade with Europe, or something close to it. Northern manufacturers pressed for tariff protection against cheap foreign imports with which they couldn't compete.

There were other hangups. For example, American maritime law restricted entry into U.S. ports by British vessels. British manufacturers, whose technology was a generation ahead of their American counterparts, could turn out industrial goods at rock-bottom prices and dump them on the U.S. market. The industrialized Northeast howled. In 1826, tired of trade wrangling, Britain again closed her West Indies ports to American shipping. As before, the Kennebec region suffered a chain-reaction recession. Where could Maine products go? Where could Maine shipowners find cargoes? Where were shipyard workers supposed to find work?

Bath was hit very hard. Some of her best local shipwrights moved to busier yards in what is now Canada's Maritime Provinces. Those who stayed home did repair and maintenance work for half their accustomed wages. The crunch continued until 1830, when the British finally reopened the West Indies. Local historian Parker Reed reported that "on the day [that] news reached Bath, all the vessels in port displayed every piece of bunting they possessed, presenting a gay scene at the wharves where numerous vessels

The ship *Palestine*, built in 1833 and active in the cotton and emigrant trades. Her principal owners were George and John Patten and Noble Maxwell. This consummate watercolor by Frederic Roux of Le Havre shows her leaving that port in 1838, displaying the Anchor Line flag. *Courtesy Peabody Essex Museum, Salem, MA.*

were lying, as well as in the stream where vessels were riding at anchor."[1]

Matters weren't as hopeful as they looked, however. Americans trading in the British Caribbean now had to pay a duty on U.S. lumber — effectively making Maine wood products uncompetitive with those of Canada. The West Indies trade would never be the same.

George and John Patten were not in mourning over the ups and downs of Caribbean commerce, for both had a knack for turning hard times as well as good times to advantage. The brothers Patten had other economic fish to fry.

In later life, John stated that the firm's most profitable trade was with the West Indies, but he undoubtedly was thinking of per-voyage profit margins, not overall profits. Indeed, the Pattens began edging out of Caribbean commerce by the mid-1820s. When the British closed their Caribbean ports in 1826, G.F. & J. Patten virtually abandoned the construction of brigs — vessels particularly suited for West Indies commerce — and shifted almost exclusively to larger, ship-rigged vessels intended for the cotton trade. Although in subsequent years they occasionally undertook Caribbean voyages, even carrying sugar products to Europe, the brother-partners had found a timely and comfortable niche.

Southern cotton had been an occasional cargo for Bath ships since 1802, when William King dispatched his brig *Androscoggin*, under Captain Nehemiah Harding, to New Orleans, then under Spanish control. The *Androscoggin*'s mission was to explore the possibilities of the cotton trade. Captain Harding reportedly was unsure about the exact location of New Orleans, but with King's assurance that it was somewhere in the Gulf of Mexico, he found an old Spanish chart that got him to his destination — no mean trick.[2]

Apparently this voyage, a first for Maine, provided the basis for King to invest in a cotton thread mill in nearby Brunswick. But not much else resulted, even after the United States purchased Louisiana in 1803.[3] The problem stemmed from the raw material. American cotton, being the short-staple variety, required processing that was too costly for the textile market.

Twenty years later, however, that problem had vanished. Britain's industrial expansion had created vast demand for cotton, and meanwhile, Eli Whitney's cotton gin, invented in 1794, had won gradual acceptance by southern planters. No wonder: The machine greatly reduced the time and expense involved in separating seeds and other matter from cotton fiber — a breakthrough that finally made American cotton cost-effective to European factories. The vast agricultural areas of the American South guaranteed a steadily increasing supply of this vital product (and, incidentally, gave the dying institution of slavery a new lease on life). By 1830, American cotton exports amounted to about 554,000 bales, increasing to 1,854,000 bales in 1850.[4] Transporting that vital cargo from southern ports to Europe became the specialty of Bath-built ships. It was also the making of George and John Patten's formidable fortunes.

According to John, "It was our custom to build one and sometimes two [vessels] every year. They were all for our own use, and we never built one for sale."[5] What made an effective cotton freighter? Bath-built examples were wide-bodied and kettle-bottomed, a compromise between the need to navigate the shallow bars of southern ports and the need to load as deeply as possible to compensate for the unusually light weight of cotton cargoes. In the early days of the trade, a single ton of cotton filled 100 cubic feet of cargo space, which meant that ships rode top-heavy and high in the water. Their speed suffered accordingly: Moving a southern cotton cargo to Europe took anywhere from four to eight weeks. Virtually all cotton carriers were full-rigged ships — that is, square-rigged on all three masts — and their overall appearance was blocky, even clumsy.[6] Such vessels became the stock-in-trade of the Patten shipyard.

Looks could be deceiving, however. The trade's peculiar characteristics inspired a functional formula for ship design: To be stable and cost-effective, a cotton freighter had to have a depth of hold measuring half the beam (width) at the main deck. Above the main deck, a vessel's sides tapered in toward her center — an aesthetically pleasing characteristic called tumblehome. This balance between light, bulky cargoes and the need for stability resulted in ships that could carry larger cargoes than their overall dimensions indicated — a fortunate outcome that reduced their port dues.

Were Patten ships well built? Yes — up to a point. Construction of any vessel was a compromise between durability and the projected economic life. For practical purposes, every vessel had to be strong enough to withstand extraordinary but inevitable rigors, such as groundings (cotton ships were forever grounding on the bars of shallow southern harbors), storms, and captains' bad judgment. But there was such a thing as overbuilding. As she aged, an indestructible vessel could eat up a fortune in maintenance costs.

By 1830, Maine's available supply of prime hardwood, such as white oak, was dwindling. To produce durable frames, local shipbuilders increasingly resorted to elm, yellow birch, rock maple, and southern live oak, or a combination thereof — called "mixed hardwoods" in the industry. With scrupulous maintenance, such vessels could be very long lasting but, even when new, they failed to impress diehard inspectors. Underwriters such as Lloyd's of London gave Patten vessels high but not top ratings for construction, probably because of the mixed woods that were used. The Pattens did not overinsure, relying on the soundness of their vessels and the judgment of their masters.

Patten-built ships enjoyed a reputation for sound, time-proven construction and avoidance of newfangled rigging gimmicks that distracted other shipbuilders.[7] Their owners, building strictly for their own account, had not skimped on the essentials. In 1838, for example, to ensure a supply of southern live oak, George Patten and William Sewall traveled to Philadelphia to procure a steady supply of this vital material.[8]

Local people had their own ways of sizing up a vessel's quality, and their recollections lingered for decades. Those who made good in sailing ships cherished countless memories that, in turn, provided newspaper copy that is still readable and evocative. For example, one day in 1890, Captain Curtis Merriman of Brunswick visited Bath and was interviewed by a local reporter. Merriman, who had enjoyed an illustrious career commanding square-riggers of Brunswick's Skolfield fleet, was under no illusions about the dim future awaiting sailing vessels.[9] But he gave the reporter a glowing account of his early days with the Pattens: "I shall always feel a pride and interest in any vessel built in Bath, Maine. In 1841, as [an] ordinary sailor before the mast, I sailed from this port in the ship *Monmouth*, at that time the largest full rigged ship ever built and sailed from this port. She was 730 tons, carried eighteen men before the mast, also the captain, two mates, cook, steward, and boy, in all twenty-four souls. She was commanded by Noble Maxwell, who died a short time ago.... The first mate was Thomas Patten, a son of John Patten, of the firm of G.F. & J. Patten, who built and owned her.... The *Monmouth* took in hay, and old stone walls, for ballast, reached New Orleans in eighteen or twenty days, took cotton to Liverpool, at nine sixteenths of a penny per pound, discharged, and took salt to Boston. She was full rigged, in all carrying twenty-six sails. Although I am over seventy years, I remember every sail on her, they were, inner and outer jibs, foresail, fore topsail, for top gallant sail, fore royal, fore topmast stay sails, double lower studden [studding] sails, double top mast studden sails, double top gallant studden sails, in all thirteen sails on the foremast.

"On the main masts were, the main sail, main topsail, main top gallant sail, royal, main topmast staysail, main top gallant stay sail and double main top gallant studden sails, in all eight sails. On the mizzen mast was the spanker, topsail, top gallant sail, royal and crochet [cross-jack] sail, which last was attached to the cross jack yard, making 5 more sails.

"Now if your memory is good you will count them up making twenty-six sails in all carried by the good ship *Monmouth* when we sailed from the Kennebec and every man on board felt...much pride in her...."[10]

In the firm's early years, it was apparently Captain John Patten's practice to command a new vessel during her shakedown, then turn her over to another skipper. For example, he skippered the firm's first ship-rigged vessel, *Catherine*, named for brother George's first-born child. (We shall hear more of Catherine.) The ship *Catherine* is a perfect example of the transition from West Indies to transatlantic trade. She measured 100 feet in length, 24 in breadth; her depth of hold was 13 feet — dimensions that, as we have seen, gave a conservative indication of her actual cargo capacity.

On the *Catherine*'s maiden voyage in November 1824, Captain John cleared Bath for Havana with a cargo of pine boards and shooks. In January 1825, after discharging in Havana, the *Catherine* loaded cotton in New Orleans. In March, she proceeded to Liverpool, arriving in late April. She carried an unknown cargo (probably emigrant passengers) from Londonderry to New York, arriving on 17 May 1825. Her next voyage was again to New Orleans by way of Jamaica.[11]

The Pattens slowly but steadily increased their vessels' tonnage. Although their policy was to build strictly for their own use, they were not loath to part with a ship after a

few years. Demand was high and, for the Pattens, replacement costs were low. In 1826, the Patten fleet consisted of five brigs and one ship that traded coastwise, to the Caribbean, and to Europe. Five years later, the fleet comprised three brigs and four ships. By 1839, it consisted of a schooner, a brig, and six ships. Cotton was king.

The fleet's tonnage was closely calibrated to the rise of the cotton trade; in fact, the Patten brothers were uncannily skilled at pacing expansion with the growing market — a talent they continued to exercise until after the Civil War.[12] That was but one of many factors that ensured their success.

The Patten brothers were close and congenial despite the fact that George's life had been somewhat sheltered compared to John's. George, remember, also held the title of captain, but he attained the rank as a militia officer; it had no seafaring connotation. The pair were so close, in fact, that they conducted business and personal affairs from a single fund, each drawing what he needed with the full trust of the other. Even in the 1820s, so casual a practice was quite unusual, and it may partly explain why written records of the firm are so sparse today. Enough information survives, however, to afford a picture

Although all successful shipbuilders and merchants kept their eyes on the proverbial bottom line, they often splurged on lavish adornments for their vessels. Here, in a rare daguerreotype, is the carved sternboard of the *Tempest*, a passenger-and-cotton ship built by David and Lincoln Patten of Bowdoinham in 1849. Records indicate that the ship also sported a decorative figurehead. They don't make them like that anymore. *Courtesy Loyall F. Sewall/Maine Maritime Museum.*

Captain George F.
Patten's elegant home at
the foot of Cedar Street,
Bath, overlooking the
company shipyard. The
house still retains much
of its original character.
*Courtesy Maine
Maritime Museum.*

of the firm's daily operations and, more important, the components of its success.

The Patten yard was at the foot of Cedar Street at the north end of Bath. Its work-force was largely local, consisting in part of farmers who sidelined as laborers. Given John's statement about the pace of the firm's shipbuilding, and keeping in mind the slump of the late 1820s, it is safe to assume that the firm shared skilled workers with other yards uptown.

George and John had gained early favor with workers by paying in cash, not in scrip redeemable at a company store, as was then customary. In fact, the Pattens did not oper-ate a store until years later. Their willingness to pay in cash was a first in Bath, and other yards eventually followed suit.[13] Skilled workers received a dollar a day — about $23 in 1995 currency.

A long, hard day's work was the accepted norm in any shipyard. The work day ran from sunup to sundown. The yard provided workers' meals, along with the customar-ily stiff ration of rum.[14] As the temperance movement gained momentum in Maine, how-ever, the Patten yard bowed to changing times. An 1830 newspaper account of the *New Orleans*'s launching assured readers that the handsome vessel had been built "without the use of any ardent spirit."[15]

Business prospered. Conspicuous symbols of success were the stately Federal houses both brothers called home. When George arrived in Bath, he lived in an old house on

the corner of North and Front Streets, just a short walk from the shipyard. When John came home from the sea and entered fully into the partnership, he acquired brother George's house. George built a new home overlooking the yard at the foot of Cedar Street. Spacious and elegant, both homes sat among ample gardens. In 1837, when the Pattens established a wharf and store at the foot of North Street, Captain John could oversee those operations from his living-room windows. Brother James lived next door to John on North Street.

But the real symbol of success, of course, was the steadily increasing number of cotton ships flying the Pattens' black-anchor-on-white house flag. That flag gave the growing Patten fleet a name: the Anchor Line.

Why did the Pattens succeed? For several reasons. One, already mentioned, was timing. Another was the tribal spirit of cooperation that they had brought from Topsham and that they continued by employing other Pattens as captains. Add to that the factor of fire in the belly: George and John clearly enjoyed what they were doing and were determined to be the first in the family to score spectacular success. The brothers' self-consciousness about success would also manifest itself in their later, conspicuous public charity and civic leadership.

Personal traits aside, G.F. & J. Patten devised very sound strategies and never flinched

Looking down North Street in Bath during the Pattens' heyday. The third house on the left belongs to Captain James F. Patten. The last house, on the corner, is Captain John's, overlooking the company wharf. The Woolwich shoreline is more distant than it appears in this photograph. *Courtesy Maine Maritime Museum.*

when times took a turn for the worse. The brothers spread their risk, including a very small number of investors in each new Patten vessel. Significantly, the circle of investors consisted largely of members of the clan. In addition, George and John Patten regularly took shares in vessels other than their own. It was this practice that gave rise to the oft-repeated error that, in their heyday, they "controlled" sixty-five ships — which would have been the largest private fleet in North America. At its peak, just before the American Civil War, the Patten fleet numbered fifteen square-riggers with a gross tonnage of more than 13,000.

In the yard and in the office, G.F. & J. Patten benefited from the learning curve: efficiency that accrues from applying the lessons of repeated experience. The yard's master carpenter, Dennis Lines, was a seasoned shipbuilder. The nature of the cotton trade was indeed repetitive, not beset by abrupt changes in technology, so the applied lessons of learning cycles were especially advantageous.

The firm may have been as steady as a rock, but, at times, the U.S. economy was otherwise, subject to periodic surges and recessions. National overexpansion in the mid-1830s led to a financial panic in 1837 and a severe depression that lasted until 1841. In the mid-1850s, the U.S. economy cooled again at the point when U.S. shipping tonnage had caught up with demand. The result was a scramble for cargoes, a rat-race made more difficult by a long spate of violent, dangerous weather in the North Atlantic. Surely, Captain John's affable, avuncular exterior masked a good deal of worry that uncontrollable forces would ruin the family. Indeed, Patten correspondence is filled with anxiety about unstable freight rates, scarce cargoes, and imminent hard times; yet the company stayed ahead of the game.

There were, of course, specific setbacks, such as the *New Orleans*'s 1834 grounding at the mouth of the Kennebec. As will be seen in chapter 3, Patten vessels took their share of hard knocks thanks to inaccurate charts, shifting and undredged channels, and the scarcity of aids to navigation. But, over the long term, the shipping market was expanding, and so was G.F. & J. Patten.

Years of coping with assorted ups and downs produced another payoff: substantial experience in ship design, seasonal timing, administrative leadership, and banking connections. Put simply, the Pattens perpetually fine-tuned their mastery of cotton-trade lore, thereby retaining a competitive edge.

For example, they managed the size and age of their fleet with finesse. By the 1830s, their increasing tonnage provided economies of scale while their private yard kept maintenance costs to a minimum. Patten vessels crossing from Europe to America often carried cargoes readily marketable in Bath — salt and iron, for example. By returning to Bath periodically, the ships could be repaired and maintained cheaply at the company yard. They could also be sold on favorable terms when the market was right, giving way to new, improved models built in-house.

More keys to success: Although the Patten brothers exploited the booming cotton market, even purchasing outright some of their cargoes, they did not become totally

dependent upon that single specialty. Beginning in the 1820s, Patten cotton ships side-lined as packets, bringing European emigrants to North America on their return voyages. And, long before the Civil War dethroned King Cotton, G.F. & J. Patten was trading in the Pacific. The brothers, moreover, did not have a hidebound commitment to maritime enterprise. As their prosperity grew, they diversified into other ventures such as banking and railroads.

Finally, we must consider the Pattens' impulse to recycle part of their earnings for the general good. As will be seen, both George and John made handsome financial contributions to charitable, educational, and religious organizations in the community. By all accounts, they did so readily, never putting on upscale airs or losing their upbeat outlook on life. If it is true that what goes around comes around, that also helps to explain the brothers' momentum of success.

From the start, their rise carried along other members of the Patten clan whose skills and toil were, over time, repaid handsomely. Younger brother James F. is a good example. Although details about his career are few, it is known that James became captain of several Patten vessels: *Andes II* (1832-35), *Manchester* (1835), *London* (1838-39), and *Monmouth* (1842). The shares he held in such vessels made him nothing less than a junior partner in the company.

Cousin David Patten, born in 1799, commanded several company vessels: the ill-fated *New Orleans* (1830-34), *Caspian* (1834-36 and 1846), *Delaware* (1838 and 1852), and *Halcyon* (1842). David also invested in other Patten ships. David's brother Lincoln,

James F. Patten, brother of George and John. For decades, James was a successful master of G.F. & J. Patten ships and an investor in the company, growing wealthy through these and other ventures. His son, Charles E. Patten, would continue that tradition. *Courtesy Maine Maritime Museum.*

who, born in 1808, was a relative youngster, likewise enjoyed a long career at sea, much of it spent commanding Patten ships. Years later, in 1858, Lincoln and David Patten would form a shipbuilding partnership of their own.

Cousin William Patten also commanded company vessels: *Statira* (1821-25), *George* (1825 and 1828), and *Globe* (1831). In 1841, William became co-owner and manager of a fleet of twelve vessels homeported in Richmond, upriver from Bath.

Presumably, the clannish nature of Patten maritime enterprise enhanced understanding between the land-bound brothers and their seagoing employees. In the days before transatlantic telegraph, captains were incommunicado for long periods, so it was absolutely essential that they understand precisely their degree of autonomy. With prices and cargo rates subject to frequent changes, captains in European, Caribbean, or cotton ports had to make quick decisions that would have a powerful impact on the firm's fortunes. Expenses incurred on voyages were covered by a Patten account with the British banking firm of Baring Brothers & Company, from which skippers drew as needed.

The most dramatic example of familial success within the Patten firm involves Noble Maxwell, first cousin to George, John, and James — a somewhat eccentric loner whose fortune grew along with those of his celebrated relatives. Maxwell and the Patten brothers were similar only in their talent for turning a buck, but Maxwell's career provides an interesting close-up of the business afloat and ashore.

Remember Captain James Maxwell of the schooner *Industry*, who before the Revolution swallowed the anchor and, with his wife Peggy Patten settled into a long life as a farmer on Bowdoinham Neck? James and Peggy had several children, cousins of George and John Patten. One of these, Noble, after a rudimentary onshore education, went to sea while still a youngster. Like his slightly older cousin John, he apparently saw action as a privateer during the War of 1812.[16] Noble Maxwell's early activities as a mariner are obscure because, throughout his surprising life, he habitually kept personal matters to himself. As his fortune grew, and grew, and grew, his secretive side occasioned no end of speculation inside and outside the clan.

Noble Maxwell's business relationship with G.F. & J. Patten was a vital element in the firm's success. And by the time that relationship ended under less than cordial circumstances, Maxwell may have been wealthier than his cousins. He continued to increase his fortune into old age and was still active in business when he died at ninety-six. Family stories cast him as a bit of an oddball. Certainly, he was different from his cousins in one significant way: For him, accumulating wealth was the central focus of life, while for John and George it was the natural outcome of prudent enterprise. Another difference is that Maxwell remained a lifelong, childless bachelor.

First things first. In the 1830s, while his career as a captain was flourishing, Maxwell is said to have had one passion other than money: George F.'s attractive daughter Catherine. According to family tradition, Maxwell fell in love with Kate Patten when she was a teenager. The fact that he was Kate's first cousin once removed probably would have been

enough to put the kibosh on a serious relationship — to say nothing of a thirty-year age difference — so it is difficult to give much credence to such a story. But matters of the heart are not driven by logic. There is no doubt that the two were close and that Maxwell took a protective interest in Kate.

For her part, Kate maintained a warm and even flirtatious correspondence with Maxwell. For example, writing to him from the Gorham Female Seminary (later Westbrook College) in February 1839, she asked him, "Pray, why have you not shown the light of your countenance upon us poor souls (nuns)? I heard from Ma, last week and she said you were coming on *soon*. Now, if there is one word in Webster's dictionary that I abhor, 'tis this word *soon*. I took it for granted that *soon* meant that week, and accordingly kept upon the tip-toe of expectation.... I really think that you must have been troubled by the blues unless you have had very pleasant company, and that can hardly be supposed unless you have taken up with the ladies.... I sometimes think you *may* take a *sudden leap* into the ditch of matrimony. Take, however, the word of an 'old maid' don't be too *hasty*. Stop until you arrive at years of discretion before you put your head in that noose. A matrimonial noose of all things is the worst. If you felt at all inclined there are not a few young ladies of 'sweet sixteen' here, and I would advise you take a look at them 'before purchasing elsewhere' as the merchants say."[17]

Composing letters of this sort was very much a part of a young lady's education in Kate's day, and it would be dangerous in hindsight to read between the lines. But Noble

Enigmatic Noble Maxwell. Son of James Maxwell and first cousin of the Pattens of Bath, Captain Noble commanded and invested in Patten-built vessels and was a key factor in the company's success until 1850, when the relationship ended melodramatically. Maxwell nurtured his capital, grew ever wealthier, and lived a long, solitary life in Boston. *Courtesy Maine Maritime Museum.*

Maxwell may have done so. Whatever the case, in 1840 Kate wed Bostonian Wildes Walker, embarking on an unhappy fourteen-year marriage. According to family members, Captain Maxwell lost his joie de vivre at that point. When, fourteen years later, Kate was divorced, Maxwell ever after kept close to hand a "well thumbed copy of a transcript of the divorce proceedings in which Kate gave a graphic account of what she had suffered as the wife of a worthless husband."[18] This tidbit is particularly interesting because, as will be seen, Kate and Maxwell had had a melodramatic falling-out years before her divorce.

It is very likely that Maxwell's relationship with Kate Patten made him wary of future entanglements, but he kept his thoughts on that subject to himself — except for a carefully copied sentiment he entered into a pocket notebook: "A good book and a Good woman are excellent things for those who know how to appreciate their value. There are men however who judge both from the beauty of their covers." Maxwell never married.[19]

Which is not to say he wasn't a good catch. Maxwell was an unofficial partner in G.F. & J. Patten and a substantial co-owner of the company's fleet. Whether he was at sea or at home, the Patten brothers kept him well advised on the nuances of the business, and advice was exchanged by all parties. An example or two will illustrate the degree of detail involving Maxwell while providing some flavor of the day-to-day decision-making that drove the company. In December 1835, the brothers contacted Maxwell in Boston, informing him that they had "concluded to take a yearly Policy on the [ship] Caspian — say for $20,000 valuing her at $25,000 for one year..., and if at Sea at the expiration of the year, the risk to continue at prorata premiums until she arrives at her port of destination. She is now insured one half at the Merchants and half at the Ocean Office; but we decline having any more business with the latter, and you can get it done at any good office that will take the risk on the best terms.... You will please forward the Policy and premium note by mail & we will sign the Note and return it."[20]

Sometimes business details were spiked with family news and even humor that illustrates the closeness of all parties. Here is an 1841 letter from the brothers in Bath to Maxwell in New Orleans, where his ship, *Monmouth*, was loading cotton: "We are sorry to see business so dull and so little prospect of there being any better here.... The [ships] Majestic & London have gone back to New Orleans and the Caspian is up for there.... Father remains very low and cannot continue but a short time.... Jane Peterson has been as crazy as a coot but is now more rational. It may be on your account or some other old bachelor."[21]

In May 1841, while unloading cotton in Liverpool and preparing for a return trip to the United States, Maxwell received this from the Bath brothers: "...you must do as you think best, only don't bring a cargo of salt to this place and it is our opinion that you had better take what freight offer for whenever you think you can get the most.... We would give cotton the preference to New York or any southern port on account of the expenses and the prospect of getting Ice in the fall if nothing better offered.... We have nothing new, only the death of our poor father who died on Thursday last. He has been a great sufferer and he had continued much longer than we expected. The rest of our friends are well. We think of writing [Captain] Decker that if he cannot get freight and passengers enough to make it an object that he had better try and get a freight of iron from Gottenburg [Sweden]....”[22]

Clearly, Maxwell was an integral, trusted part of the Pattens’ executive process, sharing in decision-making and prospering accordingly. Such mutual trust worked for both ends of the equation. The Liverpool cotton cargo mentioned above grossed 2,635 British pounds — about $311,825 in 1995 terms. Maxwell’s primage (a captain’s cut of the freight fee that constituted a bonus above his wages and other income) was 125 British pounds — about $14,800 in 1995 currency.[23] Money aside, Captain Maxwell also enjoyed warm relations with George and Hannah Patten, a devoted couple who, with their eight children, provided him with a surrogate family and a home in Bath when he needed it.

The steady rise of Maxwell’s fortune over his years with G.F. & J. Patten form an interesting contrast with the success of another Patten protégé, the talented Charles Davenport.

Charles Davenport’s career is one of those rags-to-riches tales that gladden the hearts of free-enterprise advocates and serve as object lessons for ambitious youngsters everywhere. Born in Bath in 1819, Davenport went to work as a boy with just the basics of an education. His first job was clerking at Elkanor Sprague’s store on Front Street, not far from the Patten shipyard. He earned a princely wage of six dollars a month — slave wages even in the 1820s — but he soon moved up to a better position as a clerk for J.H. McLellan, a Bath merchant and shipbuilder. Davenport’s new boss apparently taught him bookkeeping, a trade he practiced from sunrise to ten at night. When his work day at McLellan’s was at last over, young Davenport would pick up wood chips at the Clapp & Boynton shipyard, drag them home, and chop them up for fuel.

Davenport’s dutiful diligence inevitably attracted wider attention. In 1834, G.F. & J. Patten made him an offer that he was able to accept only by promising to do McLellan’s accounts after hours, work that kept him up past midnight. Eventually, all his time was spent with the Pattens. Transferring to the Patten office was a smart move — so much so that Davenport declined the position of collector of customs for Bath.

The brothers took Davenport under their wing. To fully utilize his energy, they built a store on their newly acquired wharf at North and Front Streets, across from Captain John’s home, and Davenport managed that establishment outright for the next sixteen years. They also brought their protégé along in another way: helping him to take shares in new vessels. His first venture was a $400 share in the schooner *Hamilton* that he sold two years later for $800. Davenport was a partner in the firm’s ship *Delaware* (1838) and henceforward had a share of every new Patten ship. He also became temporary cashier at Bath’s Lincoln Bank, thanks to George F. Patten, the bank’s president. Years later, Davenport too would be president of that institution.[24] Like his mentors, he would also become a civic leader and, eventually, seal his reputation as “the richest man in Bath.”[25]

Exhibiting a zest for details, Davenport quickly made himself indispensable to the Pattens, and his contribution became a major factor in the firm’s success. He was an inte-

Charles Davenport, whose industriousness as a young man made him a Patten protégé, then a partner. Davenport successfully emulated his mentors and followed in their philanthropic footsteps as well. A successful banker and a mainstay in the later firm of John Patten & Son, Davenport was known at the end of his life as "the richest man in Bath." *Courtesy Maine Maritime Museum.*

gral part of the endless network of correspondence that linked the company's Bath office with its skippers in far-flung locales. In June 1842, for example, explaining that Captain John Patten was unable to write, being "somewhat afflicted with the rheumatism," Davenport confided the latest scuttlebutt to Noble Maxwell: "You have probably noticed the arrival of the [ship] Delaware in New York. She had 264 passengers & her freight consists chiefly of Salt and Coal. She ran foul of an iceberg passing the Banks, and carried away her jibboom, but Capt. [David] Patten thinks the ship received no serious damage.... Mr. Larrabee, who fell from [shipyard] staging 25 to 30 feet, on Monday last, has today command in the yard again. They are getting along fast with the new ship [*Halcyon*]."[26]

A request posted a few months later to Maxwell in Boston indicates that the former poor boy had acquired the carriage-trade tastes (although not the literacy) of the Pattens: "We are expecting the Steam Frigate Masura here tommorrow, and I may be under the necesitay of inviting the Oficers to my House. Should I have to do so and have nothing to offer them to drink, it might not be considered very polite. I therefore ask the favor of you to purchase a baskit of the first quality of Champaign, Wine and 3 gallons Brandy, and send down by the return boat, and the bill and I wil send you the money. As there is so much desception in Champaign, I wish you to be particular. Nothing strange or new in this place. All are well."[27] By the 1840s, from accounting to socializing, Charles Davenport was the Pattens' right hand in the Bath office. He never left their side. When his son was born in 1847, he named him George Patten Davenport.

Captain Noble Maxwell, meanwhile, had also acquired formidable business acumen — so much so that he was outgrowing his place in the company. Maxwell had been investing heavily in Boston bank stock and doing very well. These and other ventures soon became the tail that wagged the dog; so in 1844, he, like his father, swallowed the anchor and devoted his time to shoreside business. He continued to prosper but became preoccupied with the details of his fortune to the exclusion of other, softer pursuits. Maxwell was no Silas Marner or Scrooge McDuck, but there is no denying that a bean-counter mindset got the upper hand after he retired from the sea. He kept his house in Bowdoinham, where taxes were lower than Bath's, living there in summer. The rest of the year, he lived frugally in Boston, where he could keep careful track of his investments.

Now a punctilious money manager, Maxwell assumed a skeptical attitude toward G.F. & J. Patten's casual business procedures, which apparently got on the nerves of his employer-partners. Witness his complaint to George F. in November 1847: "The last time I cal[l]ed on you you seamed Much disatisfied that I should want to know anything of my business further than you did Show.... You take the Interest on My Money or Exchange in Barings for your Trouble without accounting to me for It..., and further there is no act from you to me that showes when or at what Price you ever have Sold any of my exchange Which I think I have right to Know and further there has been several cargoes of salt at Bath that I was interested in...but I have had no [account of] sales nor any act of Expenses for Storage or Your com[mission] or Services...all of which I think I have a Right to know and to know it from your [account] to me.... I can't think Mr. Patten there is any Thing unreasonable in any of these demands if there is I dont ask it — and I have alwais thought was willing to do as you would be done by and I Sincerely believe If you had business with any person that Placed you in My Situation you would want those very things I have Asked."[28] *"Mr. Patten?"* By the sound of that officious address, something clearly had changed.

In the spring of 1850, an altercation between Maxwell and George F. Patten ended years of symbiotic enterprise and killed off Maxwell's goodwill with the Bath-based Pattens. The exact details are vague except that Maxwell raised some further objection to G.F. & J. Patten's recordkeeping — possibly the brothers' practice of personally drawing on company assets in which other fortunes such as Maxwell's were invested. Perhaps Maxwell was advised by newer, outside business colleagues to challenge the Pattens. Whatever the case, the dispute was a money matter about which Maxwell vented his displeasure in no uncertain terms, calling for an investigation of the company accounts and delivering a dressing-down that left George F. deeply shaken. It was the end of a lifetime, cordial, mutually beneficial friendship.

Worse, perhaps, it was the end of Maxwell's relationship with Kate. George F.'s spirited daughter, furious at Maxwell's conduct, made her feelings clear in no uncertain terms:

"Sir:

"I have no disposition to refrain from giving you an expression of my feelings, for the abusive language and conduct towards my Father on a recent occasion. To think one who has shared the hospitalities of his roof in sickness as in health should at this late day attack him in the spirit and manner that you did, is to me inexplicable. Thank heaven his character and integrity stand on too solid a basis to be affected at his age, by your foul aspersions.... Twere I a man, an investigation of not only accounts, but conduct should be more vividly impressed upon you than during your life has ever troubled you to make other than verbally.... Who that know you that does not know of your failings as well as proverbial closeness not to call it meanness...?

"...I return to you a memento of early days, given when your friendship and home were identified with those friends who taught me to respect you. The chain once attached, well worn, finally broke and was lost. And now farewell and may your present friends prove as true as those who have ever been solicitous for your welfare both temporal and spiritual if so while possessed of reason you will not have cause to complain.

"C.F.P. Walker"[29]

Assuming that Maxwell did harbor tender feelings for Kate, it is easy to imagine the impact of this frigid dismissal. He had but a few days to recover from it before Kate's twenty-five-year-old sister Hannah weighed in with even greater vehemence. Hannah's outraged kiss-off sheds a bit more light on the controversy and fully dramatizes Maxwell's banishment:

"How am I to address you, what can I say that can make you feel the cruelty of which you have been guilty toward your best friend? I know my pen is powerless to do so, for [how] could you thus forget the kindness of years as to abuse a man whose character you well know was above a shadow of suspicion, to heap insult upon insult upon a head whitened not by age alone, but by the care of *your* property as well as his.... I realize after all, by the proof of your own unmanly actions that you *did* love your gold better than anything or anybody else.... How hard to realize that *you* could be guilty of causing a whole family to suffer from your cowardly treatment of one so dear to us.... That you could thus shamefully treat one on whom so many dependant ones were leaning, could add another care or sorrow to his or her brow (for you well know, they are inseparable) shows a hardness of heart of which I supposed none but a murderer guilty. And now Capt. Maxwell we have all left you and you *know* you stand alone. I can almost hear your reply 'there are friends enough' and so there may be new ones, attracted *now* by the sound of wealth and with your coldness of heart these empty expressions may satisfy your spirit, but *never*, let me tell you, in the few short years left you on earth will you find hearts that felt for you as we have done.... Your own conduct has shown that little did you value that affection, that little did you care if you did meet us in the street to pass you coldly by, that you ceased to remember the children who for years sat upon your knee and watched your coming in and your going out with a love which nothing but your own selfish heartlessness could ever take away. Before I say *farewell*, let me express the hope, that before you go down to your grave, unwept, unloved, you may see and *feel too* the injustice which you in your frenzy did; and give to our parents who mourn over your changed nature and your hard hearted cruelty... the slight satisfaction after such an injury, of an acknowledgement of your ingratitude. With such a hope, far off as it may be in the dim future I will leave you.

"Hannah T. P. Slade."[30]

The future for Hannah Slade and Noble Maxwell is now the past, so we can follow this piquant tale to its end. Maxwell wisely diversifies his investments away from sailing vessels and into railways and banks. He enjoys holidays in posh Saratoga Springs, New York, where he occasionally is seen in the company of a female. In summer, however, he returns by steamboat to Bowdoinham, where he is catered to by his sister Peggy's family. Motivated by duty and dazzled by his enormous fortune, his closest relatives indulge the mirthless, florid-faced, white-haired loner's pinchpenny lifestyle ("Herring is the cheapest food a man can eat!") and rock-ribbed conservatism. Once, while watching from Bowdoinham the distant flash of Bath's Fourth of July fireworks display, Maxwell can think only of the city's enormous public debt. Surrounded by small fry enjoying the spectacle, Uncle Noble raps his cane "nervously on the ground and mutter[s]; 'They had better pay their debts!'"[31]

But there is another side to Uncle Noble. He is frequently sought out for financial advice by admiring acquaintances. He is also a soft touch for his relatives, whose assorted hard-luck tales bring forth generous donations. As years pass, Uncle Noble makes it clear that he intends to leave his fortune to his extended family with the hope that all hands will have as much fun using his money as he had making it. At age ninety, he stops coming to Bowdoinham, and relatives persuade him to place his fortune in the hands of a trustee. He spends his last years living in solitary elegance at the Vendome Hotel on Commonwealth Avenue in Boston, mercifully unaware of the hefty cost of his board and care.

In 1887, at age ninety-six, Maxwell dies, leaving a legacy that makes some of his family members wealthy and others at least comfortable. Sagadahoc County probate records indicate that at the time of death, the value of his property — mostly stock — totals $191,428, about $2.2 million in 1995 value.[32] This, however, is misleading, for Maxwell appears to have transferred most of his property to relatives before his death, a precaution to avoid inheritance taxes that he surely would have found obnoxious. As revealed by heirs, Maxwell's overall legacy includes stock in sixteen railroads, eight textile mills, and fourteen Boston banks, as well as substantial holdings in U.S. government bonds. All in all, his estate totals $2 million — about $34 million in 1995 currency. In accordance with his expressed wishes, he is buried next to his sister Peggy on the Decker farm in Bowdoinham.[33]

Now back to the 1850s. Aside from the personal anguish within a family that prided itself — and capitalized — on its closeness, G.F. & J. Patten suffered no serious setback from its breakup with Noble Maxwell. Patten ships and captains (some of whom were named Patten, of course) continued enjoying long-established reputations for

Mary Peterson Turner Patten (1800-1862), second wife of Captain John. Her two children both died young: Mary Paulina at age 5 (in 1836), and Captain John L. at 24 (in 1860). *Courtesy Sutherland Family.*

reliability. At home, the company's affairs were in the capable hands of Charles Davenport, thus freeing the founders — now past middle age — to pursue civic and family activities and to invest their substantial capital in ventures other than shipping.

As they aged, George and Hannah Patten were troubled by health problems (the exact nature of which is now hard to pinpoint), but both managed to maintain normal lives enhanced by a gracious lifestyle and a doting family. Their two surviving sons, James T. and George M., did not opt for seafaring careers. Parker Reed's history of Bath describes George F. Patten as "large in statu[r]e, commanding and distinguished in his personal appearance. While always possessing more than ample means, his mode of life was that of comfortable simplicity, and his house was one in which there was always generous hospitality."[34]

Captain John, blessed with the Patten genes for longevity, continued his robust, hale existence. According to one personal acquaintance's recall, John's robust constitution was strengthened by sound health habits: "Though a little remarkable for a sea-faring man, he was not addicted to the use of tobacco in any form. Although brought up in a period when spirit[u]ous liquors were used with a freedom we can hardly comprehend to-day, he never used them in any but the most moderate degree.... His even, cheerful disposition was a great moral factor in his physical life. He was a man who never allowed himself what is popularly called the 'blues.' Gloom was not a companion that he tolerated in his home."[35]

With his first wife, Betsey Bates, who died in 1826, he had had two sons, Thomas and Gilbert, both of whom became captains of G.F. & J. Patten vessels. Thomas, who trained under Noble Maxwell, died in 1847. Captain John's second wife, Mary Peterson Turner, gave birth to two children. Mary died in 1836 at age five; John Levi, born the same year, would, like his half-brothers, pursue a maritime career.

Meanwhile, life went on at the Bath office, an endless succession of circumspect decisions, each of which had to be made without a moment to spare.

NOTES

1. Reed, p. 150.
2. Ibid., p. 151; M. Smith, p. 24.
3. *American Sentinel* (Bath), 30 July 1857.
4. John G.B. Hutchins, *The American Maritime Industries and Public Policy, 1789-1914* (Cambridge, MA: Harvard University Press, 1941), pp. 236-37.
5. Captain John Patten, quoted in *Boston Traveler,* 2 December 1886.
6. Mark Hennessy, comp., Historical Files on Bath Ships and Shipping (MMM).

7. Baker, p. 347.

8. William Hutchinson Rowe, *The Maritime History of Maine* (1948; reprint Gardiner, ME: Harpswell Press, 1989), p. 121.

9. Skolfield and Martin, pp. 146-47.

10. *American Sentinel* (Bath), 13 November 1890.

11. Throughout this book, dimensions and itineraries of Patten vessels are drawn from Records of the Bureau of Customs (Record Group 36) and Records of the Bureau of Marine Inspection and Navigation (Record Group 41), National Archives and Records Administration, Washington, DC; and Robert Applebee Collection of Bath Customs District Records, Penobscot Marine Museum, Searsport, ME; as researched and condensed in Charles E. Burden, comp., Records of Patten Mariners and Vessels (MMM), *passim.*

12. Ralph Linwood Snow, "Patten Fleet Size by Year" (manuscript chart, MMM).

13. Baker, p. 312.

14. Reed, pp. 146-47.

15. *Maine Inquirer,* 10 December 1830, quoted in Baker, pp. 344-45.

16. [Wilbur F. Decker], "Notable Career of Noble Maxwell whose Wealth Reached Seven Figures," *Bath* [ME] *Independent,* 14 November 1935. Decker's article appears in three weekly installments — 7, 14, and 21 November 1935. Decker, a nephew, was personally acquainted with Maxwell.

17. Catherine F. Patten to Maxwell, Gorham, ME, 26 February 1839 (private collection; quoted at length in Briggs, chapter IV, pp. 21-22).

18. Briggs, chapter 1, p. 15.

19. Undated pocket notebook found in Noble Maxwell Papers (MMM).

20. G.F. & J. Patten to Maxwell, Bath, 29 December 1835 (Noble Maxwell Papers, MMM).

21. G.F. & J. Patten to Maxwell, Bath, 7 March 1841 (ibid.).

22. G.F. & J. Patten to Maxwell, Bath, 27 May 1841 (ibid.).

23. Account sheet, ship *Monmouth* of Bath, 1841 (Noble Maxwell Papers, MMM).

24. Hennessy Historical Files (MMM).

25. *Bath Daily Times,* 5 July 1897.

26. Charles Davenport to Noble Maxwell, Bath, 20 June 1842 (Noble Maxwell Papers, MMM).

27. Davenport to Maxwell, Bath, 5 September 1842 (ibid.).

28. Maxwell to George F. Patten, Boston, 11 November 1847 (ibid.).

29. Catherine P. Walker to Maxwell, New Brunswick, NJ?, 17 April 1850 (ibid.).

30. Hannah Slade to Maxwell, Bath?, 5 May 1850 (ibid.).

31. [Decker], "Notable Career of Noble Maxwell."

32. Inventory of the estate of Noble Maxwell, 1887 (Probate Records, Sagadahoc County Court House, Bath, ME.

33. Ibid., *Bath Independent,* 21 November 1935.

34. Reed, p. 340.

35. Ibid., p. 341.

3

"All Sorts of Winds and Weather"

The need for quick, often urgent decisions multiplied as the Patten company increased its fleet and tonnage. Like other maritime managers, the Pattens peppered their correspondence with ongoing complaints about sparseness of cargoes and pitifully low freight rates. This litany continued through good years and lean years, and today it might easily be construed as the record of a hardscrabble business one step away from bankruptcy. Just the opposite was the case.

Vast numbers of people were involved in the company's activities, either as employees or customers. In more than four decades of existence, G.F. & J. Patten ships employed hundreds of mariners. And because those ships often doubled as passenger vessels, they provided a cramped home to thousands of U.S.-bound European emigrants who probably would never forget their passage on the Anchor Line.

It is important to remember that the overwhelming majority of Patten voyages went off without a hitch and therefore excited no public notice in their day. Patten sailors, like most in the merchant service, grew accustomed to a little risk, a bit more tedium, a lot of hard work, and an acceptable payoff at each destination. The details of such routinely successful voyages were by and large quickly and forever forgotten.

The surviving written record of Patten voyages, by contrast, is preoccupied with maritime mishaps and disasters, for such occurrences unleashed a requisite flood of paperwork. Thus, the well-documented voyages are the ones where something went wrong. Although these were by no means typical, and should not be taken as typical, they do make interesting reading. They also provide some vivid glimpses into the deepwater details of the business.

Perpetually on guard against conditions beyond its control, the company was prepared to accept unpleasant surprises as part of the cost of doing business. A look at some of these surprises will demonstrate that accepted level of risk.

The 1834 near-disaster of the ship *New Orleans,* mentioned in chapter 1, was an

The cotton freighter *Italy,* built by G.F. & J. Patten in 1846, as painted by Frederic Roux during a visit to Le Havre. The white-banded imitation ports seen in this view were a popular motif in the early 1800s, originally meant to deceive distant predators into mistaking a merchant-man for a warship. *Courtesy Mr. and Mrs. Chester Brett.*

extreme but not an isolated incident. There was also the case of the Patten brig *Jasper*, under Captain Edward Oliver, which limped into Bath in December 1835. In October of that year, the *Jasper* had been bound from Laguna de Terminos, Mexico, loaded with logwood for Marseille. Off the northwest coast of Cuba, she ran into powerful north winds. According to Captain Oliver's report, the *Jasper* was "under a heavy press of sail to enable him to weather away the Colorados and Isabella Shoals, the Vessel laboring & straining heavily, discovered the Vessel to have sprung a leak, but was able to keep her free." A few days later, however, more heavy weather caused the leak to worsen. By mid-November, with the *Jasper* leaking at the exhausting rate of 900 pump strokes per hour, "It was considered expedient and necessary by the officers and crew, for preservation of property and safety of crew, to make for some Port for repairs, and they accordingly put away for Boston."[1]

More trouble: Snow and adverse winds prevented the brig from getting into Boston. With the crew approaching a state of collapse, Oliver made Bath instead. Inspection revealed that the *Jasper* was indeed badly strained and would have to be dry-docked for repairs. The Pattens sold her. Repaired and rerigged as a bark, the *Jasper* eventually made her way into the New Bedford whale fishery. She was condemned in New Zealand in 1853.[2]

Another Patten brig, *Noble*, named for Noble Maxwell, who skippered her for several years after her 1822 launching, got into trouble in July 1837. Under the command of George Mustard, she was bound from Liverpool with salt, undoubtedly expecting to load cotton at Apalachicola, Florida, her intended destination. No such luck. In mid-Atlantic, the vessel ran into heavy seas and began to labor badly, springing a leak. She stayed on course, keeping "one pump constantly going." The leak worsened. Then Mustard "discovered that the Main Mast was sprung and the Brig leaking badly it was considered... necessary to make for the nearest port."[3] The nearest port turned out to be Bath. The *Noble* was so badly damaged that she had to be stripped of her cargo and extensively repaired. She was then rerigged as a bark and continued in service under Noble Maxwell's ownership until the mid-1840s.[4]

While Mustard was commanding the *Noble*, that vessel's namesake was skipper of the Patten ship *Majestic*. Noble Maxwell turned over command of the *Majestic* to Mustard in 1840, whereupon the latter reenacted his previous mishap, bringing a leaky vessel home for repairs in August of that year.[5] The fact that damaged Patten vessels put into Bath if possible indicates a company policy of undertaking major repair jobs at home.

One of the Patten workhorses was the ship *Caspian*, built in 1834. In 1852, she left Charleston for Le Havre, loaded with cotton. Outward bound, the ship struck the Charleston bar but proceeded on her way in leaky condition. As she crossed the Atlantic, she took on so much water that even the captain had to take a trick at the pumps. Worse, as the *Caspian* approached the English coast, she grounded on a ledge. Managing to work herself into Plymouth, she was in such bad shape that Captain Gilbert Patten, John's twenty-nine-year-old son, traveled to England to oversee her extensive repairs. A later voyage took the *Caspian* from Newport, Wales, to New Orleans under Captain George Delano. Learning that New Orleans was in the grip of a yellow-fever epidemic, George F. Patten sent instructions that the *Caspian* should anchor at a distance from the city and all hands should evacuate the vessel for the duration of the epidemic. The letter arrived too late; Captain Delano and several crew had already become sick and died.[6]

The *Caspian*'s next master illustrates another point about how the Pattens recruited skippers from the local talent pool. Llewellyn Scott Wyman of Phippsburg began a long career as a captain when he assumed command of the *Caspian* in 1853 at the ripe old age of twenty-two. Subsequently, he commanded the Patten vessels *Florence*, *Champlain*, and *Canada*. Retiring in 1875, Wyman later was associated with shipbuilding in the Damariscotta area.[7]

The venerable *Caspian* met her end on the Gingerbread Grounds, Bahamas, in 1854, while carrying ice from Boston to New Orleans. The Pattens immediately built a second

The ship *Caspian* in a tight spot in the Gulf of Venice, 7 August 1847. The *Caspian* survived a number of close calls before being lost in 1854 while freighting ice from New York to New Orleans. *Courtesy Mystic Seaport Museum, Mystic, CT.*

Caspian, whose life proved as short as her predecessor's had been long. In 1855, after taking her share of hard knocks, she too came to grief. The loss of the second *Caspian* yielded a priceless story.

While the ship was lying at New Orleans in 1858, the crew purportedly was annoyed by a sad-eyed dog intent upon getting aboard. After being put off the ship several times, the hound came aboard again and was unceremoniously thrown overboard by an exasperated sailor. Undaunted, he swam ashore and came on board yet again. At this point, his canine persistence was rewarded and he became part of the *Caspian's* crew.

Fourteen days out, the *Caspian* was blown onto a reef on the north coast of Cuba. Powerful surf carried away the ship's boats. Then the masts let go, one of them killing Captain William Trufant, a well-liked veteran who also had skippered the first *Caspian*. The surf carried the ship close to land, but there was no way for the crew to get ashore or for those gathering on the beach to render assistance. Suddenly someone remembered the dog, secured a rope around his neck, and threw the pooch overboard. Sure enough, he made it to the beach. The rope around his neck had been attached to a stout line, which people ashore made fast to a tree. A bosun's chair was then attached to the secured line and, one by one, all hands made it to shore safely, including the now-widowed Mrs. Trufant.[8]

Surprises were not always bad ones, however. In 1840, the Pattens launched the bark *Florence*, a general-purpose freighter that sailed under the Anchor Line flag until 1863. In 1855, under the command of Timothy Mitchell, the *Florence* was on a transatlantic voyage when she spotted a vessel in distress. She proved to be the Neapolitan schooner *La Lucie*, whose crew was taken aboard the *Florence*. *La Lucie* sank soon after the evacuation. Mitchell carried the crew to Marseille, where the proper reports were made. The Neapolitan consul offered to compensate the Pattens for the expense involved in the rescue and provide Mitchell with a gratuity to boot, but he declined these gestures. According to the U.S. consul at Marseille, Mitchell's response was that the rescue "was but an act of humanity which seamen are always prompt to perform...I am highly gratified by the thanks of the consul and obliged by the offer of remuneration; but which latter I myself decidedly decline as I am sure would also my owners at home. I feel happy that under Providence I have been instrumental in rescuing from a watery grave the lives of His Neapolitan Majesty's seamen and those feelings are the only recompense I desire."[9] Impressed by Mitchell's gesture, Ferdinand II, King of the Two Sicilies, ordered a gold medal struck for Mitchell that was delivered through official channels to the United States.

A second opportunity for heroism came to Mitchell during his command of the ship *George F. Patten*. The twelve-year-old *Patten* was off the coast of Portugal in 1860 when she came upon boats of the British bark *Mary Bannatyne*, whose captain and crew had abandoned her in a sinking condition. The distressed mariners were taken aboard the *Patten* and conveyed to Cadiz. Mitchell, having once again declined any compensation for his rescue, received a telescope from the British government.[10]

Dramatic highs and lows were by definition untypical of everyday — or every-year — life aboard Patten vessels. Luckily, enough primary material has survived to provide a taste of that workaday routine. The most amusing source is the shipboard journal of Ezekiel Welch, who was aboard the ship *Sheffield* in 1846. Welch, age twenty-six, hailed from Topsham and may have been an in-law of the *Sheffield*'s twenty-nine-year-old master, John P. Smith. Welch had an irreverent streak and obviously got a kick out of his jottings at the time. They are still enjoyable.

The *Sheffield* was a fast sailer. Her first captain was Noble Maxwell, for whom the Pattens had built her in 1836. Ten years later, under Smith, she loaded cotton at New Orleans and sailed for Genoa. As Welch described, the outward-bound *Sheffield* "exchanged signals with the ship Caspian of Bath from Liverpool bound to Charleston…we have a fresh breeze from the S. Eastward and dark cloudy weather with some lightning, four or five ships in company but we are out-sailing all of them as usual. they cant hold a candle to the old Sheffield no how they can fix it for she is up and gone."[11]

Most common merchant seamen were too busy to keep written records of their voyages, even if inclined to do so. Officers were more apt to maintain journals, but these usually were clinical, logbook-style accounts intended for future reference. Welch's

The Patten bark *Florence* (1840), shown entering the port of Naples. With Timothy Mitchell in command in 1855, the *Florence* rescued the crew of a distressed Neapolitan schooner, an act that earned Mitchell a gold medal from the King of the Two Sicilies. The *Florence* was part of the Patten fleet until 1863 and remained active until 1875. *Courtesy Sharon Sewall.*

The *George F. Patten*, built in 1848 for transatlantic freighting. During the American Civil War, under her namesake's ownership, she eked out a living hauling guano from the Chincha Islands, Peru, to Europe. She continued her postwar career under Norwegian ownership as the *Claus Heftze*. Courtesy Maine Maritime Museum.

journal was different because, apparently, he was neither a sailor nor an officer but a passenger, which afforded him enough time to note down trivial but fascinating details: "Saturday 28th March.... at 6 PM threw the Cat over board for reasons best known to myselfe.... Sunday 29th march... at 4 PM Capt. and myself took a little Brandy punch to pass off the time sociable. he is now playing on the accordean for our amusement.... Monday 30th March.... The carpenter doing to a he pig what he would not like to have done to him selfe.... the Capt cracking nuts and jokes.... Friday April 4th.... We have four pigs on board and when the ship lays down on her side they are not able to stand on the deck and it is amuseing to see them sliding down to leward one after the other and then watch them chance to get to the windward and the first lee lurch, away they goe to leward again."

Welch apparently roomed in Captain Smith's quarters. Well into the Atlantic, the *Sheffield* was struck by a heavy sea that "knocked in all of our cabin windows and filled the Cabin half full of water which has spoiled a quantity of our stores and wet most part of our clothing." But the weather soon moderated, providing an opportunity to watch porpoises playfully keeping company with the *Sheffield*. Welch also had his journal for company, and he never missed a chance to caricature his pal the skipper: "Monday 6th

April '46.... the Capt is about going to bed he says he will take a look at his wife before he turns in. he gets the Minature [portrait and] says he thinks she looks rather cross tonight. the Capt and myselfe have just ben taken some Lemon Ade."

More heavy weather. On 12 April, "The ship is sailing at her utmost speed which is very pleasant. but she is groaning dreadfully under her very heavy press of canvass, but she must take it and she darts forward with all the mad fury of some wild annimal and hurles the waves to the right and left as her bold prow comes in contact with them and leaves them far behind in a broad sheat of undulating foam and the scene is awfully grand."

Such a description is a reminder that service aboard a merchant sailing vessel involved a steady round of strenuous tasks. One need not know the fine points of rigging to get a sense of the activity: "Friday 17th April. Today we have all sorts of winds and weather. At 6 A.M. it blew almost a perfect hurricane from the Southward and weather looks very bad. Called all hands and close reefed the topsails furled the fore and mizen topsail jibs and Mainsail and hove the ship to.... wind moderating and halling to the westward Squared away and let out close reefs. At [noon] let out all reefs and set top galant sails and one top-mast studdingsail.... At 4 PM set lower studding sails."

Three days later, in pleasant weather and with all sails set, the crew had a leisurely break. "The hands are l[o]unging about the decks in groups, some reading some sewing and some working. The Capt amuseing himselfe by tieing up Corn in pieces of Canvass and giving it to the pigs to see them work the Canvass open to get the Corn out." The rest of the account was a matter of routine. On 2 May, the *Sheffield* entered the Straits of Gibraltar, and on 14 May she took on a Genoa pilot.

The sights of Genoa exceeded Welch's expectations. "We find this a fine harbour and is easy of access. there is a Friget and several other men of war here and [a] large fleet of Merchantmen. Genoa is a very beautifull place to look at from the harbour. it is at the foot of very high Mountains, is Walled in by double walls and very Strongly fortified. In the evening we have a plenty of Music and ringing of bells & Several boats with ladies came off a long side and pulled around us &c &c...." While stevedores unloaded the *Sheffield*, her crew received shore leave in the city. On 29 May, Welch and the second mate went to the opera and took in "some great dancing and a variety of other things to numerous to mention...."

The ship took on stone ballast and prepared to head for Leghorn to load marble for New York. On 3 June, the day she was to set sail, "the Capt Recvd a letter from Leghorn stateing thus and so too which he refuses. therefore he has desided to go to Cadiz for Salt from there to Bath.... Monday June 8th. All this day we have a fresh breeze from the South Westward and fine pleasant weather. hands employed in various ways, some scrapeing ship and others trimming bal[l]est. Carpenter makeing an adition to the Transom seet in the Cabin and making bal[l]est tubs &c This Eve three Brigs in company."

The *Sheffield* loaded salt and recrossed the Atlantic without incident. Several days out of Bath, all hands were put to painting ship. Then came the challenge that had been the undoing of so many. "Sunday August 2d '46. At midnight made Monhegan [Island] light 15 miles dist. at 4 AM made Seguin. at 11 took a pilot and stood in for the mouth of the River, with a light air from the Eastward and tide runing out. at Pond Island we was becalmed [and] came very neer going ashore let go all the halyards and Anchor at the same time. we lay there a short time and got under weay again with the Boat a head, and came up to town. At 6 PM let go anchor and furled all sails."

His journal and voyage ended, we hear no more of Ezekiel Welch. The *Sheffield*, however, did not tarry long in Bath. Captain Smith took her to New Orleans for cotton, which he freighted to Liverpool, arriving there on 19 December 1846. She was similarly engaged in 1847. In that year, the Pattens sold her to a Boston firm for which she continued in the cotton and emigrant trade. During the Civil War, when American commerce was a risky proposition, she was sold to British interests. The *Sheffield* was still sailing as late as 1870.

The records of Captain Abner Wade provide quite a different perspective, dramatizing the rigors of command, a topic totally omitted in Welch's good-old-boy portrayal of Captain Smith. Between 1845 and 1859, Wade was master of several Patten vessels. In the early 1850s, while in his early thirties, he maintained an informative journal of his exploits in the cotton and emigrant trades.[12]

Abner Wade grew up on a farm on scenic Phipps Neck in Woolwich, across the Kennebec from Bath. The eldest child of a large, fatherless family, he went to sea at sixteen. In 1843, he married Sarah Ayer of Sangerville, Maine, and the young couple took up residence in that inland town. Wade's first command came two years later, at age twenty-eight. A family story tells of how the young skipper saved the life of a sailor who had fallen overboard at the mouth of the Kennebec. Like most seafarers, the unfortunate sailor could not swim; but Wade, hollering at the top of his lungs, ordered him to do so — and he did, at least long enough to be rescued by one of the ship's lowered boats.

In 1849, John Patten's son Gilbert turned over command of the 797-ton *Halcyon* to Wade. The *Halcyon*'s regular route was between New Orleans (cotton) and Liverpool (passengers). While in Liverpool, Wade bought himself a blank journal to fill with his account of the voyage back to the United States. After a minimal refit to accommodate a human cargo, the empty cotton freighter loaded three hundred emigrants, mostly Irish. For the long passage to New York, most of these passengers would be packed like sardines into extremely cramped, squalid, dormitory-type quarters in which they were expected to prepare their own food. Few who boarded knew what discomforts lay in store.

The rude awakening began on the first day out of Liverpool, when the *Halcyon* ran into heavy northwesterly winds and a current to match. Reducing sail, as seemed necessary, would probably set the ship back onto the British coast, so Wade pressed on: "Monday, 30th Sept [1850].... It was necessary to carry a heavy press of canvas to keep the ship off the shore. Anyone who knows anything of the geography of this part of

England can understand the situation.... It is well known that there is a strong in-draught into Bristol Channel; this together with the heave of the sea and the natural current...will be admitted a sufficiently critical position.

"As the gale increased in force I made up my mind that it would be impossible to weather [the hazardous Isles of Scilly, off the west coast of Cornwall] and that the ship must go ashore. I had no doubt that before morning's dawn the good old 'Halcyon' with her living freight of over three hundred souls, would be broken on the shore, and not one left to tell the tale.... Nothing but the mercy of God in causing the wind to haul saved us; the wind did haul and we were enabled to head off shore. Not however before we had carried away a Main Topsail, Fore topmast Staysail, split a Mizen Topsail & Jib — besides straining violently all the other sails. The gale and sea continued in unmitigated violence till after 12 o'c[lock midnight]....

"Wed 2nd [October].... Com[mence]d with light breeze and good weather.... Some of the passengers sick with the usual complaints of imigrants on first going to sea, viz colds, headaches, loss of appetite, indigestion, congestions (slight) etc. etc. nothing serious however and nothing but will yield probably to good medical treatment *like my own*....

"Thursday 3d.... O the beauties of carrying 'the finest Pisintry in the World' to America! Some want rice, some tea — all want medicine, and generally none are satisfied. My time is taxed to the full in the capacity of 'Doctor', But if by the use of such

Captain Abner Wade, master of the Patten ships *Halcyon* and *Falcon*. Before ill health forced his retirement in 1859, Wade experienced some tough scrapes as a shipmaster, vividly described in his personal journal. *Courtesy Sutherland Family.*

knowledge as I possess and such medicines as are at my command I can in any way amelliorate the condition of the poor creatures I shall be most happy to do it.... The more I see of the emigration system the more I wonder that agents should continue to dupe them as they do. To-day a 'Paddy' came to me for his allowance of potatoes, nothing doubting that the said praties [potatoes] would be duly served out.... he was led to the suppostition that he could have potatoes whenever he chose to demand them by the passenger broker who 'did his business' in L[iver]pool....[13]

"Thursday, 10th.... All the passengers in very good condition considering that for the last two days we have had rough weather, which generally brings on more or less complaints under various names...but which may generally [be] set down to seasickness, or debility occasioned by it.... In my 'practice', when a passenger calls for medicine and enumerates, as he is almost sure to do, a long string of ailments which he thinks afflicts his system, I never fail to prescribe for him, give him medicines with very particular directions, and very seldom fail of effecting a rapid and satisfactory cure." Wade's favorite nostrum was colored water with molasses.

Seasickness subsided among the passengers but an epidemic of measles broke out, killing one child. Another died of dysentery — all quite routine matters in the U.S. passenger trade. Wade did what he could to keep the miserable, sick children comfortable, but he resented parents' insinuations that the contagion somehow was his fault.

Shipboard tension was worsened by adverse weather, which greatly retarded the *Halcyon*'s progress across the Atlantic. On 9 November, she raised the coast of Hispaniola. Now in steamy weather, the ship steered south of Cuba and into the Gulf of Mexico. She made New Orleans about 22 November 1850.

Twelve weeks later, filled with cotton, the *Halcyon* was towed downstream from New Orleans by the steamboat *Phenix*. She prepared to set sail for Liverpool, only to ground on the bar. It took five days of effort to float her off. She then made her way through the Florida Keys, picking up the Gulf Stream off Palm Beach. The days when Bath ships were manned by expert local seamen had long since passed, and, to put it mildly, Wade was not pleased with the crew's seamanship: "Friday 21st [March 1851].... Steering East per compass, or at least that is the course given but God knows not very strictly followed, for such a set of ragamuffins for steering as the present mob on board the 'Halcyon' I never saw and hope to 'never see the like again.' I have been obliged repeatedly to shorten sail for no other earthly reason than to abate the speed of the ship so that these Johnny Raws might keep her somewhere within 8 or 9 points of the course given....

"Thursday 27th.... Com'd with fresh gale from WSW, cloudy weather but no rain. This is the first wind from S.W.d we have had without rain during the passage. I wish we could also have clear weather to enable us to obtain observations of the sun, for with the steering of the precious specimens of the genus homo under my command it will be hard work to find the mouth of the channel [between Ireland and Britain] unless by some means or other it has grown wider than it used to be....

"Friday 28th... Have now about five or six days sail to our destination and O how I wish we may have fair winds and clear weather to finish the passage which has become tedious. And then I want to hear from my wife and babies and all that sort of thing. 'Tis sweet to know there is an eye awaits our coming and will look brighter when we come.'"

After forty days at sea, the *Halcyon* "arrived in Liverpool on the first day of April, rather arrived in the [Mersey] river, for we came to anchor on the first in the evening."

Emigrants again, although apparently a smaller number than on the previous voyage. Exhausted and infuriated by the passenger trade's red tape, Wade escaped Liverpool at last, heading for New York on 17 May 1851. The voyage proceeded uneventfully until 8 June, on the Grand Bank southeast of Newfoundland, at which point Wade's daily account ends, and for good reason. A later account in his hand continues the story: "...4 AM blowing fresh from S.E. and increasing fast. From 4 to 6 close reefed Fore and Maine Topsails furled Mizen Topsail & Mainsail. [At] 8 blew heavy gale with very heavy sea running. About 8:30 ship broached to against her helm and rolled tremendously. After taking three or four heavy rolls the Fore and Main Masts went by the board — the foremast going over the side to leeward and Mainmast falling on lee side fore and aft and lodging against the house and lee rail — taking with it the Mizen Topmast and breaking the Mizen Mast off below the top. The broken spars over the side were now thump-

"Nothing but the mercy of God saved us," wrote Captain Abner Wade after the Patten ship *Halcyon* came through a fierce gale off the Isles of Scilly, outward bound from Liverpool in 1850. This portrait, painted in Liverpool about that time, shows the *Halcyon* off South Stack lighthouse, Anglesey, at the entrance to the Mersey River. The *Halcyon* was lost off the Grand Banks in 1851. *Courtesy Sutherland Family.*

ing the ship severely. Com'd immediately to cut away the wreck. All the masts being gone the ship was rolling in a mass from side to side, breaking one pump and injuring the other and starting the booby hatch so as to let the water below...."

Before they were cut away, the floating spars, held to the ship by a tangle of rigging, damaged the *Halcyon*'s rudder, leaving the dismasted vessel entirely unmanageable. According to Wade, "The ship now lay in a trough of the sea...and rolled fearfully, sea making a complete breach over her. Secured the hatches and nailed canvass about the stumps of the masts to prevent water going below." Meanwhile, a mast of sorts had been jury-rigged from a spare yard, but the ship's violent rolling prevented its installation. The crew "got the water out of between decks also remains of Passengers effects which had been mostly all broken up and destroyed."

On 11 June, recalled Wade, "[We] determined should an opportunity offer to get the passengers at least off of the wreck." After a harrowing night, two ships were spotted heading in the *Halcyon*'s direction from the west. "About 10 the first ship spoke us — Wm H. Wharton from Mobile for L'pool. Told him our situation & he agreed to assist. Got our boats into the water, the other ship did the same and commenced immediately transferring passengers, provisions & water.... Between 10 & 11 the other ship, the Connecticut, also from Mobile for Liverpool spoke and proffered assistance. Sent her boats and began the work of transferring passengers etc."

Getting the passengers off took another day. On Friday the thirteenth, after consulting the officers and men, Wade decided to abandon the *Halcyon*.

Although the incident had occurred just a few days out of New York (Eldorado to the many emigrants aboard), the rescuing vessels were bound in the opposite direction. Consequently, the *Halcyon* crew and passengers found themselves en route to Liverpool. Upon arriving, Wade was offered passage to Bath aboard the Houghton ship *Pelican State*, so he headed for home. The fate of the *Halcyon*'s hapless passengers is not known, but their state of mind can easily be imagined.

According to family tradition, G.F. & J. Patten took the *Halcyon* disaster in stride, even praising Wade's seamanship under pressure and his safe evacuation of everyone aboard. Accordingly, after Wade had rested up for three months, he was given another Patten command: the three-year-old *Falcon*. Built for the cotton trade, the 813-ton *Falcon*, like the *Halcyon*, had been under the command of John Patten's son Gilbert. On 10 January 1852, having traveled by sea from Maine to New Orleans, Wade assumed command and resumed his journal-keeping.

"New Orleans to L'pool

"Left town evening at 10.30 P.M. Friday Jan'y 15th. Came to anchor inside the bar next day at 10 AM, our crew in a drunken and disorderly state. Used such means as was considered advisable to render them subordinate and got under weigh at 1.30 PM with tow boats Mississippi and DeSoto and went over the bar without stopping. Made all necessary sail....

"February 1st [west of Bermuda].... Going along at 9½ knots. I am inclined to think that we are enough out of trim to affect our sailing materially... for it is not possible that this ship, if everything were right about it could go as little as 9½ with the pleasant wind we have now and the sail we are carrying.... [7 February 1852]: Three weeks out and not half passage. Heighho! Long passage this time as usual. Mr. Wade you drive a slow coach *generally*. Afternoon very strong breeze. Carrying a press of sail as there are no indications of immediate bad weather.... [10 February, northwest of the Azores]: Com'd with strong breeze from N.W.'d and beautiful weather for the time of year. All prudent sail set. Going along nicely, 8-12 moderate wind hauling to N.'d. Made more sail. [11 February]: Through the latter part the weather beautiful and breeze steady. Made more sail. I never have before seen so much pleasant weather in making a passage at this season of the year as we have had lately."

On 18 February, under shortened sail in rainy weather, Wade came upon a sight that undoubtedly reawakened painful memories: "At 5:30 PM passed the wreck of a Brig of about 200 tons, everything gone above the deck except stump of the foremast. Full of water and had apparently been in that condition for some time." That was the last event of note until the *Falcon* made Liverpool on 2 March 1852.

Wade's journal says little about his subsequent voyages in the *Falcon*. She crossed to New York, then headed for London via Saint John, New Brunswick, where she probably loaded deals (cut boards). At Saint John, Wade's crew deserted, precipitating a delay of several weeks while replacements were shipped from Boston. The captain's minimal coverage of the desertion is tantalizing, for there undoubtedly was a story here worthy of a chapter in itself. What was the cause of this brouhaha so unusual in the merchant service? Who was involved? With her new crew, the *Falcon* carried New Brunswick lumber to London, took on emigrants at Bremerhaven, and crossed again to New Orleans. Wade confided no opinions about his human cargo on this voyage, although it is doubtful that he had mellowed any about the emigrant trade.

Two days after the *Falcon* left the River Weser for New Orleans, another Patten packet, the brand-new *Mobile*, sailed from Liverpool with sixty passengers. She, too, was bound for New Orleans, but she never made it. The *Mobile* struck Arklow Bank on the Irish coast and was lost. Seventy-four people, including Captain Joseph Tarbox, died. Nine survivors blamed the disaster on a faulty course laid out by the ship's second mate.[14] Wade probably would not know of the *Mobile*'s unhappy fate until his arrival in New Orleans on 24 November.

Abner Wade then moved to the Patten ship *Assyria*, which, at 1,364 tons, was the largest vessel in the Anchor Line. In 1857, he suffered a heart attack, followed by convalescence in his Sangerville home. In 1858, the Pattens contacted him again: "We write to inquire with regard to the state of your health — whether you are able to go to sea again, and if so, if you would like once more to take charge of a Ship."[15] So eager for his services was the company that Wade was offered his choice of available Patten ships. He opted for the cotton freighter *Amity*. She would be his last command.

Wade's health seemed to worsen. He had consulted New York and London doctors, who assured him he had only a year to live; so, in 1859, forty-two-year-old "Cappy" Wade swallowed the anchor and returned to Sangerville, planning to spend his last year with his family. A family photograph taken some years later shows him ensconced comfortably in his rocker, reflecting on the ways of the world. An avid reader in many fields, including history, theology, archaeology, and literature, Cappy Wade has fooled the doctors. He lives quietly for another thirty-six years, during which he helps manage a woolen mill and takes an active part in town affairs. The "Sage of Sangerville" dies in 1896.

When Abner Wade gave up the *Falcon* in 1853, his replacement was Captain Jarvis Patten, destined to become one of the stars of the family's younger generation. A second cousin of George and John, Jarvis was born in Bowdoinham in 1827. During his early career, he joined the ranks of Pattens whose lives revolved around the sea. But Jarvis's generation was different, owing to the family's increasingly upward mobility. Thanks to his clergyman father, John (a Bowdoin College graduate who had inherited the Robert Patten farm in Bowdoinham), Jarvis had received a classical education that refined his genteel sensibility. He acquired fluency in French and, in later life, was an amateur poet, like his older brother and fellow captain Bardwell. A photograph taken of him in young adulthood reveals the focused gaze of a man whose eyes are on bigger, better things.

But a Patten was a Patten, so Jarvis went to sea. In 1851, he received command of the company ship *Delaware* and also married Charlotte Whittemore. The next year, the first of the couple's eight children was born. In 1854, Jarvis replaced Abner Wade as skipper of the *Falcon* and commenced a private journal of his maritime experiences over eighteen voyages — all in a single volume. A century and a half later, that document is the most informative available account of daily life aboard a Patten ship. For the most part, it reads like a logbook, being a clinical inventory of sailing tactics, weather conditions, and navigational data. Occasionally, however, personal inspiration takes over.[16]

Because some of Jarvis Patten's voyages were outside the cotton trade, his journal provides examples of how G.F. & J. Patten had diversified their ships. In April 1855, for example, the *Falcon*, having discharged her usual cargo in Liverpool, loaded a thousand tons of coal for Constantinople, a destination that surely fired the imagination of her erudite skipper. The coal was intended to supply British, French, and Turkish forces opposing Russia in the Crimean War and probably was earmarked for use by naval vessels.

The Crimean conflict was a godsend for shipowners, since the Western world had entered another period of economic recession and financial jitters — factors that cut demand for cotton and, in turn, cotton freighters. The crisis was worsened by an oversupply of vessels built during the expansionist 1840s. At the end of that decade, gold fever in California engendered a mania for speed, resulting in fast, sharp ships with reduced cargo capacity and sail plans that required large crews. Came the crunch and those "clippers" simply couldn't compete.

The Pattens, like most Bath shipbuilders, had not been seduced by the speed craze;

so, in the hard times of the 1850s, their capacious, cost-effective fleet retained a competitive advantage. At the same time, the logistical support of allied forces in the faraway Crimea created a sudden, enormous demand for shipping. Cotton traders that otherwise would have been idle got busy running to and from the Ottoman Empire. This serendipity was somewhat offset by several years' worth of miserable, dangerous weather in the North Atlantic, which used up ships, claimed lives, and of course increased maintenance costs.

Fire in his eye: the young Jarvis Patten. After a distinguished, eventful career in sail and steam, Jarvis became a broker in London, U.S. consul in Antwerp, and, in 1884, America's first commissioner of navigation. *Courtesy Maine Maritime Museum.*

By the time Jarvis Patten loaded English coal for Constantinople, he knew all about the North Atlantic's foul weather. His run from Charleston to Liverpool had been an ordeal of adverse winds, gales, and squalls. Exasperated with the *Falcon*'s slow, toilsome progress, Patten admitted in his journal on 14 February 1855 that sailing "to Liverpool is a hard road to travel I believe, this year anyhow but I am not alone in my misfortune which is a comfort." Four days later: "48 days out [of Charleston] and still an east wind that beats all the east winds for longer than I ever saw." Finally, on 27 February: "At 3 PM arrived off Lpool & at 10 PM into dock. So ends this passage of 56 days the longest I ever made and I hope ever will make."

Because the *Falcon* would be sailing into temperate waters on her upcoming voyage, Patten had her hull coppered in Liverpool. His ship loaded with coal, and with George F. Patten's eighteen-year-old son and junior partner, George M., aboard for company, Captain Jarvis departed for Constantinople on 3 April 1855. Eleven days later, she passed Gibraltar, entering the Mediterranean. Another three days, off the Algerian coast, the skipper broke his businesslike account with a rare personal entry: "O If I had my darling Lottie how much shorter these long days would seem." Although many captains sailed with their wives and children aboard, the practice was not permitted in the Anchor Line, probably because of bitter experience. The brothers' younger sister, Pauline, married to distant cousin William Patten, died in Havana aboard his ship, probably of yellow fever, a perpetual threat to Yankees visiting the tropics. Jarvis Patten was accustomed to long separations, but as a relative newlywed with a baby son, time away from home had a new poignancy. Such poignancy was hardly dulled by the fact that the *Falcon*'s first mate, William Whittemore (a burgeoning captain), was Lottie's brother. At least Jarvis could look forward to letters that almost certainly awaited him in Constantinople.

By 6 May, the ship had "run up to the Entrance of the Dardanelles.... dropped down to three miles NE by E of Cape Janisary & anchored in 14 fath[om]s water — A large fleet at anchor here and an English and French frigate. Saw a Sardinian steam frigate with troops pass up into the Dardanelles.[17] At 3 PM went ashore at the Turkish town of [Çanakkale] near the site of Ancient Troy the ruins of which we saw & the reputed tombs of Achilles and Hector — bought a sheep, some fowl & eggs & saw a Greek dance...."

So much for culture. Patten found traffic so heavy in the Dardanelles that a steam tow could not be had at any price. He therefore decided to proceed under sail through the long, narrow passage into the Sea of Marmara. The *Falcon* anchored in the Golden Horn on 10 May, unloaded unspecified goods, then proceeded three days later to the Turkish arsenal to discharge her coal. The route took her under two bridges, but, as Patten recorded, a "steamer run us into one & done some damage." When unloading began, the skipper, for whom time was money, deemed the Turks "very slow." On their best day, they managed to unburden the *Falcon* of 60 tons, so it took an entire month to empty her. On 25 June, free at last, the ship got past one of the Golden Horn bridges but was delayed alongside the second "on acct of a Man of war passing to hurry Capt Lyons wounded before Sebastopol."

Because of the vast array of vessels (including the celebrated new superclipper *Great Republic*) clogging the harbor, Patten had to secure an exit tow from a Royal Navy tug. On 1 July, the *Falcon* departed for Valletta, Malta, for a medical inspection — a precaution probably intended to contain the ravages of "Crimean fever," a wartime choleric outbreak that would prove more lethal than battle casualties. At Valletta, Patten secured the Spanish consul's certificate that the *Falcon* was fit to load salt at Cadiz. There she headed, arriving on 31 July. She departed with her new cargo and some passengers two weeks later, destination Bath, Maine. After an uneventful transatlantic passage, she raised the offshore Maine islands of Matinicus and Monhegan and made all sail, arriving at the mouth of the Kennebec at noon, 24 September, as the weather cleared. Patten's excitement on arrival can easily be imagined, for Lottie had lately given birth to a second child, a girl. Home at last!

Not quite. When the Bath pilot came aboard the *Falcon*, he had "brought with him orders from the owners to proceed to Boston with the ship, the cargo being sold there. Therefore after putting some of our passengers & effects into the pilot boat [and] hauled off to the SSW — Good bye George M P[atten] — I shall miss you *some*. At 4 took departure from Seguin bearing NNE dist[ant] 10 miles.... At 4 AM made Cape Ann Lights — At 7 got a Boston Pilot.... at 11 came to anchor in Boston Harbor —

"So ends our long voyage."

There was time back in Bath for but a short interlude with Lottie and the children, for another long voyage awaited. On 17 October, the *Falcon* took her crew aboard, "most all drunk," and left Boston for Savannah (where she loaded wheat and staves) and New Orleans (cotton). On 23 December, aided by two steamboats, the ship laboriously crossed the Mississippi bar and made sail for Le Havre.

In mid-Atlantic, on 18 January 1856, the barometer started to drop and the winds picked up. The following day, it was "blowing very hard.... Furled everything snug except my spencer & an old stay sail in the miz[zen] rigging which I find very servic[e]able in keeping her up to the wind as the sea runs very high & irregular — Shipped two very ugly ones which stove our bullwarks in & Galley doors & windows of houses & other damage — I think the ship is a little too much by the storm to lay well or has too much wheat in for she rolls badly...."

Things continued in that vein for several more days. Then, on 6 February, a few days out of Le Havre, "a *screamer* from SW" overtook the *Falcon*. The ship was dangerously close to the notorious Scilly Isles, which made for some tense sailing. Then the winds shifted again, this time to the east, blowing in the very face of Jarvis Patten. "Oh how much to[o] bad to be jamed in here & not able to get round Scillys when 40 miles more would have cleared them. Very hard very hard indeed." The ship was taking steady punishment but getting nowhere. "Oh dear," confided Patten on 20 February, "poor unfortunate Falcon When will our luck change...." It changed the next day, and the *Falcon* made Le Havre on 27 February.

She proceeded thence to Cardiff, loaded iron, and recrossed to Savannah. After a very brief turnaround, it was cotton to Liverpool (bumping the Savannah bar while departing), completed in thirty-two days, followed by a fifty-seven-day return to Savannah with salt. It is possible that Jarvis and Lottie Patten were able to spend time together at this point — but not much, if any. The *Falcon* sailed again for Liverpool on 15 December, a passage she completed in twenty-nine days. Later in 1857, a transatlantic crossing to New Orleans took sixty-five days, mostly unremarkable but for one exception: On 19 October, in mid-Atlantic, "Dan'l Henwright aged 17 yrs a native of Tralee Ireland fell overboard & was drowned." Falling overboard from a ship under sail almost always resulted in drowning because of the time required to haul aback, lower, and search. Ironically, Henwright's death occurred not in the teeth of a storm but on a fine day with a moderate breeze. Jarvis Patten's journal provides no other details.

Most of Patten's daily accounts of the *Falcon*'s voyages reveal only the meteorological conditions, the vessel's progress, and the tactics employed to keep her moving safely and efficiently. In other words, they typify the mundane details that were the very stuff of the merchant service. A close examination of the journal will provide any reader with a sense of the decision-making and muscle power required to keep a vessel out of danger and in the money. Here is a typical example, written on 3 February 1857 with the *Falcon* outward bound from Liverpool: "Breeze increasing from the SW 3 PM tacked to SSE & at 6 tacked again to WNW & shortened sail 8½ wore to SSE — Midnight all sail in but 2 close reefed topsails & blowing a gale. Woer [Wore ship] to WNW — 4 AM woer again to WNW & begins to rain — 8 AM lull & wind baffles to west. wore to SSW — Soon after which cants back to south quarter — Ends raining. Several sail in company. Holy Head [Wales] in sight bearing ESE & the Irish shore — judged our selves to be about mid channel.

"Bar. 29.40, Ther 48, 4 days out."

So it went, with unbroken attention to the nuances of sailing advantage — as usual, time was money — and an unblinking eye on the weather.

Times were tough for cotton in 1857. On 1 May, at New Orleans and apparently without a cargo, Patten received word that the *Falcon* should proceed to Bic, Quebec, an island on the south shore of the St. Lawrence River, for orders. Her cargo would be deals (lumber), probably for a European port. The *Falcon* crossed the bar on 5 May, rounded the Florida Keys, and made her way up the eastern seaboard of North America.

On 24 May, she was off the south shore of Nova Scotia in thick fog. According to Patten, "at 3 PM fogg clears of[f] when saw the land — coast of Nova Scotia." This meant trouble: The *Falcon* was inshore, possibly among granite ledges. Patten estimated his position as just off Country Harbour, Nova Scotia; then the fog closed in again. "Stationed the officer of the Deck & Watch on forecastle keeping lookout, the fogg being dense." Cautiously, under shortened sail, the vessel made her way eastward about ninety-nine miles by the captain's calculation. Soundings indicated thirty-nine fathoms and a sandy bottom, which Patten assumed was the Scatari Bank off the eastern end of Cape Breton Island, with open ocean to the east — a proper course for the Gulf of St. Lawrence.

Just before eight A.M., the crew "sounded again with 29 fathoms fine sand and the ship was paying off her course not having gone ⅛ of a mile. When saw the rocks close on board put the helm up. but the ship did not pay off half a point when she brought up on a solid ledge of Rocks staving her stem & bows badly the first blow — Hove all aback but the rocks about the ship & under her were so sharp & the sea running so high that the ship immediately bilged & filled with water. in half an hour she went ashore which was at 8 AM & before night the sharp rocks we[re] sticking up through her timbers & she was broken amidships.

"The sea was running too high to work this day, it breaking on the ship & threatening to break her to pieces every moment.

"At first [I] thought I was ashore on Scatari but when the fogg cleared away, found we were run ashore near Big Lorin [Lorraine] Head...." The vessel had piled up on the southeast shore of Cape Breton just east of Louisbourg, miles to the west of Patten's assumed position.

Captain and crew took stock of their situation: "This is a shocking wild coast although there are plenty of good Harbors — If we had fell in a mile or less to East we might have run into a fine snug little harbor and not have known it the fogg was so thick."

The next two days were spent stripping the broken ship of sails and rigging. With no chance of timely instructions from the owners and no buyers on Cape Breton, Patten hired a local schooner, *Camilla,* to take the *Falcon* remnants to Bath. The fee was $400. He also took it upon himself to auction what was left of the ship for whatever he could get. It was a bitter experience: "Saturday, May 30th. An awfull wet day & storming & wet & blowing hard from SSE.... Rather a stormy day to sell a ship but as it is the appointed day — I got up on a big rock & with the wreck of the Falcon before me the sea breaking high on her sides & the wild rocks about her & surrounded by some 30 or more Cape Breton speculators in wrecks & stolen goods — I got up on a rock...& putting on the air of an auctioneer I bid the Falcon off for $160."

The men of the late *Falcon* boarded the *Camilla* and sailed in her for Halifax on 9 June. "Went out of Little Lorin [Lorraine] harbor at 6 PM & passed the wreck of the Falcon & bid adieu to the gloomy scene of my shipwreck & the remains of our noble ship.

"Poor Falcon — one more storm & not a vestige of her will remain."

On 16 June, Patten caught the Halifax-Boston steamer. Four days later, he "arrived at Home at last in the Bosom of my family."

But not for long. And even that brief interlude was marred by the news that another Patten ship, *Clara Brookman,* had gone ashore near Squam Inlet, New Jersey, on 27 July and broken in half with an assorted cargo valued at $140,000.[18]

In October 1857, Captain Jarvis took command of the year-old, 960-ton *John Patten* — cotton again — and continued skippering company vessels during the 1860s, as did his older brother Bardwell.

Well off, well seasoned, and still in his thirties, Jarvis Patten has a distinguished career ahead of him. By 1866, he has retired from the quarterdeck, opening a ship brokerage, Jarvis Patten & Co., in Bath and, later, in Liverpool. He is a partner in the Liverpool ship-brokerage firm of Gillchrest & Patten. He serves as U.S. consul in Antwerp. He becomes a tireless writer and publicist for American maritime interests. In 1884, at age fifty-seven, he is appointed the first U.S. commissioner of navigation by President Chester A. Arthur. As commissioner, he effectively merges the federal government's disparate, disorganized maritime bureaucracy into a single unit and presses for a standardized measurement system for the world's merchant tonnage. His time in office is short-lived, however. With the change of administrations, he falls victim to the political spoils system, as President Grover Cleveland dismisses him in favor of a political supporter.[19] Jarvis Patten remains in Washington, DC, as a congressional lobbyist for American maritime interests. He dies in 1888 and is buried in Washington.

When the *Falcon* went on the rocks in 1857, she was a precursor of events that would affect the entire U.S. merchant marine. That year saw a financial panic that, for a while at least, wrote an end to economic optimism. One of the casualties was William Patten of Richmond, former master of G.F. & J. Patten vessels, whose shipowning partnership with Captain William Sturtevant built several vessels, including the clipper *Pride of America*, a ship that, true to her type, lost money.[20] The Panic of 1857 finished off the partnership. And in January 1858, cargoless in Mobile, Captain Charles E. Patten (the youthful son of James F. and nephew of George F. and John), master of the company ship *Britannia*, fretted to a friend that "I have been laying here so long now that I am afraid that we shall be obliged to lay here until spring as things look at present. Freights are mighty dull...."[21]

The Panic of '57 came at a time of trouble for G.F. & J. Patten, for in that year, disaster had struck two of the firm's ships. By the end of the decade, losses would amount to nine vessels totaling 7,107 gross tons. The oldest vessel lost, at twenty-one, was the *Caspian*. Newest was the second *Caspian*, which went ashore within a year of entering service. Most of these calamities were due to groundings, not structural shortcomings in the ships themselves.

With a loss rate during the 1850s of 38 percent, Patten ships were decidedly unlucky; losses and sales of ships (13 percent) produced an overall attrition rate of 50 percent. During the 1840s, with fewer losses and more sales, the rate had been 45 percent. Nonetheless, the Patten fleet continued to expand, from eleven vessels grossing 6,993 tons in 1850 to twelve grossing 11,169 tons in 1859 — a 60 percent increase in tonnage.

Losing ships, of course, was an accepted and expected part of maritime enterprise. Furthermore, the Patten record looks worse than it actually was. For one thing, Patten ships and cargoes almost certainly were insured for part if not all of their replacement value. For another, the Patten yard could build replacements as cheaply as anyone in the business. In some cases, such as the *Falcon*'s, part of a vessel's equipment and rigging was salvageable. Meanwhile, the partners, being kingpins of the Lincoln Bank (discussed in chapter 4), had ready access to capital in the tightest of times. Finally, George and John Patten made a practice of investing in other companies' vessels — dozens of them. To say that their eggs were in many baskets would be an understatement.

Proof of all this is the fact that the company's shipbuilding rate accelerated in time of loss. Usually, G.F. & J. Patten produced about one ship a year. Following a loss, however, the rate would double. In other words, if the Pattens lost a ship, they built two instead of one immediately thereafter. If anyone had the staying power to ride out the frustrating 1850s, it was George and John Patten and their associates.

This lithographic detail of the Bath waterfront, based on a sketch by Cyrus King ca. 1845, reveals G.F. & J. Patten's wharf on the shore to the right of the moored schooner's foremast. Farther right, just aft of the schooner under sail, is the company shipyard. *Courtesy Maine Maritime Museum.*

The U.S. economy revived again by the end of the 1850s, and Bath people resumed their phenomenal output of vessels for local and worldwide use. Despite the Panic of '57, the Port of Bath claimed registries of about 500 vessels. That collective tonnage made the Bath fleet the nation's fifth largest — after New York, Boston, Philadelphia, and Baltimore.[22]

With the coming of the American Civil War, however, the bottom fell out of the cotton trade. In fact, shipping anything anywhere on the high seas became a dangerous proposition because of commerce raiders flying the flag of the Confederacy. As American shipping duly shrank, British and Canadian vessels moved into the vacuum. Yankee shipbuilders and merchants would never recover from the damage they sustained during the Civil War.

Which is not to say that all shipbuilders and merchants went down to ruin in the early 1860s. As before, the Pattens rode above the storm, even though one of their vessels, *Ariel,* would fall prey to hostilities. Years before America's secession crisis blossomed into war, the now-venerable brothers were doing well in other enterprises, squeezing profits out of cargoes ranging from Canadian lumber to Peruvian guano. At the same time, as they moved into business prominence, the two founding fathers were enjoying local celebrity as public-spirited, philanthropic community leaders.

NOTES

1. Protest, Brig *Jasper* of Bath, 25 December 1835 (William Torrey Notarial Records, MMM).

2. Alexander Starbuck, *History of the American Whale Fishery* (1878; reprint Secaucus, NJ: Castle Books, 1989), pp. 468-69.

3. Protest, Brig *Noble* of Bath, 5 September 1837 (Torrey Notarial Records, MMM).

4. Burden, comp., Records of Patten Mariners and Vessels (MMM).

5. Protest, Ship *Majestic* of Bath, 27 August 1840 (Torrey Notarial Records, MMM).

6. Hennessy Historical Files (MMM).

7. Ibid.

8. Ibid.

9. J.L. Hodge (U.S. consul at Marseille) to Chevalier R. de Gayzucha (Neapolitan consul at Marseille), 9 March 1855 (copy, ibid.).

10. Lyons (British Embassy) to Lewis Cass (U.S. Secretary of State), Washington, DC, 7 May 1860 (copy, ibid.).

11. Ezekiel H. Welch, Journal kept on board ship *Sheffield* of Bath, 1846, with subsequent onshore accounts (MMM). All quotations about the 1846 *Sheffield* voyage are from this source. For clarity's sake, some of Welch's quirky spelling has been standardized.

12. Wade's journal is quoted at length and annotated in John H. Sutherland, ed., "The Journal of Captain Abner Turner Wade, Transcribed with a Commentary by A. Edward Conover" (typescript [copy], 1991, Charles E. Burden Collection, Bath, ME). Sutherland was Wade's great-grandson. Facts about Wade's career and quotations from his journal are taken from this carefully researched source.

13. Some packets (apparently not the Anchor Line's) did provide potatoes to steerage passengers to supplement the customary ration of bread and water. Any foodstuffs beyond those basics were the passengers' responsibility (Baker, p. 393).

14. *Weekly Mirror* (Bath), 3 October 1852.

15. G.F. & J. Patten to Abner Wade, Bath, 20 October 1858 (quoted in its entirety in Sutherland, p. 40).

16. Jarvis Patten, Journal kept on board ship *Falcon* of Bath, 1854-57 (MMM). Facts and quotations regarding the *Falcon*'s voyages are from this source. For clarity's sake, Patten's casual punctuation has been corrected in a few quotations.

17. The northern Italian Kingdom of Piedmont-Sardinia was another Turkish ally in the Crimean War.

18. *American Sentinel and Bath Daily Times*, 7 August 1857.

19. *The Marine Journal* (New York), 18 December 1886.

20. Baker, p. 295.

21. Charles E. Patten to "Uncle Ned" [Captain Edward P. Stinson], Mobile, AL, 13 January 1858 (Manuscript Collection VFM 801 ["Uncle Ned" correspondence], G.W. Blunt White Library, Mystic Seaport Museum, Mystic, CT).

22. Owen, p. 202.

4

"Constant Personal Attention"

In the most jittery days of the 1850s, Bath citizens could look back on the previous decade with pleasure. During the 1840s, the community hit its stride as a ship-building center, and physical evidence of civic pride was everywhere. Captain Jarvis Patten put those years in perspective: "Encouraged by the profits of a lucrative commerce, ship building continued to increase...beyond all precedent; 369 vessels of 118,732 tons were constructed, the average tonnage being 321.... The Mexican War which occurred toward the close of this epoch increased the demand for tonnage, and the freighting commerce of the country was prosperous throughout."[1]

The town of Bath was growing up. In fact, in 1847 it ceased to be a town and was rechartered as a city by the Maine legislature.

In America, prosperity and growth beget status symbols. One of the best symbols from the 1840s is a view of Bath by H.A. Hilling, believed to be an immigrant from Britain. Sitting atop a hill on the east bank of the Kennebec, Hilling produced a detailed panorama of Bath's waterfront. If you look carefully at this remarkable painting, you'll see that the view is necessarily compressed; yet the overall scene is entirely convincing. Just as important, the artist has conveyed a wholesome picture of peace and plenty, enterprise and progress. That impression is accurate, for a spirit of reform has taken hold in Bath. The temperance movement is gaining strength, and Maine will soon go Prohibitionist. Solid citizens are determined to improve the community's quality of life in other ways as well.

Look at the many vessels passing by or docked along the waterfront in Hilling's painting. Patten vessels, perhaps? Alas, for our purposes, the span of Hilling's canvas stopped short of the Patten wharf and shipyard, too far north of the downtown for inclusion, so you must use your imagination. Now look at the downtown. Especially charming and eye-catching are the white church steeples that give a lift to the skyline and inject a note of spirituality. Most imposing of these is the newly completed Winter Street Church, a

Bath in 1844: a growing, lively community. This folk-art panorama of peace and prosperity typifies American optimism of the 1840s. The artist, H.A. Hilling, meticulously crammed this painting with details, some of which still define the cityscape. Unfortunately, the Patten wharf and yard were too far upriver to fit into Hilling's delightful view. *Courtesy Maine Maritime Museum.*

voguish Gothic masterpiece whose construction was overseen by a committee of leading citizens that included George F. Patten. Images can be deceiving, however, for two of these steeples are not long for this world. The Universalist Church in midtown Bath will be torn down for commercial redevelopment in 1849. South Church, used by Catholics, will be gutted by xenophobic arsonists in an 1854 riot, leaving Captain John Patten and two other uninsured owners poorer in property and spirit.

Things come and things go, but as the details of the 1844 panorama confirm, Bath's townscape had been influenced mightily by Patten enterprise.

Now listen to Hannah Patten, and you will pick up the buzz that lay behind the lively activity seen in Hilling's painting. Like her charming sister Kate, George Patten's daughter Hannah was a walking social calendar who enjoyed keeping traveling family members up to date. Her reports reveal that Bath's gossip mill, alive and well nowadays, was firmly in place by the 1840s. In Hannah's time, well-to-do families like the Pattens had plenty of grist for the mill.

Here is Hannah's slice of Bath life, breathlessly written for Noble Maxwell when he was still in the family's good graces. In March 1841, the Pattens were in a mood to celebrate the Whig party's successful campaign to put William Henry Harrison in the White House. But that was by no means the only topic of interest: "I thought I would let you know how all the old maids of our town get along. In the first place I just tell you that Jane Peterson is crazy, they say it is not caused by the opposition of her friends to her marriage with J. Bright, but of religion which she has studied so much on the subject as to be insane.... 14th of March, we had a great ball, Mrs. Randall and her sister were there. Mr. E. Clapp was as fond of it as he could be; he danced two or three times. Mr. Holmes and wife were there. Capt. Thomas & wife, Dr. Wales & wife, Dr. Putnam, & Dr. Waldron & wife, Mrs. Marston of Augusta were there.... James Hall (the widower) is the bear of Bath. He seems to feel as if he could choose from among them all, and I do not think him far from wrong. But, to Miss Sarah McLellan & to Mrs. Marston he seemed most attentive. They both went to the ball with him. Mr. Drew goes to Mrs. Randall's quite often. Some think him engaged to her. I don't know who he is, but perhaps you do. Cyrus King still goes to Mrs. Robinson's. I forgot to mention that the evening of the 4th some of the Whigs' houses were illuminated — ours among their numbers. Mr. Clark & Pa went to Washington. They have not yet returned but I think they will in a day or two. At Washington there were some 50,000 to 60,000 people. Harrison was nominated on a white horse.... [His] address was long and eloquent. He delivered it in a loud and clear voice and did not seem at all fatigued....[2] There were two balls there over the 4th. Pa said he should go, but I do not know whether he did or not. Ma concluded not to go to Washington with him as she was so sick.... Mr. Bowman fails fast."[3]

Obviously, except for Mr. Bowman, life in Bath was lively indeed. Here is the picture Hannah paints for Maxwell a few weeks later: "Clara Houghton is engaged to Otis Kimball! So there is another to add to your list of lost girls.... Catherine [Kate] calls her daughter 'Catherine Patten Walker.' They say it looks like its mother. Pa & Ma have had

their portraits taken & they are very good ones.... There is a great temperance reforma-
tion here. The drunkards have a meeting by themselves every night & of their own accord
& now 120 have joined the teetotal society; it is among the higher as well as the lower
class. You do not meet with an intoxicated person on the street. Grandpa [Thomas Patten]
died the 20th. He died very easy, went to sleep & did not wake again.... Mr. Davenport
takes his place at the bank till October. He willed $600 to Mrs. Osgood McLellan; he was
not at all acquainted with her, so it makes a little talk in our town.... Paulina and I are
going to Boston in a few weeks. Mr. William Sewall broke his leg about a fortnight ago
— a stick of lumber rolled on it. But he is about again now.... We have lots of steam boats
on the river this summer.... Our new carpet is made & looks nicely.... Ma says if it is con-
venient she would like you to get for her two pairs of good thick blankets — 2 yards
wide..., a nice piece of linen sheeting also if you can find it, 6 yds of pink & white checked
linen gingham. She sends much love...."[4]

Take Hannah's word for it: There was never a dull moment in Bath. Meanwhile, her
father George and uncle John were quietly moving their business and community forward, producing visible changes in Bath. If H.A. Hilling had waited a decade to paint
the Bath skyline, the result would have been much different.

George F. Patten was, to put it mildly, a deep-pocketed donor whenever asked to support a worthy cause. He also made his mark as a public servant. Like brother John, his
politics were Whig, and in 1856, he was proposed as a gubernatorial candidate by members of Maine's crumbling Whig party. With old parties giving way to new, he became a
Republican, which did not win him much favor among his cotton cronies in the South.
In 1838-39, George represented Bath in the Maine legislature. He would return there
near the end of his life, in 1864-65, when there was glory in belonging to the party of
Lincoln.

John and George Patten enjoyed unusually long professional lives, but politics was
at most their avocation. In George's case, health problems interfered. As for John, his
interests were more local. He was a member of Bath's first city council and, in 1852-53,
was elected mayor. Both brothers, certainly, could have pursued more active political
careers had the spirit moved them, but times were changing. Despite — or because of
— the reformist spirit that gripped the nation, party politics were getting ugly by the
1850s. Picture ex-mayor John Patten contemplating the ruins of his South Church property, gutted by rioting members of the Know-Nothing party in 1854. That sight alone
probably was enough to make a man rethink any further political ambitions. As another
painful reminder, Captain John undoubtedly studied a celebrated series of paintings by
John Hilling, who had witnessed the South Church conflagration and got the sequence
down on canvas. The local press, putting a good face on a bad situation, applauded
Hilling's work as "perfect representations of the house and its destruction," and indeed,
the paintings did go on to become folk-art classics.[5] But John Patten may have seen things
differently. Whatever his feelings, he never again held elective office.

When it came to informal types of civic leadership, however, John and George Patten neither hesitated nor stinted. Instead, they set an example for the community by affirming the same values that had brought them so much success in business.

The Patten approach to business, public service, and philanthropy revolved around a single, nonpolitical objective: to improve Bath's physical plant and infrastructure so that the community — including the Pattens, of course — would stay abreast of change and benefit thereby. Neither reflective, spiritual George nor outgoing, worldly John ever lost the common touch. Though they were big fish in a small pond, they were always approachable and receptive to new ideas, whether commercial or charitable. As the pond enlarged, so did their influence.

One distinctive characteristic of G.F. & J. Patten was the company's hometown orientation. Patten ships, after construction, did not simply disappear forever into transoceanic traffic, plying between large commercial population centers. Instead, they often carried cargoes to and from the Kennebec, returning home also for essential repairs. This localized focus made George and John acutely sensitive to Bath's strengths and weaknesses as a seaport. Accordingly, the brothers committed themselves to new ventures that promised to upgrade the city's commercial capabilities.

Bath may have been a good spot to build ships, but the surrounding waterways, wetlands, islands, and hills were major barriers to the city's development as a manufacturer, marketplace, or export-import center. These shortcomings seemed especially pronounced in the 1830s and 1840s, when all America developed a mania for economic expansion. Confident that progress and growth were here to stay, entrepreneurs floated countless "internal improvement" projects: canals, bridges, turnpikes, railways, steamship lines, land development. The Pattens were drawn into that mania. Like investors everywhere, they learned that glamorous, sure-fire projects could take forever to pan out — if they panned out at all.

Take the case of Merrymeeting Bay Bridge. In 1835, a company was incorporated to construct a wooden toll bridge across Merrymeeting Bay between nearby Brunswick and Topsham. Such a bridge would greatly simplify and shorten the transport of farm products from towns such as Bowdoinham and Topsham — Patten country — to the wharves at Bath. The Bay Bridge would cost $20,000 — equivalent to almost $450,000 in 1995. Stockholders expected bridge tolls to provide a healthy return on investment and cover the structure's maintenance costs in the bargain. The charter proprietors included George and John Patten and ex-governor William King.

Soon the project took on a political cast. Anticipating a $10,000 refund from the 1836 federal surplus, Bath selectmen bought into the Bay Bridge project. When Uncle Sam's money arrived, however, taxpayers elected to distribute the windfall among themselves. Undeterred, town fathers honored their bridge commitment by borrowing the promised sum.[6]

Upon completion, Bay Bridge did indeed benefit the local economy. Unfortunately, though, it was seldom used in winter, when people could avoid tolls by moving goods across the iced-over bay. It was also subject to severe damage when bay ice went out in the spring, which increased maintenance costs. Later, improved roads and rail facilities further reduced the bridge traffic. In other words, Bay Bridge lost money. And because it had increased the city's public debt, the issue became especially controversial.

The ever-deteriorating bridge proved a financial and public-relations headache for decades. In 1863, private investors were ready to call it quits. Bath's city council passed a resolution thanking venerable Captain John Patten, who, "in the four years past has devoted much of his time, together with other benefits, in making the repairs on the Bay Bridge without charge to the city."[7] The next year, the state legislature vested the entire bridge franchise with Bath, and the city acquired all the bridge stock. But the dilapidated bridge went from bad to worse, at one point becoming impassible after the collapse of one span. In 1878, city fathers served notice that they would abandon it unless other communities helped with the upkeep. Accordingly, the legislature conveyed the property to Sagadahoc County. Repairs were made and the bridge survived more or less until 1896, when spring floods destroyed it altogether.[8]

Other Patten ventures had a happier outcome. In 1853, ex-mayor John Patten was one of four original incorporators of the Bath Gas Light Company, organized to provide illumination for the city. James F. Patten served as one of the directors. The company was capitalized at $150,000 but raised less than half of that amount. Its success was assured, however, when city fathers awarded it a thirty-year consumption contract that could be (and was) extended beyond that date. The company's gas house was at the foot of North Street, near the Patten company wharf.[9]

The biggest investment story in the community, however, was the arrival of the railroad. Linking Bath overland to Portland and points west was of course essential if the City of Ships was to maintain her prominence as a port. During the 1830s and 1840s, the state of Maine was inundated with proposals for ambitious private railroad projects, yet none were designed to serve Bath.

The closest proposed line was the Kennebec and Portland, chartered in 1836 by citizens upriver in Gardiner.[10] Capitalized at $1.2 million, the Kennebec and Portland's anticipated route was from Augusta and Gardiner to Portland via Brunswick, Freeport, and Yarmouth.[11] Under the supervision of Reuel Williams of Augusta, work proceeded, but rising expenses, technical problems, and the Panic of 1837 created formidable, time-consuming barriers. Meanwhile, where did Bath stand?

Bath was heard from in 1847, when three of the city's maritime leaders, George and John Patten and William D. Sewall, revitalized the Kennebec and Portland with an infusion of cash and the insistence that a branch line be constructed from Brunswick to Bath. Reportedly, Patten and Sewall each put up $100,000 (about $2.4 million each in 1995 value). John Patten invested $80,000 (about $1.95 million in 1995 value).[12] The deal went through; the railroad was coming to Bath. George Patten, who became the company's president, officiated at festive ceremonies in Bath. Having reportedly rehearsed his shoveling technique in his backyard, he hefted the project's first spadeful of earth, setting things in motion.[13] The community's consensus was that Patten's gesture would usher in a new era for the City of Ships.

The line from Bath to Yarmouth Junction opened in June 1848. According to Bath historian Parker Reed, the first train left on Independence Day, 1849, pulling flatcars fitted with seats so that citizens could have a free ride.[14] In subsequent years, a linkup with a compatibly gauged railroad was achieved in Portland, in effect connecting Bath by rail with Boston and points south. All in all, a sound investment — in the long run.

In the short run, the Kennebec and Portland ran up massive repair costs, staying alive via bond issues. Funding the linkup with southwest-bound rails in Portland necessitated a separate mortgage.[15] To the railroad's manager, Reuel Williams, the line was a series of headaches; to the directors, it must have seemed like a bottomless money pit. Stockholders in various towns along the route became restive. In 1857, matters reached a point where Williams, after falling out with George Patten and William Sewall, brought a stockholders' suit against them.[16] The dispute was resolved out of court, and George F. remained active on the board of the company.[17] In 1859, the state legislature authorized town governments to provide financial help, and the company survived. It also changed its name to the Portland and Kennebec Railroad.

From the start, Maine's assorted, undercapitalized private railroads had engaged in costly, wasteful squabbling over route rights, shipping charges, tariffs, and gauge widths. Instead of a systematic network, the result was a series of literally incompatible, sometimes hostile operations.[18] Meanwhile, deciding which standard to accept became a political issue in the state capital. It is well that the Pattens and Sewall were honored for bringing the railroad to Bath, for they received little else for their effort. In 1863, the local press revealed that the Pattens' $180,000 commitment to the railroad had been a major public service but, thus far, a total loss to the investors.[19]

Inevitably, railroad consolidation became the only practical solution. In 1870, more than twenty years after George Patten shoveled that historic spade of earth, the Portland and Kennebec was unified with the recently consolidated Maine Central Railroad. Little good it did George F. Patten: He had died the previous year.

Every good railroad deserves a fine hotel at the end of the line. At least that was how the Patten brothers saw things in the hopeful days of 1849. Thus was born the Sagadahock House, a colossal new facility befitting an important transportation hub. When the Kennebec and Portland's first train arrived in Bath, disembarking passengers could take refreshment and lodging in Bath's newest, biggest building, which had opened that very day.[20] Captain John Patten headed the Sagadahock Company, the syndicate that built the hotel. George F. also was part of the syndicate; others included shipbuilders Levi Houghton and sons and chandler Green Richardson, a future mayor of Bath. Needless to say, the hotel cost a fortune. The Patten brothers' share was between $40,000 and $50,000 — about $1 million in 1995 currency.[21]

Sagadahock House was expensive beyond a doubt, and looked it. Inspired by the Tremont House in Boston, and located across from the Bath Customs House at the hilltop intersection of Front and Centre Streets, the new brick hotel was four stories high and had eighty guest rooms. Its classic symmetry made it compatible with Bath's other commercial buildings, but it was half again as big as anything else in the downtown. On the street level were four stores, two banks, and the city post office. In addition to rail connections, stagecoaches to and from points east stopped twice daily, pulling up to the hotel's lofty pillared portico. Inside were a ball room and a dining room. George Washington never slept there, but Jeff Davis did.[22]

Given its location and scale, the Sagadahock House quickly became the social center of Bath. Parties and meetings without number were held there for decades. A number of permanent residents also made the hotel their home. But despite its imposing presence, usefulness, and contribution to Bath's public image, the hotel was not a moneymaker. In 1860, John Patten acquired full ownership, prompting the local press to comment that the building "could scarcely fall into better hands unless it should be purchased by some good man with a view to keep the hotel himself, and to give to it the benefit of his constant personal attention."[23] The implication was that only John Patten had the requisite blend of enthusiasm and wherewithal to oversee the building's needs.

John, however, did not go it alone. Somehow, he persuaded George to take a half interest in the property.[24] By early 1863, while the Civil War malingered and Bath citizens debated bridge and railroad problems, the aged Patten brothers admitted that the return on their Sagadahock House investment was nil.[25]

J.D. Lang, a wood-burning locomotive of the Portland and Kennebec Railroad, built in 1854 and shown here on the wooden bridge at Augusta. Thanks to George and John Patten and William D. Sewall, the railroad came to Bath in 1849; George Patten became president of the P&K. *Courtesy Charles S. Given/Maine Maritime Museum.*

Their loss was Bath's gain, however, because the hotel provided the setting for count-less gala occasions. One of those is of special interest to this story: the wedding recep-tion of Mr. and Mrs. Edward Warden on 18 April 1867. The mother of the bride is Kate Patten Walker, daughter of George F. and Hannah, and much-beloved/estranged confi-dante of Noble Maxwell.

Kate's marriage to Wildes Walker of Topsham was a nightmare relieved only by the drastic step of divorce in 1854. In awarding that bitter decree, a New York judge forbade Wildes Walker to remarry until after Kate's death. But years later, in April 1867, Walker succeeds in getting that proviso overturned by the Sagadahoc County Superior Court when Kate fails to appear at the scheduled hearing.[26]

Aside from her personal feelings, Kate Patten Walker has more important things on her mind in April 1867 — namely, her daughter's wedding and reception at the Sagadahock House. Since her divorce, she and her now-grown daughters have lived at her parents' Front Street residence. Now, at age forty-six, Kate watches her daughter marry Edward Warden, former owner of the Bath Iron Foundry, in a ceremony at the genteel Patten home, after which the wedding party and guests retire to the Sagadahock House, where there is "dancing and the festivities usual on such occasions," which are "enjoyed as they could only be enjoyed by a bridal party."[27] Kate soon becomes a grandmother. She dies in 1875, in Ischia, Italy.

Kate Patten Walker's granddaughters illustrate how wealth and gentility provide status to American females in the late nineteenth and early twentieth centuries. One becomes Baroness Leicester and lives in England. The other marries Franz Hans von Wauttenburg, Austrian military attaché in Bern, Switzerland. As for Katie Warden, their mother: She will live until 1917, when, forty-seven years after tripping the light fantastic at her wedding celebration in the Sagadahock House, she dies in Switzerland, probably among members of her extended family.[28]

Meanwhile, the Sagadahock House has continued as a city focal point and source of fond memories, operating until 1896, when it is gutted by fire.

Bay Bridge, the Kennebec and Portland Railroad, and Sagadahock House provide two insights into the Pattens' shoreside investments. One is that the brothers were willing to commit capital to projects that might take a long time to pay off (the railroad) or, possibly, never pay off (Sagadahock House). The other is the single criterion the Pattens applied consistently throughout their long careers: Long-shot or long-term, an investment had to make a positive difference in Bath. When confronted by the grim financial results of some of their huge ventures, the brothers could (and probably did) console themselves that they had done some good for the community.

Most of the time. One possible exception was the creation of the Bath Whaling Company in 1841, an incident worth including for its bizarre qualities alone.

During the 1840s and 1850s, the Noble Maxwells and Pattens of the world were constantly importuned by moneyless, ambitious individuals peddling get-rich-quick schemes. Men of means soon developed effective defenses against such "opportunities." But it was well known around Bath that the Pattens, especially Captain John, were approachable, kindly people who remembered when all they had going for themselves was know-how and raw ambition. That may explain how the Patten name became associated with the Bath Whaling Company.

The Bath Whaling Company was the brainstorm of twenty-eight-year-old David C. Densmore. Born in the inland town of China, Maine, Densmore was a poor farmboy who went to sea at thirteen, eventually winding up on a Nantucket whaler on which he rose to a second mate's berth, learning the esoteric, complicated business of whaling along the way. David Densmore was not a very lucky person, but he had come through his share of dangers and misfortunes unscathed, a circumstance he attributed to spiritual guidance. Densmore was positively certain that when he got in a tight spot, a "spirit voice" of some departed soul literally whispered in his ear, pointing the way to safety.[29]

Safety, but not prosperity. In 1841, broke and unemployed in Hallowell, Densmore borrowed enough money to take the steamer to Boston but missed the boat during a stopover in Bath. That meant spending a night in a cheap joint in the south end of town, which was enough to make him wonder where he'd find his next meal. At that low point, he later recalled, a ghostly voice gave him the answer: Densmore should start a whaling company right here in Bath. Where would the money come from? "Subscription," said the ghost.

As Densmore knew well, whaling was a regional specialty that had not taken hold outside of southern New England, partly because its peculiar procedures and trade secrets were very difficult to emulate. It was also a business that, despite its overall size, was dominated by small-time entrepreneurs. The hundreds of Yankee vessels whaling out of Nantucket, New Bedford, and adjacent ports were not owned and managed by corporations. Instead, each voyage involved a complex process in which owners held percentages on a voyage-to-voyage basis and shared proportionately in any profits. During the 1830s, however, a few nonwhaling towns tried to break into the business by incorporating companies that bought vessels and equipment and hired talent from established whaling ports. Densmore and, if you like, his spirit guide, would have heard about two such companies in Maine: one in Wiscasset, the other in Portland.

Because whaling was truly a regional specialty based upon decades of accumulated know-how, these wildcat companies proved to be more trouble than they were worth and had lately called it quits. So much for Wiscasset and Portland. But who was to say that Bath couldn't prosper with a whaling company? Certainly not Densmore. Certainly not the spirit voice whose advice he heeded. On a tip from his innkeeper, Densmore headed for the north end of town in search of a Patten to help him build his dream.[30]

Looking back years later, Densmore remembered calling on John Patten in the captain's North Street home. His host considered the proposition of raising capital, buying a ship and equipment, and finding a crew with the requisite expertise. How much would it cost? Twenty thousand dollars. Who would be master of such a vessel? Densmore, of course. He had never been a captain, but, at twenty-eight, he had years of experience under his belt and was competent in navigation. And wasn't it Patten tradition to give young men command? But whaling.... Patten agreed to participate, provided Densmore could convince a sufficient number of other investors to get similarly involved.

That conditional yes was all it took. Using the good name of Patten, Densmore had no trouble finding thirty-seven other investors.[31] As he later recalled, "The affair had been gotten up so quietly, that hardly any outside of those engaged in it knew any thing about it...."[32] Thanks to a voice from a ghost and a nod from a Patten, David C. Densmore was now a whaling captain.

What is curious about the Bath Whaling Company's shareholder list is that John Patten's name does not appear. The name of John's brother and neighbor James does, however. Is it possible that Densmore's memory confused John with brother James, John's next-door neighbor? That would seem unlikely, for Densmore's published account of his maritime career is remarkably accurate. Could it be that after steering Densmore toward other investors, John cleverly excused himself from the oddball venture? Perhaps — especially if Densmore let slip the ethereal source of his inspiration. We may never know exactly what happened.

With the requisite funds subscribed, the fledgling company bought a three-year-old, 206-ton brig, *Massasoit,* which was rerigged as a bark and equipped at bargain-basement rates with gear auctioned off by the defunct Portland Whaling Company. When she at last set sail, the *Massasoit's* unruly complement included some very green local boys, some very drunk able seamen, and assorted former gentlemen now down on their luck. "As a whole," said Densmore, "the crew was an average one for a whaler."[33] So, in October 1841, Bath's only whaleship left the Kennebec to hunt sperm whales in the North and South Atlantic.

She did not do well. Although Densmore's spirit voices kept him out of trouble, they were mum as to the whereabouts of whales.[34] Thus, when the *Massasoit* returned to the Kennebec in March 1843, she was only a quarter full. At that year's slumping prices, the gross value of her meager take of sperm oil was about $8,000.[35] To make matters worse, on her way upriver to Bath, the *Massasoit* grounded. Densmore reported that he had "anchored at Parkers Flats, in consequence of the wind and tide being ahead, and on his passage up the river the same day got on a rock just below Fiddler's Reach where said vessel remains, notwithstanding all the exertions he could make to get her off...."[36] Removing the stuck ship's cargo lightened her sufficiently to float her off and up to Bath. Luckily, she was not badly damaged.

The outcome of the venture, however, was discouraging enough for Bath's investors to get cold feet. Accordingly, the cargo, vessel, and gear were sold, generating enough combined proceeds to allow the company to claim it had finished in the black. The *Massasoit's* short career on the Kennebec gave her the honor of being Bath's first and Maine's last deep-sea whaler.

After a stint as a merchant vessel, the *Massasoit* whaled out of Mattapoisett, Massachusetts. She was condemned in 1851. David Densmore was finished as a shipmaster, but, by his own account, spirit voices led him to other callings. For a few years, he holds various jobs around mid-coast Maine. Comes the Gold Rush and he is off to California. By the 1860s, he has become a full-time faith healer, always guided by the voices of deceased but sympathetic spirits. Those spirits also persuade him to establish a newspaper, *Voice of Angels,* in Boston. The paper's columns carry the dictated musings of his spirit voices. In 1876, to inspire others, he publishes his autobiography, *The Halo.* More than a century later, it will remain the only primary account of the Bath Whaling Company.

Not all Patten investments were in innovative but chancy ventures. George, John, and James all put their money into bank stock, primarily at the Lincoln Bank, organized in 1813 and located on the corner of Front and Centre Streets. That original building was razed in 1849 to make way for the Sagadahock House, but when the hotel opened, the Lincoln Bank's new offices were on its ground floor.

Both George and James served as presidents of Lincoln Bank; Charles Davenport was a cashier. All three Patten brothers invested in the bank, but George was by far the most heavily committed. In 1854, he held $21,000 worth of stock — 217 shares at $100 a share (equal in value to $437,000 in 1995 currency). John held 145 shares (worth $301,600 in 1995), and James had 75 (worth $156,000 in 1995).[37] Perhaps taking a cue from cousin Noble Maxwell, George Patten spread around his investments in bank stock. He held 48 shares of the Augusta Bank at $80 per share (close to $80,000 in 1995 value), and at the time of his death in 1869, he also held shares in the Bath National Bank and the Globe Bank in Boston.[38]

Meanwhile, in 1852, George Patten, Charles Davenport, William D. Sewall, Zina Hyde, and several other blue-chip businessmen formed a group to incorporate the Bath Savings Institution. In 1855, David Magoun, first president of the Bath Savings Institution, was succeeded by Davenport, who continued to preside over the institution for more than forty years. John Patten also served as a director. The Pattens' substantial commitments to new businesses and bank stock underscore the immensity of their fortunes, especially by local standards. And all these ventures, remember, were subsidiary to their maritime pursuits.

Because of their impact on the community, George and John Patten's shoreside investments would have secured their reputations as public-spirited citizens. But in the meantime, the brothers also led the way in local philanthropy.

In early 1843, members of Bath's Old North Church empowered a building committee to erect a new Congregational church. George F. Patten was part of that committee, which tackled the assignment in a manner befitting a whaling company or a hotel syndicate. As local historian Parker Reed put it, the group "inaugurated the undertaking as 'proprietors,' independent of the parish, the necessary funds to be raised by subscription, depending upon the sale of pews for reimbursement. This was readily accomplished, as on January 31, following, $5,250 had been raised and eight pews subscribed for. The site for the church was selected at the northwest corner of Washington and Winter Streets, for which $1,350 were paid. The committee on building had full powers.... By selling the pews at auction the proceeds fully repaid the outlay incurred by the proprietors, 'the house to be called the Winter Street Church.' Its dedication took place February 1, 1844."[39] When, a few months later, H.A. Hilling painted the Bath townscape, beautiful Winter Street Church was the latest addition to the skyline. You can't miss it.

Conspicuous charity has a way of spreading. It spread, for example, to Charles Davenport, who had prospered with G.F. & J. Patten and was now an active partner in that firm. Davenport made a practice of emulating his mentors, and charitable activity was no exception. In 1852, when Methodists in Bath's North End resolved to start a church of their own, they found themselves initially short of funds, so the new congregation considered appealing to the Methodist missionary board. Enter Charles Davenport,

who offered to meet the following year's expenses. Davenport's gesture was contagious; other donors then came forward. Thus, says Reed, "during the winter of 1854-5, notwithstanding the general depression in business, the society purchased an organ at an expense of $600. In 1857, when banks were breaking and business firms suspending, the church nevertheless raised $867.41."[40] Beacon Street Church was on its way. And Charles Davenport, its first Sunday-school superintendent, was on his way to becoming another important community benefactor.

Although his formal education consisted only of the basics, George Patten was devoted to higher learning. He was a member of Bowdoin College's board of overseers and, evidently, a financial supporter of that institution.[41] Closer to home, he and his brother John were charter members of the library that today bears the Patten name. Every respectable town needs a public library, but Bath's efforts in that direction were modest and sparse until the Patten brothers provided the catalyst for change.

Surprisingly little is known about this intriguing story. Apparently, the community's first circulating library was a collection of books available in the mid-1820s at Dr. Nathaniel Weld's apothecary shop. The collection was kept cased and, according to tradition, included "all the volumes of the old English Encyclopedia." Henry Hyde, who ran a bookstore at Front and Centre Streets, also kept a small circulating library. In 1836, Bath's Mechanics Association, an organization of tradesmen, set up a small library collection

Isn't that Captain John Patten chatting with a friend in front of Zina Hyde's chandlery at the corner of Front and Broad Streets? And why are millstones leaning against the storefront? Note also Front Street's unpaved thoroughfare, the wooden sidewalks, and the impressive trade sign overhanging the photographer's studio. *Courtesy Maine Maritime Museum.*

consisting of books contributed or purchased for general use by members.[42]

Meanwhile, in 1827, steps had been taken to incorporate a town library, with David Magoun, Joseph Sewall, and Freeman Clark acting as trustees.[43] How far these intentions got is not known. They may have generated what was briefly known as the Bath Public Library, for such an institution did indeed exist, though it probably was no more than a downtown reading room supported by membership fees.

No records of the Bath Public Library have survived, but it is safe to say that it came on hard times; otherwise, no one would have felt a need to take the library issue in hand. People felt just such a need, however, by the mid-1840s, and on 8 November 1847, eighty-six of them met in the office of Dr. Israel Putnam to create a privately funded library.

The start-up assumed the now-familiar form of a subscribed corporation: Each charter member took one $5 share. Topping the list of charter members were the names of George F. and his two sons James T. and George M., and, inevitably, Captain John Patten.[44] Just as inevitably, perhaps, the new group called itself the Patten Library Association. Four directors (no Pattens) were elected. At the outset there were 132 subscribers.

By the time the directors had their first meeting two weeks later, whoever was in charge of the Bath Public Library had suggested that the new association take charge of the old institution's books. The exact outcome is not known, but the proposed transaction smacks of a foregone conclusion. The Patten Library Association may even have been created precisely to take over the previous organization.

In June 1852, eighty-four-year-old General William King — Maine's first governor and Bath's leading celebrity — died. The entire city was draped in mourning. King's funeral procession included the Bath Brass Band, the Bath City Grays (the local militia unit), contingents of several local Masonic lodges, Mayor John Patten, the city council and aldermen, and other VIPs, who made their solemn way along a lengthy, circuitous route from downtown to outlying Maple Grove Cemetery. On instructions from the city government, Mayor Patten kept the bells tolling from the start to the finish of the long procession.[45]

Shortly after the funeral, King's widow moved to Portland and the late governor's furnishings were put on the auction block. Just before the sale, Bath's Whiggish newspaper, *The Weekly Mirror,* drew readers' attention to General King's collection of books, about to be sold, and called for someone to rise to that occasion: "We suggest to our liberal citizens that an effort be made to purchase them for the Patten library. An effort should be made immediately."[46]

Whereupon George and John Patten made just such an effort. As they told the association after the sale, "Having purchased the library, cases, maps and globes which were the property of Gen. King, we present the same to the Patten Library Association on the condition that the same revert to the donors should the association ever be dissolved, and on the further condition that a suitable room be procured for the whole library."[47]

For $300 (about $6,250 in 1995 value), George and John Patten had purchased a very eclectic set of middle-brow books, heavy on political history and law but with something for everyone. Years later, Reed characterized King's library as "large and well selected for his time. The greater number of books are such as a public man and statesman to be well informed would need, containing as they do the proceedings of Congress and the Massachusetts and Maine legislatures. There are many volumes of standard literary works, although he was not a man of culture. There are some works that have been long out of print and of rare merit."[48] The entire collection, numbering more than 500 volumes, reflected the needs and tastes of a man of humble education who, as he rose in station, had made a valiant effort at intellectual catch-up.[49] How interesting it must have been for those who had known the late governor to peer into his mind via his book collection, and to discover how wide-ranging his reading had been.

If a member of the Patten Library Association had a bent for classical history, Thirlwall's *History of Greece* or, better still, Gibbon's *Decline and Fall of the Roman Empire* would fill the bill. Someone with an affinity for business (a Patten, for example) could try Smith's *Wealth of Nations* or Alldridge's *Universal Merchant in Theory and Practice.* For flag-wavers, there was Major Dobson's *Monuments of Washington's Patriotism.* For the military mind, how about Charnock's biography of Nelson? At the other end of the literary spectrum, a romanticist could try Scott's *Ballads and Lyrical Pieces.* And if no reformers were lurking about, *Tom Jones* or *Tristram Shandy* were always good for a few bawdy laughs.

Despite its variety, the King collection constituted a body of mainstream editions quite common then and, with few exceptions, now. But the Pattens certainly understood that purchasing the lot would preserve a priceless piece of local history. The terms they set for the association's acceptance were met. In November, the association set up in second-floor quarters in the former Elliot House, a hotel building at Front and Arch Streets that had been remodeled into stores and offices.[50] The King collection has been part of the Patten Library ever since.

The Pattens' generous gesture was in keeping with the public mood of the early 1850s. With Prohibition now in place, solid citizens probably felt more than ever the need to provide a wholesome, morally uplifting infrastructure. Toward that end, the Pattens added an uplifting component to their business, placing mini-libraries aboard their newest vessels. Witness this item in the Bath *Weekly Mirror,* 19 June 1852, which reported that G.F. & J. Patten's brand-new ship *Marshfield* came equipped with "an excellent library at the expense of the owners. The ship Caspian belonging to the same gentlemen, had also been fitted with a library. All honor to those who recognize that seamen possess minds and hearts. A few years since a ship would not have been deemed properly founded without a large quantity of ardent spirits. Let us hope that the time will soon come when no vessel's outfit will be considered complete without a well stocked library."[51]

On 16 November 1852, about three months after receiving King's collection, the Patten Library Association legally incorporated, with George Patten as president. Funding was obtained through annual assessments of a dollar or two on the membership and by

John Patten's marble bust presides over a corner in the Patten Free Library. The bust was received by the Library Association after brother George declined to provide one of himself for display. *Courtesy Patten Free Library, Bath.*

fees charged to borrowing nonmembers. Twenty-five dollars would buy a life membership free of assessments.

In 1857, George Patten retired as library president. To recognize his service, the association asked that he provide a bust of himself for display in the library room. Such a grandiose gesture was foreign to George F.'s nature, especially in a year when businesses around the city were going belly-up. And of course there was the detail that he, not the library, would pay for the sculpture. No bust of George F. Patten was forthcoming, but the association did not have to go bustless. Brother John provided a likeness of himself to the library.

The Patten Library Association, which was the work of public-spirited private citizens, set a pattern for local philanthropy. Bath people became famous for their deep pockets — so much so that the city government was spared the chore of providing facilities that other towns accepted as municipal obligations. Why, for example, establish a free public library when the town's private institution filled the bill? And when it came to other worthy public services, Bath's leading citizens usually could come up with the money on their own.

John Patten lived so long that he had an extra share of opportunities to come up with the money to seed worthy causes. At seventy-seven, he became active in the creation of an asylum for children orphaned by the American Civil War. When that war commenced in 1861, people in Bath, mercifully ignorant of the horror that lay ahead, promised departing soldiers and sailors that, should they die in service, their children would be looked after. Fulfilling that promise was the inspiration that led to the Bath Military and Naval Orphan Asylum.

After the war, a committee of women undertook to raise the necessary funds. The start-up goal of $7,000 was reached, thanks partly to John Patten, who contributed $1,000. The asylum incorporated in February 1866, its first board consisting of John Patten, George F. Patten, Charles Davenport, Oliver Moses, and J. Parker Morse, the last of whom had also donated $1,000 to the cause. Those trustees promised to raise an additional $20,000 within two years, which would entitle the organization to $6,000 in annual support from the state treasury. That goal was met.[52]

The asylum, which cared for orphans from surrounding towns as well as from Bath, opened in a rented house on Walker Street. In 1870, it became a state institution, moving to an 1800-vintage mansion. Patten, Davenport, Morse, and other Bath notables continued to serve as trustees.

At age eighty-six, John Patten was asked to help establish the Bath Old Ladies' Home, a project that had begun with an 1875 bequest from Mary Ledyard for such a purpose. Records show that the shipbuilding partnership of John Patten & Son provided a gift of $3,000.[53]

Posterity will remember the Patten Library Association as the crowning example of Patten family charity, partly because the effort pioneered by George and John was carried on by their descendants.

Years have passed since the library got on its feet. The institution now resides in a Centre Street building owned by John Patten. In 1879, a decade after brother George's death, Captain John, now ninety, conveys ownership of the building to the association — with one condition. Hoping to plant the seeds of future library expansion, he stipulates that the building will go to the city of Bath "whenever said city shall institute a public library and appropriate funds for its support."[54] The city takes no action, but, as before, private citizens do.

In 1887, Bath banker and businessman Galen C. Moses donates $10,000 (equal to $170,000 in 1995 dollars) to the association for the purpose of erecting a library to serve all Bath citizens without charge: a Patten *Free* Library. Twenty-four citizens come forward to buy a site on which to build the new library. They choose a lot at Front and Summer Streets, adjoining the city's parklike green and looking across to Winter Street Church. A younger generation of Pattens is well represented in that group: Captain John's grandson John O. gives $200; James F. Patten's sons Fred H. and Charles E. each give $100.[55] Charles, erstwhile master of Patten ships, is just a year away from becoming Bath's mayor. In 1896, he will donate another $1,000 (equal to almost $18,000 in 1995) to the library's permanent book fund. His bequest to the library in 1908 will be ten times that amount. Another future generous supporter will be Charles Davenport's son George.

Meanwhile, Galen Moses makes good on his promise, securing the donated services of New York architect George Harding (a Bath native) and shooting the works on the new building regardless of cost. The Patten Free Library's stylish, yellow-brick building opens on 6 January 1891, issuing borrower's cards to any interested citizen — free of charge. Those using the reading room can make a selection from the Governor King collection and, under the impassive gaze of Captain John Patten's marble bust, curl up by the fireplace with Baroness von Minntoli's *Recollections of Egypt*, or Holland's *Life of Martin Van Buren*, or perhaps even Beaumont's *Experiments and Observations on the Gastric Juices*. Something for everyone, and it's free.

As years passed, John Patten's openhandedness made him a steady target for supplicants from near and far. How far — and how far-fetched — may be seen from a mysterious episode that occurred in 1883. In March of that year, the old captain received a long letter in Spanish datelined Ceuta, Spanish Morocco. The writer was one Alberto Patten y Balderrama, a disgraced Spanish bureaucrat, who solicited John Patten's help. Balderrama claimed to be a distant relative through his father's line: "My father, in his youth, left his native country, and passed...to the service of the Spanish Army in which he made a career as a Colonel."

Balderrama described himself as the former custodian general of military funds for the Greater Antilles. During his service in Havana, a substantial sum of money had disappeared. Court-martialed, Balderrama claimed to be innocent, framed by whoever actually embezzled the lost funds. He was nonetheless found guilty, stripped of his office, and exiled to house arrest in Ceuta, where he had taken ill. Now near death and recalling his father's glowing accounts of the family's Maine relatives, he was appealing to Captain John to assume guardianship of his motherless young daughter. He had, he wrote, taken confidential steps to overcome the legal hurdles to this goal, and furthermore had established a secret bank account for his daughter's financial care. In true melodramatic style, the particulars of that account were "kept hidden and reserved in a secret [compartment] of a trunk that is in the pavillion I occupy...." If Captain Patten would answer his call, arrangements could be finalized through a secret intermediary, Balderrama's parish priest and confessor.

"I beg of you," Balderrama wrote to Patten, "in memory of our ancestors, my dear relative, a prompt reply, in order that with your response my conscience will be put at ease in view of the seriousness in which my existence is found if the Supreme Maker does not remedy it.

"I again reiterate that for no reason should you deviate from those instructions given you by my Confessor, for even though he is only a poor priest, he is truly the human personification of honor and self denial, and besides he knows the injustice of which I have been the victim and of the Government's desire to take all that I possess.

"Meanwhile, remaining impatient and meditating until the receipt of your reply, this afflicted and disgraced relative lies here in his bed of pain.

"[Signed] Alberto Patten y Balderrama."[56]

What was the meaning of all this? The truth? We shall never know for sure. What is

certain is that Patten at first resolved to answer the call. He provided Jarvis Patten with power of attorney "to act in my name and stead in all matters pertaining to the guardian-ship of Julia Patten y Gutterrez, now residing in Ceuta, Spanish Africa...."[57] Jarvis pre-pared to depart for Ceuta by way of Gibraltar, first securing from the secretary of state the necessary bona fides for his mission.[58] Everything was set, but at that point the adven-ture sank like a stone. In view of the good captain's generosity and careful preparations, it is clear that Balderrama's story was not taken lightly. Did Captain John get wise to a confidence game? Did Balderrama, as expected, die? And what fate awaited Julia? Whatever transpired, it did not take place in Bath, Maine. But the Patten y Balderrama affair surely must have been the most bizarre appeal ever made to John Patten's philanthropy.

Given the uneven returns on Patten onshore investments, it is likely that George and John's philanthropy flowed from the profits on their shipping empire. Besides making big money, the casual nature of that business permitted the brothers to draw whatever

The Patten Free Library, overlooking the Bath city park. Bath's leading citizens shot the works on this privately funded insti-tution, which opened its doors in 1891. More than a century later, thanks to careful archi-tectural expansion and the peculiarly generous character of Bath phil-anthropy, the building is still in everyday use. From a postcard ca. 1910.

they needed for whatever purpose they saw fit. But those days were numbered.

Notice that the Patten donation to the Old Ladies' Home was a corporate gift from the firm of John Patten & Son. In the years since the Civil War, many changes had overtaken the Patten fleet. In fact, just before the Civil War, G.F. & J. Patten had been dissolved as a company, its outmoded, clannish business style giving way to the next generation of Pattens — people with more diverse and complex objectives.

This was, of course, quite proper, and part of the brothers' plan. For reasons of age alone, George and John Patten were prepared to move into the background and let their sons carry on in different directions. But, as we will see, George and John remained close and were still engaged in partnership ventures years after the official termination of their firm. Only death would separate them.

NOTES

1. Jarvis Patten, "A Century of Shipbuilding," *Bath Daily Times*, 19 March 1881.

2. William Henry Harrison's age had aroused concern for his presidential longevity. At sixty-eight, he was the oldest serving president to that time. He died after one month in office.

3. Hannah Patten to Noble Maxwell, Bath, 13 March 1841 (Noble Maxwell Papers, MMM).

4. Hannah Patten to Noble Maxwell, Bath, 28 May 1841 (ibid.).

5. *The Weekly Mirror* (Bath), 18 May 1855, quoted in Jean Lipman et al., *Young America: A Folk-Art History* (New York: Hudson Hills Press and the Museum of American Folk Art, 1986), p. 78.

6. Owen, p. 182.

7. *Bath Daily Times*, 30 January 1863.

8. Reed, p. 237.

9. Ibid., p. 290.

10. *Act Incorporating the Kennebec and Portland Railroad Company...1836, with Additional Acts....* (Augusta, ME: Severance and Dore, 1845), pp. 1-4.

11. Ron Johnson, *The Best of Maine Railroads* (Portland, ME: Portland Litho, 1985), p. 15.

12. *Bath Daily Times*, 30 January 1863.

13. Hennessy Historical Files (MMM).

14. Reed, p. 516.

15. Johnson, p. 18.

16. Minutes of a meeting of Kennebec and Portland Railroad Company stockholders, Augusta, ME, 5 September 1857 (Document 567/7, Sewall Family Papers, MMM).

17. *Bath Daily Times*, 4 January 1860.

18. *Report of the Directors to the Stockholders of the Maine Central Railroad Company* (published annually; Bangor, ME: Samuel S. Smith), 1866, p. 4; 1867, p. 5.

19. *Bath Daily Times*, 30 January 1863.

20. Mark Hennessy, "Bath's Grandest — the Sagadahock House" (1951; reprinted in *The Times of Bath, ME* [October 1993]), p. 1.

21. *Bath Daily Times*, 30 January 1863.

22. Ibid.

23. *Bath Daily Morning Times*, 4 January 1860.

24. Inventory of the estate of George F. Patten, 1869 (Probate Records, Sagadahoc County Court House, Bath, ME).

25. *Bath Daily Times*, 30 January 1863.

26. *Walker* v. *Walker* (SVC-SCSJC, Records of the Sagadahoc County Superior Judicial Court, Maine State Archives, Augusta, ME).

27. *Daily Sentinel and Bath Daily Times*, 19 April 1867.

28. *Bath Daily Times*, 8 February 1911.

29. David C. Densmore, *The Halo: An Autobiography* (Boston: Voice of Angels Publishing House, 1876), pp. 120-22.

30. Ibid., pp. 129-43.

31. Register, Bark *Massasoit* of Bath, 18 October 1841 (Robert Applebee Collection, Penobscot Marine Museum, Searsport, ME).

32. Densmore, pp. 143-44.

33. Ibid., p. 151.

34. The voyage is summarized in Kenneth R. Martin, *Whalemen and Whaleships of Maine* (Brunswick, ME: Harpswell Press, 1975), pp. 34-36.

35. In 1843, sperm oil averaged 63 cents per gallon (Starbuck, p. 660). The *Massasoit's* gross catch was 400 barrels ("Ship Massasoit of Bath," in Dennis Wood, Abstracts of Whaling Voyages from the United States, 1831-1873 [New Bedford Free Public Library, New Bedford, MA]).

36. Protest, Bark *Massasoit* of Bath, 3 March 1843 (William Torrey Notarial Records, MMM).

37. *List of Stockholders...in the Banks of Maine* (Augusta, ME: William T. Johnson, 1854), p. 69.

38. Inventory of the estate of George F. Patten.

39. Reed, p. 471.

40. Ibid., p. 503.

41. *Bath Daily Times*, 29 September 1869.

42. Reed, p. 222.

43. Owen, p. 176.

44. *Patten Free Library, 1889-1940* (Bath, ME: Patten Free Library, 1940), p. 3.

45. Marion Smith, pp. 140-41.

46. *The Weekly Mirror* (Bath), quoted in Mark Hennessy, "Maine's First Governor — A Man of Many Interests," *Portland Sunday Telegram*, 5 January 1958.

47. George F. and John Patten to the Patten Library Association, Bath, 6 August 1852, quoted in Reed, p. 222.

48. Reed, p. 223.

49. Inventory of the William King collection (Patten Free Library, Bath, ME).

50. Hennessy, "Maine's First Governor."

51. *The Weekly Mirror* (Bath), 19 June 1852.

52. Owen, pp. 226-27.

53. Ibid., p. 242.

54. Reed, p. 224.

55. *Patten Free Library*, p. 4.

56. Alberto Patten y Balderrama to John Patten, Ceuta, 23 March 1883, with attachment (translation [copy], Jarvis Patten File, MMM). In this quotation, a few phrases of the translation have been rephrased into idiomatic English.

57. Power of attorney: John Patten to Jarvis Patten, Bath, 3 July 1883 (ibid.).

58. Protection Paper for Jarvis Patten, Washington, DC, 11 July 1883 (ibid.).

5

"A Loss Severely Felt"

In 1860, with fourteen vessels in service, the firm of G.F. & J. Patten was officially dissolved. George F. continued to operate the shipyard, building five new vessels over the next decade. John and his thirty-eight-year-old son Gilbert opened up a similar business several blocks to the north, on the site of the former Jenks and Harding shipyard. The new firm, John Patten & Son, kept the old house flag with its anchor motif. Brother James, longtime Patten skipper and junior partner in the dissolving company, retired but continued to invest in ships built by each of his brothers.

Terminating G.F. & J. Patten meant only that the Patten brothers began separating their shipbuilding assets. They remained partners in their existing vessels and, as we will see, undertook some new maritime investments together. Although the Patten brothers continued their close association, their intention in old age had been to give way to the younger generation.

Youth must be served, but in the Pattens' case, "youth" was a relative term. By 1860, the sons of George and John Patten, hardly small fry, were deep into careers of their own. And they also had ideas of their own about how their generation should do business. Nonetheless, they made a stab at continuing the family's clannish business tradition. The results were mixed.

The generational transition was a long, drawn-out affair, owing in part to the outbreak of the American Civil War, which created severe economic fallout on the Kennebec. Summing up the war and its aftermath some years later, Jarvis Patten tried to paint a positive picture of the disastrous 1860s, starting with "the blockade of the Southern cotton ports, and consequent cutting off of the customary trade of our Maine ships. Although at first looked upon as a death blow to our commerce, the result was that our ships sought employment in other occupations instead of depending almost entirely upon the cotton trade.

"The California wheat trade, which has since grown to such important proportions, began to develop during this period, and the guano, rice, and other East India business,

The *Britannia* off Perch Rock lighthouse, Liverpool, about 1855. Built in 1853 by G.F. & J. Patten, the *Britannia* carried cotton to Europe and emigrants to America in the 1850s. She also ferried military cargo to Constantinople during the Crimean War. When the American Civil War disrupted the cotton trade, she switched to cargoes of guano, coal, and iron under the command of the young Charles E. Patten. *Courtesy Hart Nautical Collections, MIT Museum.*

together with the transport service, afforded employment for the greater part of our shipping.... Many of the old vessels were sold abroad, others were made bonfires of by the Confederate cruisers.... While ships belonging elsewhere were some of them transferred to foreign ownership, our ship owners with very few exceptions, preferred to fly the stars and stripes and pay the war [insurance] premiums.... After the war commerce was slow to resume its former channels. The cotton trade had been diverted and the adoption of steam vessels for freighting purposes made it possible for British steamers to do a large part of the carrying trade."[1]

Captain Jarvis had to admit that, compared to the previous decade, Bath shipbuilding went down dramatically in the 1860s: 36 percent fewer vessels, half the overall tonnage, and a 24 percent reduction in tonnage per vessel. Furthermore, Bath's stock-in-trade, the wooden sailing vessel, was now being superseded by British-built steamers, by iron square-riggers with more capacity and durability, and even by traditional wooden ships built cheaply in Canada's Maritime Provinces. The trend would continue. Iron shipbuilding involved an entirely new technology. Should Bath adapt itself in that direction? Could it? Could wooden vessels be refined to make them competitive? What about steam power? These were the questions facing the next generation of Bath shipbuilders.

Meanwhile, the Civil War claimed one Patten ship, the nine-year-old *Ariel*, seized by Confederate authorities while attempting to leave New Orleans in 1861 and later destroyed by fire in that port. Otherwise, true to Jarvis Patten's claim, Anchor Line vessels operated out of harm's way under the Stars and Stripes, resisting the temptation to adopt neutral flags of convenience that might save them from Confederate raiders (but deny them postwar repatriation) and battling rumor, confusion, and rising operating costs. Some idea of the difficulties can be seen from G.F. & J. Patten's advice to Jarvis Patten in London. Jarvis, master and co-owner of the ship *Transit*, built in 1860, had gotten one cotton cargo out of New Orleans to Le Havre, but with the opening of hostilities, the vessel was at loose ends. The word from Bath was that "the rates in England for long voyages still rule low, besides domestic insurance being required in American Ships; and as the expenses for a long voyage...could be heavy, we think it would be an object to charter for a long voyage at the present rates. If you cannot secure any paying business, we know of no better course than for you to come this way in ballast; and if [you] can come into Bath as easily as to any other place, we prefer the Ship should come in here.... if you should be obliged to haul up awhile, it could be done cheaper at Bath than in Boston or New York. You however, can see how things look just before you leave, if you should conclude to come this way in ballast."[2]

Other prewar Patten ships successfully soldiered on in wartime. The *George F. Patten*, a general-purpose freighter built in 1848 and owned by her namesake, entered the guano trade, loading that natural fertilizer in the Chincha Islands off Peru and carrying it to Europe by way of Cape Horn. Cape Horn weather was always potentially hazardous, and the *Patten* got into trouble en route from the Chinchas to Antwerp in 1864. On 27 July, her barometer dropped ominously, prompting Captain Timothy Mitchell to reduce sail drastically. Early in the morning, the ship was hit by a gale that carried away the fore-sail, leaving the vessel rolling almost helplessly as the storm intensified. The next day, strengthening winds almost tore out the bowsprit. A cabin boy, homeward bound to his native Antwerp, was washed overboard and of course lost. On 29 July, the storm weakened enough for the crew to make emergency repairs to the leaky vessel. When the weather cleared, the *Patten* proceeded safely to her destination.[3] After the war, George Patten sold her to Norwegian interests. Renamed *Claus Heftze*, she hailed from Arendal, a port that would prove adept at squeezing profits out of aging square-riggers for decades to come.

Operating during the Civil War was risky and expensive, but it still paid off, thanks to rising freight rates, and investors in Patten ships did very well. Jarvis Patten, for example, who owned one-eighth of the ships *Halcyon, John Patten,* and *Transit,* in wartime earned $4,897 on the *Patten* over 51 months, $2,141.62 on the *Halcyon* over 34 months, and $5,922.20 on the *Transit* over 42 months. His net profit on these three holdings was $13,888.32 — about $213,880 in 1995 value. Such earnings were of course in addition to whatever salary and primage he earned as a shipmaster.[4] Inasmuch as George F. and John Patten had stakes at least twice as large as those of Jarvis, their profits thereon were proportionately greater — as would also be the case with their other vessels.

Although G.F. & J. Patten undertook no further shipbuilding after 1860, the Patten brothers came together for a final, very ambitious project: construction of the twin steamships *Montana* (1865) and *Idaho* (1866). Bath had built a few small steamers before, but these vessels were monsters by comparison: almost 200 feet in length, more than 1,000 tons apiece, and driven by propellers, not paddles. Both were built — of wood, naturally — in George's yard.

Inasmuch as this ambitious project commenced before Appomattox, the sister steamers might originally have been intended for sale or charter to the U.S. government. George's son George M., whose foundry supplied the vessels' engines and boilers, was part of the small group that financed their construction; so were Charles Davenport and John's son Gilbert. Upon completion, the *Montana,* under Captain John Kelley, went around the Horn to San Francisco. She made one charter trip to Honolulu and another to British Columbia, then was acquired by the California, Oregon & Mexico Steamship Company for coastwise service.

The *Idaho,* financed by a partnership that included most of the *Montana* principals plus James F., James T. (George's son), and Jarvis Patten, first headed for San Francisco under Jarvis Patten by way of Cape Horn. The *Idaho*'s registry indicates that despite the dissolution of G.F. & J. Patten, she was the property of that firm until the California, Oregon & Mexico Steamship Company bought her in 1867, after which she operated under a U.S. government mail contract to and from Honolulu, then engaged in coastwise service.

Both steamers kept busy hauling freight and passengers and both eventually were lost. The *Montana* met her end after becoming the property of the Colorado Steam

Navigation Company. In December 1876, she caught fire and was lost without casualties in the Gulf of California near Guaymas, Mexico. Her insured value was $60,000 (about $984,000 in 1995 currency). That same year, the *Idaho* changed hands for $50,000 ($770,000 in 1995 dollars), eventually winding up with the Oregon Railway & Navigation Company. In November 1889, en route from Port Townsend, Washington, to Portland, Oregon, she ran hard onto a reef in the Strait of Juan de Fuca. When a diver determined that her entire engine and boiler had been torn out of her and that she in fact had no bottom, her remains were towed to Port Townsend and broken up.[5]

The Pattens built no other commercial steam vessels. George F. went back to what he knew best, wooden square-riggers. In 1868, he and brother James were partners in building the 1,252-ton *Japan*, which entered the Cape Horn trade under Captain S.P. Emmons. Emmons previously had commanded the *John Patten* but had come home in 1866 to

The wooden, propeller-driven Montana *was built by George and John Patten in 1865, while their partnership was undergoing liquidation. George M. Patten's Bath foundry supplied her engine and boiler. One of two Patten-built commercial steamers, the* Montana *rounded the Horn to operate as a passenger and freight vessel on the West Coast. Courtesy Maine Maritime Museum.*

open a grocery store downriver in Phippsburg. The grocery business being what it was, Emmons needed little convincing to go back to sea in 1868 as master of the new *Japan.*

Off Cape Horn in August 1870, the grocery business began to look good again. Somehow, the *Japan* had caught fire. Emmons and the crew tried for five days to smother the flames without success. They abandoned the big ship, going aboard the assisting *Matchless,* which carried them to Pernambuco, Brazil, for medical attention. Once home, Emmons went back to his old command, the *John Patten,* which was sold in Boston in 1872.[6] By 1881, rigged as a bark, she hailed from Liverpool.

Meanwhile, the old (and old-fashioned) G.F. & J. Patten ships were disappearing. But they did not all go quietly. Take the case of the *Amity,* launched in 1858, a vessel that had spent most of her life in transatlantic trade. She was sold in 1874, to be delivered to Antwerp. The captain for her last Anchor Line voyage was James M.W. Patten of Bowdoinham, age thirty-six — "the Handsome Patten," as he was justly called. James M.W. had credentials to match his looks. His formal English education was unusually strong for a Yankee shipmaster, and he possessed a British license under which he had commanded English as well as American vessels. He had lately retired but was persuaded to deliver the *Amity* to her new owners in Antwerp.

Three weeks out of Philadelphia, the aging *Amity* encountered heavy seas and sprang a leak. She became waterlogged and was fit for abandonment, but the weather looked too threatening for the crew to lower boats. What to do? There was no choice; the order came to abandon. As feared, the *Amity*'s lowered boats capsized and the crew disappeared — except for four desperate sailors who had refused to leave the ship and were found clinging to the *Amity*'s rigging by the passing Norwegian bark *Norge.* According to a later, published account, "Two of these became insane and refused to leave the rigging when assistance was offered.... The other two were rescued by means of a line thrown from the long boat and were taken to Queenstown [Ireland], being the only survivors."[7]

Because many of the *Amity*'s crew were local, the loss hit Bath and Bowdoinham particularly hard. A few months after the news reached home, James M.W.'s Masonic lodge published a memorial to the lost captain that was a masterpiece of earnest Victorian sentiment:

"*Whereas,* it has pleased the Great Giver of life to remove by death our much esteemed brother, Jas. W. Patten, thereby severing another link of that fraternal chain which binds us into one common band of brothers and fellows, therefore,

"*Resolved,* that by this dispensation of divine Providence, this lodge has lost a worthy brother, society one of its brightest ornaments, and his family an affectionate and devoted husband and father.

"*Resolved,* that we tender our sincere sympathy to the widow of the deceased, in this her great bereavement, and confidently recommend her to the kind care and protection of him who 'tempereth the wind to the sho[r]n lamb,' whose chastisings are tempered with mercy; who doeth all things well.

"*Resolved,* that these resolutions be published in the Bath Times, and copy be pre-

"The handsome Patten": James M.W. of Bowdoinham. After retiring from the sea, this popular captain agreed to make one last voyage as master of the *Amity*. En route to Antwerp in 1874, the old ship sank in heavy seas. Patten and all but two of the crew were drowned. *Courtesy Maine Maritime Museum.*

served among the records in the archives of the Lodge, and another be presented to the family of the deceased."[8]

The wartime trend by which steamers and iron ships edged into Bath's niche continued. In 1869, the ever-watchful Jarvis Patten, writing from London, attempted to dramatize the changing maritime world for the hometown press: "The Cry is that steamers do not pay but still they are increasing yearly, the formerly valuable Baltic trade is now almost entirely done by steam, and for the ports of Holland, Belgium, & France steamers are running every day almost entirely precluding the small sailing craft that formerly found employment in this once lucrative traffic…. Iron ships are also increasing…. They carry more of measurement & less deadweight according to tonnage than wooden ships hence they pay better…. Just now there is some excitement in commercial circles as to the success of the Suez Canal and there are various speculations as to the effect it is going to have on the carrying trade of the world. Some anxiety is felt among ship owners that it will result in a reduced demand for sailing vessels cutting short as it does the voyage to the East over one half…."[9]

Anxiety. To retain its prosperity, Bath would have to modernize its shipbuilding capability or diversify into other types of industry. Leading the search for diversification were the sons of George F. and John Patten.

Captain Gilbert Patten had built a handsome career as master of G.F. & J. Patten ships. He had gone to sea at fifteen, and, in 1847, became skipper of the *Halcyon* at age twenty-two. Patten had much more going for him than nepotism. Someone who served with him during his first captaincy stipulated that Gilbert "exhibited abilities far in advance of his years: sound judgment, coolness and self-possession in danger, and a faculty to command.... I remember him in his second voyage as master in a most perilous situation, one which called for the best qualities of the seaman to extricate his ship and save her from imminent wreck. He was equal to the emergency. With quick decision, he adopted the course which the event proved was the only one that could have brought him out of the jaws of destruction, and the decision, made with a coolness and precision that would have done honor to a veteran, carried his plan to a successful issue. Even in those early days, he was governed in his dealings and in his intercourse with men by principles of high honor, and I well remember the impression he made upon those with whom he was thrown in business relations in different countries, and the many words I heard spoken in praise of his trustworthiness and integrity."[10]

In 1849, Captain Gilbert took the Patten brig *Fawn* to California with a cargo of gold hunters, becoming the first in his family to round Cape Horn.[11] Several voyages after that, he quit the sea and, following the breakup of G.F. & J. Patten, became part of John Patten & Son. (Captain John originally planned a partnership with both his sons, but John Levi, Gilbert's younger brother, died in Bath in 1860.) Gilbert's memories of going

"Love of justice, straight forward dealings, honor and strict integrity": Captain Gilbert Patten, son and partner of John and co-founder of the Patten Car Works. Gilbert's failing health curtailed family shipbuilding by the 1870s, but Patten & Son stayed afloat with ships contracted in another yard. Like his father, Gilbert was a generous philanthropist. *Courtesy Maine Maritime Museum.*

around the Horn in 1849 may have inspired the name of the first vessel built by the new firm: *Fawn*, launched in 1860. The new *Fawn* was an 874-ton cotton trader whose career was cut short by the Civil War. She was sold to New York interests and put into transatlantic service, remaining active under various owners until 1902.

During the 1860s, John Patten & Son built seven vessels. Thanks to the clipper fad, ships had gotten sharper, shapelier, and more rakish as builders merged streamlining know-how with traditional skills. The Pattens had never been known for experimentation, nor had they dabbled in clippers, but the visual evidence of the John Patten & Son ships reveals that they were up-to-date if not experimental. The company's vessels sported double topsails, a rig that could be managed handily by a reduced crew. Some were bark-rigged, a further concession to economy. In 1862, Patten & Son completed the *Hudson*, the first Bath-built ship equipped with wire standing rigging, a vast improvement over traditional hemp.[12]

Because of wartime pressures and the changing nature of world trade, the *Hudson* became a true tramp freighter. Leaving New York in December 1862, she did not return to the United States until March 1866. Meanwhile, she had sailed to Europe, India, the Persian Gulf, the East Indies, and Australia. The *Hudson* stayed active until 1876.

Another Patten & Son ship was the *India* of 1,295 tons, completed in 1869. Her captain for ten years thereafter was Lincoln Patten, Captain John's cousin, who had started as master aboard the original *Caspian* in 1839. Also on board was twenty-one-year-old Charles Rogers, who, despite his tender years, had served in the Civil War and then risen to mate on the *India*. A Topsham native who aspired to a master's ticket, Rogers took sailing very seriously. Accordingly, he kept a shipboard journal that affords us a look at life on a Patten & Son vessel. In the years since Abner Wade and Jarvis Patten recorded their shipboard experiences, some things had changed; others hadn't.

Like many Bath ships, the *India* earned her keep as a long-distance bulk hauler, sailing if necessary to the ends of the earth. On 9 January 1869, she left Bath loaded with hay and ice for New Orleans, arriving on 11 February. On 28 March, she was ready for sea again, and the crew came aboard in various stages of sobriety. On her way out of New Orleans, she got stuck on the bar that had frustrated so many Patten vessels over the years. Eventually, she made her way in ballast to Baltimore, where she went into dry-dock for coppering prior to heading around the Horn to San Francisco. On 7 May, fit and loaded with Appalachian coal, she began her long journey.

Rogers's journal on board the *India* was kept for future professional reference and meant for his eyes only. His style was much like Jarvis Patten's: a daily record of the *India*'s progress that included latitude and longitude, details of wind and weather, and sailing activity. Occasionally, something unusual would prompt a personal confidence. For example, fifteen days out of Baltimore, Rogers noted that the *India* "spoke a Russian Brig short of provision from Bounas Ayres [Buenos Aires] 100 days out, cargo of Sheep Skins. Gave him some flour & Bread, Potatoes & Peas."[13] On 10 June, the *India* crossed the Equator.

For the crew, every day promised a round of hard work. Here is a typical example, recorded on 9 July, well east of the River Plate: "This day begins with a strong wind & a heavy head sea.... at 4 PM stowed mainsail [and] inner jib. Reefed topsails, close reefed foresail. Water coming over the ship at all parts (Baro falling). at 7.30 furled fore Topsail. at 10 PM furled Main Topsail & mizzen lower topsail & hove the ship to, heavy sea running, strong wind with Passing Rain squalls. at 8 AM set the Spanker Reefed. Ends with squally weather and strong sea running."

The *India*'s progress was uneventful — much too uneventful for Charles Rogers, who took exception to Captain Lincoln Patten's caution and the crew's bumbling. Time was money. Why, then, didn't the skipper crack on sail? In fact, he did the opposite. On the Fourth of July, 1869, Rogers fumed in his journal that "they are a bunch of old women to carry sail here." On 22 July, after furling sail in light winds and fine weather, he decided that "I never see such a fraid man to carry sail as Capt. Patten. he does not deserve a fair wind at all. when he has the Top Gall[ant] Sails furled he ought

This fascinating slice-of-life photograph shows the Patten ship *India*, probably in San Francisco. Built in 1868, the *India*'s rakish lines and complex rigging dramatize how far sailing-ship technology had come by the late 19th century. The *India* stayed under the Patten flag until 1887. *Courtesy Maine Maritime Museum.*

"Coming alongside: 'See, take this line with you. Then do it god damn you. Do it now!'" This captioned sketch of a bucko mate appears in Charles Rogers's *India* journal, 1869. It may be a portrait of Rogers himself. *Courtesy Maine Maritime Museum.*

to have Studdingsails on her, all sail. Getting Old & carefull."[14]

Sailors, of course, had good reason to fear Cape Horn weather, especially when serving under an aggressive, risk-taking captain. On this voyage, however, Rogers found that there was nothing to fear, for the weather stayed pleasant and the skipper stayed cautious.

On 2 August, nearing Cape Horn, he noted with pleasure that "this day begins with a light breeze from the NW. at 4 PM wind WNW off the Land. still breezing up at 8.... we are now 140 miles from Cape Horn. Strong Wind all night some time 10 knot breeze all sail set excepting the Main Royal nice clear weather. the water [is] as smooth as it is in the Kennebec River at Bath. at 6 lost sight of Staten Land and at 8.30 AM next morning made Cape Horn dis[tant] 26 miles a splendid run, still a fair wind."

Once in the Pacific, however, Rogers found much to grumble about regarding the Old Man's progress, for the previous routine of proceeding under shortened sail resumed: "Wednesday August 4th... This day begins with a strong wind & sea from the west NW. at 4 P.M. Close Reefed Mainsail & Furled it & Main Topsail. Reefed Foresail. Furled fore upper Topsail. Reefed Mizzen Topsail. Stowed Spanker & Maine Top Mast staysail and the lower topsails. Close reefed Main & Mizen topsail & Reefed foresail & fore Topmast staysail. *Scared.* it is a shame. pretty soon comes along a ship at 7.30 PM with her Courses & all sail set excepting mizzen Top Sail, Main Royal & Flying jib. She went by us all a flying and so close you could heave a stone aboard of her. the Capt. did not hardly know what to say at that...."

By 21 August, Rogers had his mind on something else: "I was taken sick yesterday morning vomiting & the flying ax handles. very sick. The Capt standing my watch until this morning. at 4 PM went on deck." The rest of the voyage proceeded without incident until, on 30 September 1869, 145 days out of Baltimore, the *India* made San Francisco and "came to anchor in the Bay obsit [opposite] the city."

She discharged her coal, took on wheat in sacks, and set sail for Liverpool on 16 November, rounding Cape Horn again without incident in January 1870. On that passage, Rogers was either too busy or too uninspired to write down much more than weather and navigational data. Occasionally he amused himself by making hasty marginal sketches of passing ships, which he identified whenever possible. Nothing of consequence seems to have occurred until 15 February, when, just north of the Equator in mid-Atlantic, he "caught a shark 5½ feet long."

On 31 March, entering the Celtic Sea in warm weather, something interesting and grisly turned up: "At Noon passed by a *Dead Man*, floating on the water, face *downward* hair all off his head, left foot gone & the bone sticking out. awful to look at. worst condition I ever see a man being in yet." Three days later, the *India* raised Kinsale lighthouse on the south coast of Ireland, and on 6 April 1870, 146 days out of San Francisco, she "took a steam tug. at 8 AM made Holyhead [Wales], at 6.30 came to anchor oposit Queen's dock, Liverpool."

While the *India*'s California wheat sacks were being removed from her hold by means of tackle (falls) running to a donkey engine, a mishap occurred: "Boy got nearly killed by the donkey engine fall. caught him broke his arm & tore his side all to pieces." Once unloaded, the ship was painted and salted, then filled with iron, coal, soda ash, hides, salt, rags, and paper for Boston.

After a thirty-five-day passage, the ship made Boston on 23 July, and Rogers took a steamer home to Maine. After ten days, he returned to the *India* for her transfer to the Donald McKay Wharf in East Boston for repairs. While that work proceeded under Gilbert Patten's supervision, Rogers squeezed in another trip to Topsham via the Bath boat. On 1 September, the *India* sailed in ballast for Saint John, where for sixteen days she loaded lumber, departing on 26 September for Penarth, Wales. Twenty-five days later, she was in Penarth Roads. After unloading, she was towed to Bristol for orders, took on iron at Cardiff, and then cleared for New Orleans.

We will leave her to pursue her busy schedule. The *India* will tramp for cargoes worldwide under the Patten flag until the late 1880s, and still will be active a decade thereafter. Captain Lincoln Patten, a widower, will marry Maria Tarbox, widow of the ill-fated *Mobile* skipper, in 1872. Young Charles Rogers will marry Jennie Roberts, a Liverpool girl, in 1873. He will command several steamships, and his wife will often accompany him at sea. By the time of his death, in 1927, vessels like the *India* will be all but extinct.

In the wartime year of 1864, while teenager Charles Rogers was in military service, George Patten returned to the state legislature. Much had changed, including George Patten, since his last term back in 1838-39. A colleague provided a portrait of the venerable gentleman near the end of his long life: "Captain Patten is probably the wealthiest man in the House. He has for a long series of years been engaged in ship building out of which he has amassed a splendid fortune. The city of Bath owes more to Capt. Patten, than any other man for its material wealth and prosperity. It has been his enterprise more than that of any other man, which has made it a great mart of business.

"Ever since the commencement of war he has stood by the administration like a rock and contributed largely both of his means and influence to sustain it. In olden times he was a whig, now a staunch republican. His excellent business qualifications, large experience and sound practical judgement, render him one of the most valuable, and influential members of the House."[15]

George F. Patten —
former shipbuilder,
bank president, legisla-
tive representative,
militia captain, mis-
sionary commissioner,
railroad director, and
philanthropist — in old
age. On his death in
1869, the local press, in
an understatement,
noted that "the decease
of Mr. Patten will be a
loss severely felt in this
community." *Courtesy
Maine Maritime
Museum.*

Unfortunately, George Patten's term in the legislature would go unfinished. In 1865, the year his political stance was vindicated at Appomattox, he had to resign his seat because of ill health. Widowed since 1862, he had for some years suffered various physical complaints that now were catching up with him. He hung on a few years longer — the *Montana* and the *Idaho* were testimony to his resolution — but his death on 26 September 1869 came as no surprise. In the words of the Bath press, "For some time his advanced years have kept him confined to his house, and he had been gradually sinking, retaining, however, his full senses to the last."[16]

It was, however, a milestone, and everyone in Bath knew it. Citizens had acquired the habit of marking important milestones by unusually elaborate parades and ceremonies, a tradition that may have started with Governor William King's funeral. So it was with the funeral of George F. Patten. On that solemn day, flags on public buildings and on vessels in the Kennebec were lowered to half-mast. The service, held at home, where the body was on view "within an elegant metallic casket, covered with a profusion of immortelles [everlastings]," was attended by a throng of friends and admirers, including political VIPs, the president of Bowdoin College, and board members of the Portland and Kennebec Railroad. Reverend J.O. Fiske, minister of Winter Street Church, eulogized the deceased, after which a male quartet sang songs befitting the occasion.

After one last look at the remains, the pallbearers, including William D. Sewall and three sea captains, bore George's casket out of his gracious home. "The remains were conveyed to Maple Grove Cemetery, where they were buried in the family tomb. The funeral cortege numbered nearly forty carriages, one of the largest funeral processions that ever was seen in this city."[17]

A newspaper editorial following the funeral reviewed George Patten's illustrious maritime career and put the whole man in perspective for those too young to know the story: "Mr. Patten was largely interested in railroad enterprises, and in all public improvements. He was one of the original projectors of the Kennebec & Portland railroad, as well as one of the first members of the board of directors, a position he held at the time of his death.

"In the war of 1812, he was a captain of a company of militia.

"For four years he served as a member of the State Legislature, and, in 1856, he was the candidate of the Whig party for Governor.

"For many years he was president of the Lincoln Bank of this city.

"He was a trustee of the American Board of Commissioners for Foreign Missions, and trustee, and many years vice-president of the Maine Missionary Society.

"He was a member of the Board of Overseers of Bowdoin College.

"He was a member of the Winter Street Congregational church, and a liberal supporter of every Christian enterprise.

"In 1820 he was married to Hannah Thomas.... Of his eight children, two sons and five daughters survive him, one of the sons [James T.] being our present mayor.

"The decease of Mr. Patten will be a loss severely felt in this community...."[18]

George Patten's will was uncomplicated. Except for codicils that left $2,000 to the Maine Charity School and $1,000 each to the Maine Missionary Society and American Commissioners for Foreign Missions, his estate was divided equally among his seven living children, with the daughters' portions placed in trusts. The size of the estate was remarkable. Appraisers valued his real estate (including the Patten shipyard and wharf) at $34,175; his share of ship property came to $157,400; his stocks and bonds amounted to about $220,000; miscellaneous rights and credits came to another $10,600. The estate's total value was $434,000, equivalent to $6.7 million in 1995. Each of his children received $62,000 ($950,000 in 1995 value).[19]

In 1871, George's son George M. built a steam yacht named *Twilight* in his father's yard. The *Twilight* was not a significant vessel except in the symbolic sense. Her recreational character emphasized the carriage-trade tastes of a younger generation of Pattens accustomed to wealth. And the fact that she was engine-powered signaled the changing

Downtown Bath about 1870, looking west along Centre Street, where something special appears to be in the offing. One of the white buildings on the right, near the elm tree, will become the site of the Patten Library Association after its donation by Captain John in 1879. Atop the hill in the distance is the Sagadahoc County Court House. *Courtesy Norman Howard/Maine Maritime Museum.*

technology that was overtaking the City of Ships. Finally, she was the last Patten vessel launched in the old family yard. In 1872, that property was sold and added to the adjoining yard of E. & A. Sewall, a firm that was expanding thanks to its ability to adapt to changing times. In more ways than one, the Sewalls were becoming the successors to the Pattens.

Although George Patten's two surviving sons, James T. and George M., had not gone to sea, they were active in the shipbuilding community during the heyday of the Anchor Line. In 1854, at age twenty-four, James was an importer and dealer in bar iron and steel in Bath. The next year, he and his nineteen-year-old brother became partners in a spike factory that was destroyed by fire, causing a $3,000 loss.

George M. then set up a venture in new technology — for the Pattens, at least. The business, named G.M. Patten & Company, was a brass foundry and machine shop on Commercial Street that produced deck equipment. In the wartime year of 1864, it also built the engine for the *Fearless,* a tug sold to the U.S. government for service as a towboat in occupied Charleston. Other projects included supplying engines for the *Montana, Idaho,* and the Bath-built excursion steamer *Falcon.*[20] The shop was sold in 1869 to Francis Torrey of Richmond, who established the long-lived Torrey Roller Bushing Works.

In 1866, George M. Patten acquired an interest in the Bath-built steam packet *Eastern City,* designed to compete with the Kennebec Steamship Company's *Daniel Webster* between Gardiner and Boston. Competition was keen, but there was not enough freight and passenger business to sustain two such steamers. So the *Falcon* and the *Webster* put each other out of business. After idling uselessly in Bath for a few years, the *Falcon* operated between Baltimore and West Point, Virginia, under the command of cousin Jarvis Patten. She, as well as the *Webster,* ended up on the St. Lawrence River.[21]

While it was not a dramatic success, G.M. Patten & Company gave its owner valuable experience in heavy industry, paving the way for the Patten clan's next venture, G.F. & J. Pattens' Sons.

The *Bath Daily Times* reported the good news on 20 September 1872: "The late firm of G.F. & J. Patten, so long and favorably known almost the world over, has been succeeded by the firm of G.F. & J. Pattens' Sons, and it is by this firm that the Patten Car Works are being erected. The persons in the firm are, James T. and George M., sons of the late Capt. George F. Patten, and Gilbert E.R., son of Hon. John Patten."

The founding of the Patten Car Works constituted a poetic rollover from the old to the new generation of Pattens. Once again, congenial relatives and neighbors were assuming risk, pooling resources, and pioneering a promising new industry in Bath. And a rollover it was. The new company's founding date coincided with the sale of George F.'s yard to E. & A. Sewall — a transaction that probably provided some of the new company's start-up capital. Poetic justice aside, the logic of the new enterprise was as timely and auspicious as the rationale by which John and George Patten had formed their partnership more than half a century earlier. Through the Patten Car Works, G.F. & J. Pattens' Sons proposed to manufacture railroad cars "of every description, from the commonest dirt car to the most superb Pullman car."[22]

Consider the factors that led to this decision. For some time, Bath had struggled to augment its highly specialized maritime trades. Leading citizens had enhanced the region's economic potential by bringing the railroad to town. In 1870, the Portland and Kennebec Railroad had consolidated with the Maine Central system. Obviously, railroads, a growth industry, would be in constant need of improved rolling stock. Here was opportunity.

Creating a car foundry required major capital, but, in the early 1870s, the Patten sons had plenty of that. If more were needed, family connections at the Lincoln National Bank would open doors. Such a business also required know-how in heavy industry. George M. Patten had acquired just that while operating his erstwhile foundry on Commercial Street. Business expertise? No problems there, either. Connections? Already in place, thanks to the older generation's key roles in the Portland and Kennebec Railroad.

(Captain John, in fact, was a director of the Maine Central Railroad after 1870.) Location? Plenty of land available on North Street above High, near existing railroad tracks. All in all, an exciting and clever prospect.

G.F. & J. Pattens' Sons started from scratch and went first-class. In May 1872, the firm acquired the North Street plot, which ran 531 feet along North Street and was 515 feet deep. Francis Fassett, a celebrated Bath-born architect, was retained to design the car foundry. Construction began in June, when a 2,000-foot track was laid from the Maine Central right-of-way to the North Street site.

The plant buildings were nearing completion by fall. The press followed the construction enthusiastically, and with good reason, for the new, high-tech operation was, by Bath standards, colossal. Beautiful, too. The Car Works, remember, went up at a time when foursquare industrial buildings, smokestacks, and rail sidings were regarded not as eyesores but as symbols of progress and prosperity. Thus: "The wood machine shop is 150 by 75, and is two stories high. The lower story being devoted to heavy machinery…; the upper story will contain light machinery and benches for the workmen; adjoining this is the erecting shop 220 by 75, containing 8 tracks, and having room for setting up 9 passenger or 16 freight cars at a time. The whole length of the two buildings extending north from North street is 370 feet, the whole being heated by a steam apparatus…. Two inch water pipes run the whole length of the building…, with rubber hose on the posts, ready for instant use in case of fire, the whole being connected with one of Wright's steam pumps in the engine room." The complex also included an office building, blacksmith and machine shops, and a paint shop where "6 passenger or 12 freight cars can be painted at once." All the structures had gravel roofs. To superintend the operation, Pattens' Sons hired J.W. Trussel, master car builder of the former Portland and Kennebec Railroad.[23]

Although the company's records unfortunately have disappeared, it is obvious that the Patten Car Works constituted a major, long-term financial commitment by Pattens' Sons and a dramatic demonstration of confidence in economic growth. In accordance with Patten tradition, it would also be good for Bath, whose citizens were feeling the shipbuilding pinch. Demand for big wooden ships was slumping. Yards had turned to smaller schooners, construction of which was not enough to keep the workforce occupied year-round. To many, the Patten Car Works looked like a godsend.

The *Times* perfectly caught the mood of the moment by stating that "too much credit cannot be given to those spirited and energetic gentlemen, the Messrs. GEO. F. PATTEN'S SONS [sic], who have demonstrated that the decline of one business in Bath does not necessarily involve the decline of all, and we can but wish them all the success due to their perseverance and liberality. The works will be in full operation about the 1st of October and will give employment to some 200 men."[24] When the plant opened, the rush of workers into Bath created a housing shortage in the city. George and John Patten's sons were truly local heroes.

Theoretically, the Patten Car Works was an idea whose time had come. Practically speaking, however, the timing was undone by economic forces beyond the company's control. The American economy began to go sour precisely at the time the company opened for business.

For a while, the Car Works took the economic climate in stride. The Maine Central Railroad placed orders, and the plant quickly acquired a reputation for quality construction. And when demand for railroad equipment began to sag in the United States, the Car Works aggressively and successfully pursued contracts north of the border. For example, in mid-1874, it went to work on three first-class passenger cars for the Canadian government's new Inter-Colonial Railway, which linked Ontario with the Maritime Provinces.[25] Later that year, the firm built ten similar cars for the St. Francis & Megantic; three others, "beautifully finished inside and warmed with the 'Baker steam heater,'" were completed for an American line, the Portland & Rochester.[26] Between the glamour contracts, the company produced freight cars that won acclaim for their efficient storage capabilities.

In 1876, the Quebec, Montreal & Ottawa took delivery of a string of passenger cars. As reported in the *Times* on 28 August, "The second class [cars] are painted inside a light drab with head linings in blue and gold, relieved by black walnut mouldings. The first class cars are finished inside with bird's eye maple, black walnut and rose wood with blue and gold mouldings."

Such opulence, of course, depends upon a strengthening, expanding economy. But that did not occur in the mid-1870s. Domestic orders remained scant and, despite state-of-the-art facilities and a solid reputation, the Patten Car Works closed its doors in 1877. The doors remained closed. Eventually, some of the company machinery was sold and shipped to Canada. The impact of the shutdown on the community was more than a matter of lost jobs. Gone also was the hope for diversification represented by the grand investment of G.F. & J. Pattens' Sons.

The impact on the Pattens is also complex. Captain Gilbert, involved with the management of John Patten & Son, has more on his mind than the Car Works in 1877. In addition, he is in failing health. Bright's disease, perhaps? Tuberculosis? Whatever the affliction, it causes him considerable suffering and requires periodic visits to gentler climates.[27] He continues to go downhill and, in January 1882, dies at fifty-nine. Noting his passing, the *Bath Daily Times* describes Gilbert Patten as having the same qualities of character that distinguished his celebrated and hale father: "None have had business relations with him, but to respect his love of justice, straight forward dealings, honor and strict integrity.... To young men in need of assistance, to those pinched by poverty or want, to the public interests of the city, to all good men and good causes, to all friends dependent or needing his advice and help, he ever stood ready to afford the help of a brother."[28] High praise, even for the *Times*.

The brothers George M. and James T. Patten survive the Car Works failure, although James T. has a rough go of it and by 1880 is on hard times — surely a humiliating ordeal for the former mayor. In January of that year, having tried in vain to obtain financial help from his parents' friends, he requests a loan from shipbuilder Arthur

The buildings of the Patten Car Works on the far side of North Street, Bath. *Courtesy Maine Maritime Museum.*

Sewall. "I am trying hard to get something to do," he writes, "and my sisters tell me to keep up a good heart and something will turn up."[29] Something does. He becomes a New York agent for the Wasson Company, another railway-car manufacturer. Within three years, he has his own office at 18 Broadway, New York, representing Wasson and the Portland Company.[30] He also enters the oil business but dies in Waynesville, North Carolina, in 1888.

James's brother George M. is not wiped out by the Car Works failure, but he is perhaps burned out. In any case, he does not resume his former engineering business, although, in the mid-1880s, as a representative of the Maine Central Railroad, he superintends the fitting of the *Sappho*, a luxurious steamer that makes passenger connections to Mt. Desert Island. George M.'s private life is also flawed. In 1895, in an accident laced with irony, his teenage daughter Katherine is killed when a carriage in which she is riding is struck by a passing train at the Centre Street crossing, a block from the Sagadahock

The pride of the Patten Car Works, elegant railway passenger carriages such as this one served on several railroads in the United States and Canada. This one is Maine Central no. 51. Such cars were state-of-the art and opulently finished inside and out. *Courtesy Harris Rodick/Maine Maritime Museum.*

In the 1870s, second-class passengers rode in the lap of luxury, as this Patten Car Works railway coach proves. The seatbacks apparently are reversible. *Courtesy Maine Historic Preservation Commission.*

Good fences may make good neighbors, but with a neighbor like John Patten, these were purely ornamental. Here are the venerable captain, his attendant, his horse and buggy, and his handsome North Street home.
Courtesy Charles E. Burden, M.D.

House. George M. will live quietly until 1901, when, at age sixty-five, he is felled by a sudden heart attack at his Bath home. His obituary in the *Times* dwells on his father's prominence, acknowledges his participation in the Patten Car Works, and describes him simply as "an expert mechanic and a courteous gentleman who will be missed by many friends."[31]

The exciting Car Works venture retains its local mystique even in failure, but the abandoned plant presents a dismal sight until 1887, when Addison & Strout opens an oilcloth factory in some of the buildings. In 1898, the site will be taken over by the Brunswick & Bath Electric Street Railway Company and used as a carbarn until the 1930s. In 1949, as part of a celebration marking the centennial of the first train's arrival in Bath, city fathers will bring a few rolling curios to town: creaky old coaches built by the all-but-forgotten Patten Car Works.[32] Some things last forever.

Some people last forever, or seem to — John Patten, for instance. In September 1885, more than twenty years after losing his second wife, and having outlived the last of his children, Captain John's apparent indestructibility was honored in a formal manner when seventy-five friends and relatives visited the old gentleman at his North Street home to celebrate his ninety-sixth birthday. John's servants and the well-wishers had prepared a memorable evening. According to the local press, "The reception room was prettily decorated with flowers. Over the mantel were the figures 96, enclosed in a horse shoe of immortelles. During the evening Capt. Patten conversed with nearly all present. Those present sat down to a bountiful repast. It was nearly 11 o'clock when the reception came to a close.

"Among those present with their ladies were, Capt. Chas. Patten,... Capt. William

Jarvis and Lottie Patten's home, Washington Street, Bath, 1883. Outside, a study in classical formality; inside, a warren of Victorian plush and bric-a-brac from the family's world travels. The youngster peering from the third-floor window is probably son Goldwin — later Goldwin Patton, professional actor. *Courtesy Maine Maritime Museum.*

Torrey, Capt. P.M. Whitmore [Whittemore], Gen. T.W. Hyde, Galen C. Moses, Mrs. Gilbert Patten and family, Mrs. Geo. M. Patten and daughter, Miss Victoria Reed and Geo. Davenport."[33] The Jarvis Pattens, whose home was two doors up from Winter Street Church, a short walk to Captain John's, had a good excuse for their absence: They were in Washington, Jarvis having lately become the nation's first commissioner of navigation. In hindsight, one of the more interesting guests was Thomas Hyde, a heroic general in the late war and, in 1883, an organizer of the Bath Iron Works — which, in another decade, would become a leading builder of sophisticated engine-powered steel vessels. Although it was not clear at the time of Captain John's birthday party, Hyde's new company would provide the City of Ships with something the Patten Car Works had not: a recipe for future economic survival.[34]

But on that day in 1885, all eyes were on the past, not the future. It is easy to imagine the onetime War of 1812 privateer in characteristic dark suit and flowing white hair, surrounded by well-wishers and flowers, reminiscing about his long, illustrious life and, no doubt, providing an inspiration to anyone who had intimations of mortality. Having far outlived all his partners and his immediate family, he was still energetic and mentally sharp at ninety-six. And he was still in business.

Patten & Son continued after the death of Gilbert, thanks in part to the participation of Charles Davenport, president of the Lincoln National Bank and a major investor in Bath-built vessels. But the days for wooden square-riggers were numbered, and old Captain John knew it. At the end of 1886, he told a newspaper reporter that sailing vessels "have nearly all been driven from the cotton carrying business by the steamers, and the English vessels get the greater share of it. Our shipbuilding business is now languishing and the opening of the Suez Canal has completely revolutionized the East Indian carrying trade."[35] Patten & Son operated as a holding action against the revolution.

In the 1880s, Bath was again busy building ships; during that decade, the number and tonnage turned out by local shipyards broke all previous records. But most of these new vessels were small to middling coastwise schooners and steamers. Construction of large square-riggers dropped by almost 75 percent from the 1860s.[36]

As the number of big wooden ships fell, the survivors filled the shrinking niche, cutting costs to stay competitive on long-distance routes such as the Cape Horn and Australia trades. Commissioner Jarvis Patten, who knew a thing or two about freight rates and ship maintenance, saw the writing on the wall. In the mid-1880s, he admitted that "it has been difficult and expensive during the late decline of our tonnage for the American ship-owner to maintain the high reputation of the flag. He must sail his ship with fewer men, depending on quality to make up for numbers, which naturally leads to a practice of going to sea short-handed. The inducements held out to our young men to go to sea for a living have fallen off, too..., so that the average crew of the American ship to-day is probably over two-thirds made up of foreigners, lately landed from all kinds of vessels and from all quarters of the globe. Under such circumstances it can scarcely be expected that the standard efficiency of American crews will not continue to deteriorate. It is the consequence of a declining merchant shipping that the maritime spirit should decline with it."[37]

John Patten & Son's *Nimbus,* launched in 1869, was the last ship built in-house, probably because Gilbert's failing health prevented further active supervision. Thereafter, Patten & Son ships were built by Goss & Sawyer (later Goss, Sawyer & Packard), an expanding Bath company that turned out wooden vessels of all sizes, almost on a mass-production basis. After Gilbert's death in 1882, however, no further ships were commissioned.

As in earlier years, Patten ships were not the luckiest. The *Nimbus* lasted eight years, meeting her end off the Columbia River on Friday, 28 December 1877, under the command of Reginald Leonard. Loaded with grain for Cork, she and two other ships, *Pilgrim* and *Aberystwyth Castle,* had departed Portland, Oregon, each under tow by a tug. The procession crossed the Columbia River Bar in a line, *Nimbus's* tug taking the lead. Conditions appeared generally favorable for going to sea, but, according to a later report, "There were heavy rolling swells breaking on the bar, which lifted the Nimbus high and caused the vessel to thump heavily twice. Both the [other] ships... thumped also as they crossed."

How many bars had been thumped by how many Patten ships? This time, "the heavy blows received by the Nimbus started her seams and caused her to leak badly. When the pilot left the Nimbus..., there were only eight inches of water in the hold. Capt. Leonard thought his vessel was all right, and making sail bore away." A few hours later, the ship's carpenter reported three feet of water in the hold. All pumps were put into operation, but within two hours, the water had gained another three feet. Hopeless. With the *Aberystwyth Castle* standing by, and with seventeen feet of water in the hold, Leonard gave the order to abandon the *Nimbus.* All hands "stayed near in small boats and watched the sinking ship until 12:55 on Saturday morning, when the Nimbus took her final plunge, and faded from sight. As near as can be determined, the Nimbus sunk 25 miles from shore. Capt. Leonard and crew were saved...."[38] The ship and her cargo were fully insured.

Another Patten & Son ship, the 1,395-ton *Astoria,* built by Goss & Sawyer in 1875, had a long and productive life as a tramp freighter. She was sold foreign in 1887 and continued in active service another six years.

But the vessels that technically were the last word in high-tech wooden-ship design and, incidentally, the last Patten & Son ships, were the *Florence,* a 1,684-ton giant launched by Goss & Sawyer in 1877, and the *Tacoma,* 1,739 tons, in 1881. John Patten and Charles Davenport owned half of these ships; other investors included Davenport's grown son George and the ships' first captain, John R. Kelley, a longtime Patten master. The *Florence,* named for Captain Kelley's daughter, was noted for speed. She spent her Patten years hauling grain and coal between the West Coast and Britain. In 1898, she was sold to West

Coast owners. She disappeared on a passage between Tacoma and Honolulu in 1902.

On her maiden voyage, under John Kelley, the *Tacoma* went around the Horn. On board as a passenger was John Owen Patten, Gilbert's son, of whom we will soon hear more. The ship's second master was Parker Sheldon of Newcastle, Maine, who had gone to sea at eighteen and worked up from there, lately serving on the *Florence* under Reginald Leonard of *Nimbus* fame. Over his long career, Captain Sheldon twice circumnavigated the earth, went around the Cape of Good Hope six times, and made twenty-six round-ings of Cape Horn. Twelve of his Cape Horn passages were on board the *Tacoma*, a vessel he deemed "the best wooden ship ever built."

The *Tacoma* was a fast sailer but, like all Cape Horners, subject to extreme variations of performance depending on conditions. Once, Sheldon got the ship from Liverpool to San Francisco in 106 days, fast sailing by any standard. On another passage, she took a full 204 days, an endurance contest that made even Lincoln Patten's diffident style in the *India* seem hell-bent by contrast. As captains do, Sheldon blamed his crew, a bunch

Patten & Son's ship *Alameda* in a Philadelphia drydock. A Cape Horn grain trader, the *Alameda* was built by Goss & Sawyer in Bath in 1876. John Patten's grandchildren/heirs, John Owen and Clara Patten, held shares in her until 1890; Charles Davenport was her principal owner until 1895. She lasted until 1920, ending her days as a storage hulk in Dunedin, New Zealand. *Courtesy Maine Maritime Museum.*

A wharfside view of the big, fast *Florence*, one of the last Patten & Son ships. The scene probably is San Francisco. Built in 1877 at the Goss & Sawyer shipyard in Bath, the *Florence* was a bulk hauler, transporting grain from the West Coast of North America to Britain. She changed hands in 1898 and was lost in 1902. Note the elaborate carved figurehead, presumably a likeness of namesake Florence Kelley, daughter of Captain John Kelley. *Courtesy Peabody Essex Museum, Salem, MA.*

so landlubberly, he said, that it was a wonder they made it to San Francisco at all.[39]

Sheldon retired in 1893 at age fifty-six, settling down on a farm in Richmond, upriver from Bath. The original owners of the *Tacoma* gradually sold out of her, and she was taken over by a group of Sewall associates. In 1898, she was sold to San Francisco owners and, eventually, was used to supply Alaska Packers Association canneries on the Northwest Coast. She also made three trips to Manila with horses for U. S. Army forces occupying the Philippines.

After Gilbert's death, Captain John Patten built only one vessel. But, despite his advanced years, he continued, with Charles Davenport's help, to manage his numerous business affairs. In 1887, at ninety-seven, he was the oldest man in Bath and — with the possible exception of Davenport — the richest, a fixture on the streets of the city, and an institution. On Monday, 21 February 1887, Captain John ventured downtown to Davenport's office and signed off on a stock transaction. The next day, he suddenly became ill. Two days later, he was dead. The death of anyone at ninety-seven cannot be deemed tragic, yet the news and its implications came as a shock in Bath. Needless to say, it was front-page news. A brief, surprisingly unsentimental *Times* editorial paid him this tribute:

"Capt. Patten's large wealth while he lived was in good hands. While he was liberal in giving to worthy objects, his money was never wasted upon the undeserving, nor would he allow himself to be imposed upon by those whose object was questionable and who merely sought his aid because of his wide reputation for benevolence."[40]

The real outpouring of sentiment began on the morning of 28 February, when the entire city turned out for Captain John's funeral. "Out of respect to the distinguished deceased," the *Times* reported that same day, "all places of business were closed during the forenoon, and the entire business community attended the ceremony at the house. Long before ten o'clock the ample mansion was filled with the representative people of Bath."

A steady stream of mourners passed through one parlor of the captain's North Street home. "In the subdued light, caused by the drawn curtains, could be distinguished the rich, dark casket of mahogany, open for half its length, to allow a last look at the peaceful features of the venerable deceased.

"A cross of myrtle, and a wreath of the same, with two sheaves of wheat were placed upon the coffin.... In the long procession that paid their last respects to the dead, almost without exception, passed the people of our city who are best known in every department of life.

"Both boards of the city government, a large delegation from the Board of Trade, the ministers of all the churches, and a countless throng of sea captains were noticed. Many a venerable citizen came with bowed head and feeble steps to look once more upon the features of one whom he remembered from his earliest infancy.... there was not one so old that he could remember Captain Patten other than as a man grown."

The eulogy required two ministers, one of whom attested that, although Captain Patten was a member of no church, he possessed a "'deep religious character.... He was good to the poor; none in need have applied to him in vain. One hundred thousand people could rise to bless him for his charity. All that have gone away to other cities, when their thoughts turn back to Bath, think of Capt. John Patten.'" Charles Davenport and Captain John Kelley were among the pallbearers. As the coffin started on its way to the family vault, every church bell in the city began to toll. Every hack in the city had been engaged to bear mourners to the cemetery, so extras had to be imported from Brunswick. Among the large crowd of family and friends at graveside were the George M. and James T. Patten families; Captain Charles E. Patten, John's nephew; Gilbert's children John O. and Clara with spouses; Jarvis's brother Captain Bardwell and son; even Captain Lincoln Patten and his son Frank, who would be the clan's last shipmaster.

Throughout Bath, flags flew at half-mast and all work stopped until the afternoon.

Although not a soul in Bath remembered the late Captain John as a youngster, one old-timer in Boston harbored just such memories. Did the equally ancient Noble Maxwell, ensconced and isolated in his Vendome Hotel suite, hear that his illustrious cousin, one-time confidant, and longtime castaway had crossed the bar? Probably, but we shall never know for sure. Noble Maxwell died seven months after John, in September 1887, taking his brooding secrets with him.

For years, Captain John Patten had lived without any immediate family, which may explain why, surprisingly, he died intestate. His grandchildren and only direct relatives, John O. Patten and Clara Patten Goodwin, requested a direct division of the estate between themselves. The probate court granted their request.

How much was involved? Another puzzler about Captain John's estate is that no inventory was taken. An approximation of its total size can be derived from the bond required by the probate court: $400,000, about $6.8 million in 1995 value.[41]

Every death is a milestone of sorts, John Patten's more than most. With the old captain's passing, the rich nautical tradition that had propelled the clan to prominence is all but ended. Among the "countless throng of sea captains" honoring Captain John, few bear the Patten name, and those who do have long since swallowed the anchor. Only one mourner, Lincoln's son Frank, will carry the family tradition into the next century. Bath's maritime affairs are now in the hands of other clans and companies. Henceforward, Pattens will make their mark on dry land far from Bath.

NOTES

1. Jarvis Patten, "A Century of Shipbuilding," *Bath Daily Times,* 19 March 1881.

2. G.F. & J. Patten to Jarvis Patten, Bath, 1 October 1861 (Jarvis Patten File, PP/MMM).

3. Hennessy Historical Files (MMM).

4. Jarvis Patten, list of balances credited, 1863-66 (Jarvis Patten File, PP/MMM).

5. Burden, Records of Patten Mariners and Vessels (MMM).

6. Hennessy Historical Files (MMM).

7. *Bath Daily Times,* 21 January 1875.

8. Ibid., 18 April 1875.

9. Jarvis Patten to [unnamed Bath newspaper] Editors, London, 16 April 1869.

10. Reed, p. 343.

11. Baker, p. 366.

12. Receipts for the construction of ship *Hudson* of Bath, 1862 (MMM).

13. Charles J. Rogers, Journal kept on board ship *India* of Bath, 1869-70 (MMM). All details and quotations regarding the *India*'s voyage are from this source. For clarity's sake, Rogers's irregular punctuation has been standardized.

14. Captain Lincoln Patten, a lifelong mariner, was sixty.

15. *Bath Daily Times,* 26 February 1864.

16. Ibid., 27 September 1869.

17. Ibid., 30 September 1869.

18. Ibid., 27 September 1869.

19. Inventory of the estate of George F. Patten.

20. Baker, pp. 591, 722.

21. Ibid., p. 717.

22. *American Sentinel* (Bath), 30 May 1872.

23. *Bath Daily Times,* 16 September 1872.

24. Ibid.

25. Ibid., 29 July 1874.

26. Ibid., 24 November 1874.

27. Ibid., 17 May 1870.

28. Ibid., 18 January 1882. Reed's 1894 history contains a similarly detailed account of Gilbert Patten's character (p. 343).

29. James T. Patten to Arthur Sewall, New York, 24 January 1880 (Sewall Family Papers, MMM).

30. Ibid., 7 February 1884.

31. *Bath Daily Times,* 10 April 1901.

32. Ibid., 4 May 1949.

33. Ibid., 28 August 1885.

34. Ralph Linwood Snow, *Bath Iron Works: The First Hundred Years* (Bath, ME: Maine Maritime Museum, 1987), pp. 35-45.

35. *Boston Traveler,* 2 December 1886.

36. Owen, p. 245.

37. Jarvis Patten, Report of the Commissioner of Navigation, 1884 (copy; Hennessy Historical Files, MMM).

38. *Bath Commercial,* 12 January 1878.

39. Hennessy Historical Files (MMM).

40. *Bath Daily Times,* 25 February 1887.

41. Records of the estate of John Patten, 1887 (Probate Records, Sagadahoc County Court House, Bath, ME).

6

"The Last of His Generation"

In the mid-1930s, Bath historian Henry Owen reminisced about the so-called Gay Nineties in the City of Ships. "In 1891," he wrote, "the water works were four years old and the electric lights something less. Quite a number of houses had bathrooms, but they were by no means universal. Many of the richer and more pretentious houses were still lighted with Welsbach gas burners, and many of the poorer ones with oil lamps." With the passing of the roller-skating fad, many people had taken up recreational bicycling. And, "after the local trolley line was opened in August, 1893, one of the popular diversions was a pleasure ride in the open cars. In 1898 it became possible to 'trolley ride' to Lewiston, and in 1900, to Portland and beyond."[1] Owen's fondest memories of the 1890s, however, were the gala affairs held at the Alameda.

The Alameda — an immense, cavernous downtown building not far from the shopworn, soon-to-be-gutted Sagadahock House — had been built as a roller-skating rink in 1882 by a consortium of local investors that included John O. Patten, young son and heir of the late Gilbert. When the skating fad faded, the Alameda became an all-purpose social center considered the best spot in town for dances: The floor held five hundred people and the galleries a thousand more. The facility also had a stage for theatrical productions.

In October 1892, a five-day extravaganza was organized to benefit the Patten Free Library. In Owen's opinion, it was "without a doubt the biggest and most successful entertainment ever held in this city." Mrs. Gilbert Patten was a member of the planning committee. George M. and Charles E. Patten served on a seventeen-man executive committee. A New York producer was brought in to design the event, which took a month to prepare; local talent did the rest. On opening night, people from near and far were treated to staged tableaux and dances from around the world — a monumental production that required 250 costumes. The entertainment also included group singing and band concerts. In addition, paying spectators could browse among booths featuring exotic refreshments and souvenirs, or stroll through an indoor orange grove "with a prize

Spanking new and ready for sea: *Kineo*, the first and only steel five-masted schooner. Built by Sewall & Company and commanded by Frank Patten, the last Patten skipper, she made a grueling, perilous, round-the-world voyage to see if large schooners were viable in the Cape Horn trade. They weren't. *Courtesy Maine Maritime Museum.*

The rewards of two generations of saltwater enterprise: The genteel John O. Patten (right), a confirmed landsman, relaxing at home with a friend. Born with a silver spoon in his mouth, and co-heir of his grandfather's prodigious wealth, John followed his own pathway to prominence in the 1890s as a crusading newspaper editor, progressive politician, and focus of a damaging divorce scandal. *Courtesy Maine Maritime Museum.*

in each orange," or dine at an English inn on the premises that served good old American roast turkey. To Owen, "The beauty of the whole thing cannot be described."[2] The proceeds of this spectacular event were $1,900, of which the promoter took a third, leaving the library with $1,400 — about $25,000 in 1995 currency.

As the library gala proves, the Pattens were in the forefront of Bath society in the 1890s. Occasionally, their activities made headlines. One family member, in fact, was literally creating the city's headlines: John Owen Patten, who in 1893 acquired the *Bath Daily Times* and its weekly sister, the *Independent*.

In his youth, John O. Patten was not exactly a chip off the old block. Given the size of the old block, that fact was an important key to his character. He, like his father Gilbert, had been born into affluence, but Gilbert had not been spared the rigors and responsibilities of seagoing life. With John O., things were different. Growing up in his parents' imposing Italianate home on upper Washington Street, he and his sister, Clara, were groomed for a more genteel life.

At the time of Captain Gilbert's death in 1882, John was twenty. His participation in the Alameda venture may have been funded by an inheritance. Twenty is not a tender age to go fatherless, but John's fretful, socially conscious mother, Emma Owen Patten, worried about the direction John's life might take without Captain Gilbert's guiding hand. For a while, she prevailed upon family friend Arthur Sewall to take young John under his wing and keep him in the right sort of company. "Why not propose to John, that he should accompany you to Boston tomorrow," she asked Sewall shortly after her husband's death, "in view of the rare opportunities to see you & to extend even a brief recess from associations we dislike so much. I venture to ask this favor on the strength of [your] many kindnesses & believing you might...give him a hint or two upon matters of immediate practical interest to him."[3] In Emma's mind, John needed to settle down.

That, however, took years. Someone, Sewall perhaps, convinced John O. of the benefits of travel. Accordingly, in 1884, he shipped out — as a passenger — aboard the new *Tacoma,* in which he owned one-sixteenth, sailing around the Horn with Captain John Kelley. He then returned east to attend Johns Hopkins University, where, during a short stay, he studied economics and history, emerging with a social conscience firmly grounded in the Progressive values of the day.

Thus prepared for professional life, John O. took a job as a reporter on the *Boston Post.* By the end of 1885, he already was the newspaper's owner and editor. In 1887, however, he suddenly left the *Post* for an extended trip abroad with his bride, the former Lucy Larrabee of Bath. Having lately come into half of Captain John Patten's estate, the newlyweds could of course do whatever and go wherever they chose. Reed's Bath history indicates that they chose "many countries in Europe, as well as Turkey, Greece, Syria, Palestine, Egypt, India, Ceylon, Java, China, Japan, and California, and in 1892-3 passed a winter in Spain in the study of the Spanish language."[4] Between trips, John Patten was president and manager of the Atlantic Publishing Company of New York, struggling to find circulation for the company's magazine, *The Bostonian.*[5]

In hindsight, John O. Patten's early career appears to be a story of a dilettante whose high ideals and fat pocketbook did not mesh with the rigors of big-city life. But in 1893, the couple returned to Bath, where everything changed. Taking up residence in his late grandfather's North Street home, John O. Patten, director of the Bath National Bank and the Maine Central Railroad, branch president of the Sagadahoc Loan and Trust Company, and co-founder of the exclusive male Sagadahoc Club, purchased the *Bath Daily Times* and the weekly *Independent,* taking over as editor of the former. Like Pattens before him, he found himself a big fish in a little pond, and he quickly made quite a splash.

True to his ideals, Patten improved the content of the *Times,* giving readers a lively, candid look at city affairs that had previously received only perfunctory coverage. He also upgraded the newspaper's physical plant and made himself popular through his sensitivity to employees' welfare. A *Times* staffer paid him this compliment: "One day [Patten's] attention was called to the need of a vacation of one of the boys employed in the Times Job Printing Department.

"The boy was paying his board and being dependent upon his wages, felt as if he could not afford it. The expression on Mr. Patten's face when told of the matter is indescribable. 'My God' said he 'is there anyone working for me who can't afford to take a vacation? Tell the boy to take as long a vacation as he wishes and his pay will go on.'

"Is there any wonder that all the Times employees learned to respect and honor such a man?"[6]

Meanwhile, John O. had become politically active as a liberal Republican, using his family's long-established connections in that party. In 1894, he was elected Bath's representative to the Maine legislature. He won reelection two years later, despite the active opposition of right-wing elements in the community, and he was an outspoken supporter of Thomas Reed's 1896 presidential aspirations. This record of accelerating achievement went on the rocks because of a personal crisis that, given John O.'s high public profile, excited much gossip in the city.

Although the John O. Pattens were, on the surface, a convivial, social couple, their marriage had in fact gone sour. The couple's decision to part apparently was mutual. In the manner of the day, Lucy received a financial settlement and the two divorced quietly. Although divorce was by no means as rare as in Kate Walker's day, it was still considered an extreme measure and would not have gone unnoticed in the city.

Soon afterward, another divorce action raised the eyebrows of Bath society. Dr. Percy Roberts, a recent arrival from New York who had been treating John for suspected tuberculosis, brought a divorce action against his wife Irene, charging cruel and abusive treatment and alienation of affections. Roberts asked for a $15,000 settlement. In court, Roberts alleged that Irene's neglect, along with public comment on his marriage, had impaired his health and caused him suffering. He settled for $600, and his decree was granted in April 1897. What was not mentioned in court, however, was the gossip now making the rounds in Bath. Months before the Roberts divorce, the *Times*'s competing newspaper, the semiweekly *Bath Enterprise,* was alluding to a "Patten-Roberts scandal" in its gossip column.[7] The Patten part of that equation was John O., who married Irene Roberts shortly after her divorce.

Because no sensational testimony was given at the Roberts divorce hearing, the "Patten-Roberts scandal" might have remained at the whisper level — except that a heated contest erupted over custody of the Roberts's five-year-old twins. In September 1897, Percy Roberts and his ex-wife, now Mrs. John O. Patten, went back to court. This time, Bath probably learned more than it wanted to about the matter.

The *Times,* predictably, did not cover the Roberts custody case and its revelations. Neither did the weekly *Independent,* which declined to involve itself in "matters of sensational scandal in their too suggestive details and unsavory odors and does not regard such 'news' as necessary to add interest to its columns or pennies to its pocket book...." Although Bath was a first-class gossip mill, with newspaper columns devoted solely to that subject, the *Independent* was aligning itself with the mores of the city's establishment. "The INDEPENDENT is not excruciatingly prudish but has an honest ambition to merit the confidence and esteem of respectable families; to be deemed a fitting paper for an honorable place upon the library table; to be a journal that each week may be read by any lady or child...."[8] Indiscretions of Bath's "respectable people" might excite lurid curiosity, but printing such matters was beyond the pale. In a city as cozy as Bath, where

everyone was a neighbor, a newspaper's responsibility was to present a constructive —
and instructive — community image. This approach to local journalism would remain
in force for a century.

Inasmuch as the paper was owned by John Owen Patten, the *Independent*'s chosen
course was perhaps a foregone conclusion. The competing *Enterprise*, however, adopted
a totally different policy, exploiting the news blackout in other papers by printing special extra editions loaded with the latest developments in the unfolding Patten-Roberts
story. ("THE BATH SENSATION.... an Unsavory Mess Is Made Public.")[9] Editorially, the
Enterprise supported Dr. Roberts.

What emerged from the *Enterprise*'s detailed coverage was a picture of the Robertses
as an incompatible couple and the suggestion that Dr. Roberts, a former newspaperman
with an 1891 medical degree, had been disappointed with marriage and with his lack of
upward mobility in Bath. What also emerged was that John Patten and Irene Roberts
had met at a Theosophical Society gathering late in 1896, had seen each other at subsequent Bath events, and had fallen passionately in love. Lucy Patten's departure had been
with full knowledge of that circumstance. John O. appears to have considered breaking
his silence, for, at one point, the *Times* cryptically editorialized that "'unctuous recti-
tude' is an able phrase and is quite appropriate to certain worthies in our town who are
so anxious about the morality of others that they are hypocrites themselves."[10] That,
however, was all, for in the custody hearing, John O. himself became a focus of interest.

At the hearing, Irene Patten testified that "I intended to be married to Mr. Patten
before the doctor got his divorce. At one time I realized the possibility that we might run
away together.... Mr. Patten has been in my case since the spring of last year. We had
agreed to marry last winter, with the congratulations of Mrs. Lucy Patten, who was then
his wife."[11]

Because Irene Patten was seeking custody of her children, John O.'s financial condition was deemed a relevant issue. Under questioning, John gave his annual income as
"$2,500 a year at least." Had that income decreased of late? "Yes, some." Had he not
recently inherited $300,000 or $400,000? "I decline to answer." Was it true that three-
fourths of that sum was now gone? "I decline to state."[12]

The crux of the hearing was the question of Irene's maternal fitness. And on this
point, the Pattens scored a coup of sorts. Emma Patten, John's distraught and protective
mother, asked her friend Mrs. Thomas Hyde to testify to Irene's upstanding motherly
character. Emma undoubtedly knew that an appearance by the doyenne of Bath society
in a crowded courtroom would carry great weight and move public opinion. Mrs. Hyde
complied. In her brief court statement, Mrs. Hyde stipulated that she and Irene Patten
were acquainted and that, in her view, Dr. Roberts seemed indifferent to his children, an
opinion corroborated by a subsequent witness.[13] Then, lest anyone be in doubt about
which side of the controversy Bath's upper crust favored, and to what extent, Mrs. Hyde
leaked to the *Independent* the news that "she felt it right and proper and a duty to sustain her lifelong friend, Mrs. G.E.R. Patten, during the latter's hour of trial, with her

Clara Patten, who with her brother, John O., inherited grandfather John's substantial estate. Clara's wedding to Richard Goodwin was one of the most elaborate society events in Bath history. Like her brother, however, Clara died young, in 1898. *Courtesy Maine Maritime Museum.*

friendly offices and attentions, and these she gladly gave as a true friend should and would. In her testimony she truthfully gave her recollections of the plaintiff as a mother and did *not* defend social indiscretions of any nature."[14] The court awarded Irene custody of the twins except for summer months, when they were to join their father.

With that ruling, the media circus ceases, leaving the Honorable John O. Patten and his wife with whatever is left of the new life they sought. They do not have long, for John is now ill with the tuberculosis Percy Roberts spotted the previous year. Prior to the custody ruling, he has sold his newspapers to Frank Nichols and announced his departure from Bath.[15] On 5 September 1897, a few days after Irene wins her case, the Pattens depart Bath for Boston.

The story continues to play out like a twentieth-century soap opera. In 1898, despite his social setbacks, Percy Roberts makes an amazing comeback by marrying George M. Patten's surviving daughter, Hannah! There will be no children. Meanwhile, John O.'s socialite sister Clara Goodwin, a victim of chronic illness, dies at age thirty-four.

In April 1899, in Phoenix, Arizona Territory, time runs out for John Owen Patten: He dies of tuberculosis at the age of thirty-eight. Reporting his death, his former *Times* employees extol his travels, political career, and of course his editorial leadership — gracefully avoiding the story the paper had always declined to report.

Some readers familiar with the nuances of his social tribulation will be surprised to learn that "Mr. Patten was deservedly one of the most popular men in Bath and wherever he was known. He was genial, generous, and a boon companion. Every public work interested him and no appeal to his charity was ever made in vain. His purse was always open when anybody was to be benefitted. He was one of the largest givers to the Old Couples' Home and to many another public charity.... During his residence at Bath his home at North and Front streets and his summer home at Cape Small were two of the most hospitable homes of Bath. He entertained much and from sheer love of entertaining." In one important way, and despite his short life, John O. Patten has proved to be a chip off the old block, a point that the *Times* deems relevant: "By the death of Mr. Patten, one of the most respected, prominent and public spirited families of this city is brought to an end."[16]

The *Times* epitaph for the Patten line is dramatic but premature. Captain Charles E. Patten, a nephew of the late Captain John and a Patten of the old school, is still alive and kicking. Furthermore, he is one of Bath's leading citizens.

We have already met Charles E. Patten, whose father, Captain James F., was a partner and brother of George F. and John Patten. In 1850, at age sixteen, Charles went to sea aboard the ship *Italy*. He made captain by the time he was twenty-two, starting with the *Britannia*. Shortly after receiving his master's ticket, he married Jessie Jones of London and brought her home to Bath. Unlike most Patten shipmasters, Charles often sailed with Jessie as company. Throughout their long marriage, the couple remained extraordinarily devoted. They had no children.

Charles moved to the *Moravia, John Patten,* and the Houghton ship *Samaria.* He thus made a considerable fortune the old-fashioned way. Upon the death of his ninety-two-year-old father in 1883, he and brother Fred came into considerable wealth. James F.'s estate consisted entirely of government bonds, which indicates that he had transferred much of his property to his sons before his death. The bonds themselves were worth $167,000 (more than $2.7 million in 1995 value).[17] Fred, who was in the shipping business in New York, returned to Bath to administer his share of the estate. Likewise, Charles retired from the sea, investing his money in shipping. Like his father before him, he became a director of the Lincoln National Bank. Within a few years, he was one of Bath's heaviest taxpayers.[18] In time, he also became Bath's most generous benefactor.

Charles Patten's years on the quarterdeck had accustomed him to exercising authority, so life ashore must at first have seemed bland by contrast. By 1886, however, he had found an outlet for his assertive, candid proclivities: He was drawn into Bath's smoldering political climate. The results were flamboyant.

For a city of fewer than 9,000 souls, Bath's politics were surprisingly partisan and amazingly complicated. The nuances have grown cold with time, but the local press carried enough details to clarify the high and low points and afford posterity a fascinating look at small-city politicking at the end of the nineteenth century.

When Captain Charles came home from the sea, he found the political climate not to his liking. Patten was a lifelong Democrat, and City Hall was dominated by Republicans who looked as though they were there to stay. Bath's Republicans, in turn, were dominated by James W. ("Emperor William") Wakefield, a machine boss for whom politics was a profession. Wakefield operated through a band of loyal cronies, becoming the broker of city offices, elective or appointive. Generous and genial, he nonetheless hoarded information on friend and foe alike and knew when to use his knowledge to advantage. In historian Henry Owen's assessment, Wakefield was the most powerful local politician since Governor King. His domination amounted to "a local dictatorship in political affairs which was as nearly absolute as humanly possible and which endured for many years."[19]

By 1884, however, some Republicans had grown uncomfortable with machine politics, and the GOP ranks began to crack. In February of that year, when city Republicans held their annual pre-election caucus, party regulars nominated Charles Davenport for mayor, but dissidents broke with the organization, resolved "that the times demand and favor the removal of the machine method in the conduct of party management." These self-styled Independent Republicans (including Jarvis Patten) thereupon fronted a mayoralty candidate of their own.[20] The result of the Republican schism was that for the first time since 1854, a Democrat, George Nichols, became mayor. This victory was short-lived. In 1885, Nichols's proposed successor, Galen Moses, was defeated by none other than James W. Wakefield, who had reasserted party discipline.

Wakefield served four consecutive one-year terms as mayor (1885-89), and, in or out of office, was the party's local power broker. As mayor, his claim to fame was bringing to fruition a long-discussed plan for a municipal water supply, which was accomplished in 1885 by a chartered corporation whose members included John O. Patten, Fred Patten, Charles Davenport, Arthur Sewall, Thomas Hyde, and Galen Moses. The water company commenced operations in 1886, operating under contract with the city. Meanwhile, however, other aspects of the city's welfare, notably schools, had been neglected. Moreover, despite statewide prohibition, Bath was becoming notorious as a den of alcoholic iniquity. The complicated system by which a state agency licensed local agents to sell spirits for medicinal — not recreational — purposes was manipulated to guarantee a ready supply of liquor in Bath. In addition, eating establishments and social clubs found covert ways to serve liquor without harassment. Those who took temperance seriously, as well as law-abiding citizens in general, found such salutary neglect offensive.

Being a devout Democrat (unlike most of his relatives), and a strong temperance advocate, Captain Charles E. Patten found Bath's political climate frustrating, even obnoxious. He was in good company, for, in 1886, a groundswell of opposition to the Republican "ring" was building. Diverse dissenting voters coalesced into the Citizens' party, consisting of Democrats, maverick Republicans, and the working-class Knights of Labor. The Citizens' party caucused at City Hall in February 1886 to strategize the overthrow of the Wakefield machine. Who could lead them? Charles E. Patten! Speaking on behalf of Captain Patten was David Foye: "I do not believe that there is a gentleman in the city of Bath that feels more interested in the prosperity of our city than Mr. Patten. He is not a politician. To be a politician he would be a bad man. He is not generally known in the city, but I will leave it to the business men of Bath who are well acquainted with him to judge him. He is a banker; so am I. In the Knights of Labor in this city there are three directors of a bank."[21] Foye's point was that Captain Patten could be all things to all people, or at least a suitable alternative to the Republican "ring."

The Independents duly assembled a slate of candidates to run in Bath's seven wards. Although the purpose of the Citizens' party ticket was clear, the pro-Republican *Times* attributed the whole episode to "personal spite against mayor Wakefield."[22] Spite did indeed play a role, but it was by no means the opposition's sole gripe. For his part, Boss Wakefield took the high road. Whoever ran against him, he told the press, would "no doubt be a gentleman of unquestioned character and fitness, in whom the public will have confidence, and I trust that all will refrain from casting any reproach upon him or his supporters...."[23] On 1 March 1886, with the temperature hovering around zero, Bath voters turned out in their usual small numbers. Wakefield won handily, with a majority of 249 votes: 775 to Captain Patten's 526.

On 8 March 1887, Wakefield defeated Charles Patten a second time. This year, temperance enforcement had become a hot political issue. Bath was full of gossip, sermonizing, and wild claims about the rampant illicit use of alcohol. One clergyman, claiming to be in the know, excited public interest by insisting that Wakefield's regime had shut down no fewer than fifty secret gin mills. Another pundit insisted that, whatever Wakefield may have done, there were easily that many still operating in the city.[24] Given the controversy, temperance advocates ran on their own ticket, drawing votes away from Patten and his reformers. The 1887 election took place only a week after the reverential funeral honoring Captain John Patten, Charles's uncle. But if there was magic in the Patten name, it didn't work for Charles that year. Wakefield won by an astounding 508-vote majority.

The voters had spoken, and Captain Charles got the message. Accordingly, he did not run in 1888, when, in a three-way contest, Wakefield demolished Democrat George Hughes by a margin of 333 votes. And the next year, when the temperance caucus approached Captain Charles to run for mayor, he declined. In 1889, Bath politics had splintered into four tickets, Republican, Democrat, Temperance, and Labor, conditions that favored the GOP. Accordingly, George Moulton and other Republicans won handily.

In 1890, Bath's various dissidents at last decided that there was strength in unity. Shortly before the March election, a large, diverse crowd gathered in City Hall to discuss a united Citizens' party front against the Republicans. As before, opposition to the "ring" ruling Bath was alive and well. But there were other issues, too. For decades, Bath's public debt had been unusually high because of the city's investment in a ruinously expensive coastal railroad, the Knox & Lincoln. By 1884, Bath's per-capita debt was the largest of any U.S. city, which hindered municipal improvements and provoked anger about high taxes. What to do about Knox & Lincoln was a never-ending debate. Another sore spot was the allegation of malfeasance in Bath's fiscal administration. This charge was technically accurate, because funds earmarked for specific uses were clumsily applied elsewhere and replaced as needed from other accounts. But the city's accounting and administrative irregularities were attributable to unbusinesslike procedures, not an intent to cook the books.[25] The sorest spot of all, perhaps, was personal animosity. Some people simply despised Emperor William Wakefield, and Charles E. Patten was one of them. At the 1890 caucus, when temperance advocates denounced the city's lackadaisical enforcement of anti-liquor laws, things began to get personal.

The caucus identified strong candidates to run in each city ward, and Charles Patten was the general choice for mayor. As before, he declined, reportedly admitting that "I am not sufficiently acquainted with the city's affairs.... Were everything running smoothly in the city affairs I perhaps would not be so decided, but the condition of things at present, as I look at them, is such, that even were I quite positive of success I should not care to be elected to the office and have to assume its responsibilities."[26] Was the good captain saying that the mayor's office was above him or beneath him? Whatever he meant, he played into the Republicans' hands by admitting he was too green to hold office.

Patten also played hard to get, but the Citizens' party would not be denied its choice. A week later, the party recaucused, and, after a number of "ringing speeches," Charles Patten agreed to head the new ticket. In his acceptance speech, he showed that he had learned much in a week. He also set the tone for the upcoming campaign by lashing out at his political nemesis. Wakefield had been an army quartermaster officer in the Civil War, a position that, in Patten's opinion, had made him indifferent to the evils of strong drink. Patten went further, characterizing Wakefield's war record as that of a booze-happy supply officer.

Patten began his acceptance speech by saying that he had "never attempted to make a speech in public before. Forty or forty-five years ago, I tried to deliver a declamation at the Bath High School.... I started out..., then I stopped and I have never fired off yet. I wish to thank you for the honor conferred upon me, in choosing me as your candidate. Mr. Wakefield saw fit to compliment me the other evening, for my modesty in acknowledging I was ignorant of city affairs. I didn't go to war the same as Mr. Wakefield; I never drew rum out of the tail end of a cart." Patten and Wakefield had tangled on temperance issues before. Thus, "When I said to Mr. Wakefield 'you don't care if the streets of Bath run with rum,' he turned around and said 'I never denied it.' ...if there is a man in the democratic party, citizen or temperance party who is such a damn scoundrel as James Wakefield I pity him. (Applause.) I don't care who knows it; if Mr. Wakefield is here let him come along. (Continued cheers and applause.)"[27]

Captain Patten's manner of speaking was a new development in Bath politics, and it did not go unnoticed in other Maine communities. Reacting to his remarks, the *Bridgton News* called his words "exceedingly unfortunate.... That such language was tolerated if not enforced in an assembly of gentlemen in a Maine city is a marvel...."[28] Outraged, Wakefield announced he would sue Patten for libel and slander to the tune of $25,000. Patten tossed aside the threat with a quip that $25,000 wasn't enough.[29] Emperor William was at last on the defensive ("The city books are public property and open to the inspection of all.").[30] So was Mayor Moulton, renominated by the Republicans.

On 3 March 1890, the Citizens' party got out the vote. According to the bemused *Times,* "Men were coming in from far and near, ploughing through the snowdrifts to get to the polls."[31] The result was an upset: Patten won the mayoralty by 236 votes, a better margin than Moulton's the previous year. About 200 of those votes came from dissident Republicans. Moreover, members of the Citizens' party swept five out of seven Bath wards. The night after the election, the winners celebrated musically in the streets of the city by blowing jubilantly into two hundred tin horns.

Addressing the new city council on his inaugural day — an annual ritual stronger in form than content — Mayor Patten announced that he had found the city's condition to be reasonably sound, a surprising admission in the wake of the accusatory campaign just waged. He advocated fiscal conservatism, Bath's perennial motherhood issue. Time would tell if the Citizens' party would make good its agenda of enforced temperance, debt reduction, and progress without high taxes.

As his year in office drew to a close, Mayor Patten could point proudly to several positive developments during his administration. One was a fat U.S. Navy order for high-tech warships to be built at Thomas Hyde's Bath Iron Works — a real economic shot in the arm. Another was the imminent debut of the lavish Patten Free Library, open to all. The third was the sale of the old Knox & Lincoln Railroad to Maine Central Railroad — a transaction that yielded Bath $74,918 in cash (about $1.3 million in 1995 value) and eliminated the pressure for a city bond issue.[32] It hardly need be added, however, that these developments were not the work of the Patten administration. On another campaign issue, temperance reform, the mayor could point to an increase in arrests for drunkenness, a sign the city was doing its duty. But Patten was embarrassed by the city marshal's practice of arresting drunks and, without due process, immediately releasing them upon payment of a fine. This police practice apparently was endorsed by Patten, and when it was brought to light, the mayor showed the same sort of indifference for which he had attacked Boss Wakefield.[33] As for all those arrests: Didn't they prove that illegal liquor sales were increasing?[34] Meanwhile, the reigning Citizens' party had exposed none of the scandalous malfeasance hinted at in 1889 and 1890. They had, however, raised property taxes, a move that could send renegade Republicans heading for home.

As the 1891 elections drew near, Republicans launched an effective letters-to-the-editor attack on the incumbents, calling for their ouster in the sympathetic local press. The *Enterprise* characterized Patten's government as "A Record of Weakness, Do-Nothingism and Shilly-Shallying."[35] The *Times*'s position was that "a good clean man nominated by the republicans of Bath will at the present time assure an election."[36]

The *Times* was right. Patten was renominated by the Citizens' ticket, but he and his colleagues were running against a Republican organization determined to retake City Hall by presenting a new, boss-free image. Thomas Hyde, whose success with Bath Iron Works had doubled his prestige, and who had voted a straight Citizens' party ticket in 1890, was prominently in the Republican camp. To escape the "ring" stereotype, the GOP passed resolutions recognizing "the need and necessity of a pure and honest administration of all the affairs of the city government" and condemning "all illegal and unjustifiable acts in any department thereof."[37] The caucus passed by Wakefield's hand-picked choice for mayor, instead nominating a young progressive, Fritz Twitchell.[38] This time, the Citizens' party was on the defensive.

On 2 March 1891, the Republicans scored a spectacular victory, taking six of the seven wards. Twitchell trounced Patten by 316 votes. Bath's press applauded the victory, although the *Enterprise* warned that the incoming Republicans "must be true to the interests of the people, and the arrogance of bossism, so called, must be restrained, or there may be another overturn next spring."[39] Perhaps the Citizens' group had served its main purpose.

Twitchell's prudent administration managed to instigate some municipal improvements and still end 1891 with a cash surplus. Twitchell ran again. His Citizens' party opposition had now been whittled down to registered Democrats, with whom Captain Patten was still immensely popular. Would he run again? A Democratic insider told a reporter, "You can lead a horse to water but you can't make him drink. Capt. Patten has said he doesn't want it and he means it."[40] The Democrats' choice for mayor was Patten's sea-faring colleague, Captain John Kelley.

Election day, 1892, brought another Republican victory, and the winners let the whole town know it. On victory night, the *Enterprise* reported on 9 March 1892, "it seemed as if every small boy in Bath as well as some of the older ones had armed them-selves with tin horns and until nearly ten o'clock the blowing of these horns drowned every other sound. The kids formed a regular brigade, visited the locality of many of the prominent Democrats' homes and gave a regular serenade. Beside this a number of young men here who have good voices formed a glee club for the occasion and gave a serenade in front of several residences."[41] If Charles Patten's home was the object of a Republican "serenade," he surely didn't mind. Sportingly, he had run for alderman in a Republican ward and won.

By 1892, Bath's mood had switched from muckraking and temperance to prosper-ity. Bath Iron Works contracts had given the city the long-sought key to the future, and people wanted an infrastructure to match: better schools, better services, more paved streets with electric lighting. They had been given a head start in this direction by the new Republicans, who had made themselves synonymous with progress and had spent liberally to update city facilities. With the electric company and the water works (both privately owned) in place, the next step was a sewerage system — a massive, expensive prospect.

But in the early 1890s, another depression had spread over North America. Shipyards were again idled along the Kennebec and money was tight. Where would the city find funds for its rising expenses and service contracts? In that atmosphere, conservatism and tax jitters re-emerged. Suddenly, citizens were in a cost-cutting mood. Meanwhile, the water works had proven totally inadequate to the city's needs, becoming a threat to fire safety and a major headache to paying users. Citizens also grumbled about the new service contracts Twitchell's administration had awarded the Bath Electric Light com-pany, for Twitchell was treasurer of that firm.

In 1893, with economic prospects darkening, Bath's Democrats and dissidents held another crowded, noisy Citizens' party caucus. The highlight of the meeting was the presence of the *Times*'s new editor, John Owen Patten. By his own account, John O. — a Republican, remember — had been pressured by the GOP machine to be especially kind to the party. Those were fighting words to any liberal journalist, so John O.'s loyal-ties had swung in the opposite direction.

At the Citizens' party caucus, John O. mounted the rostrum and addressed the assem-bled group, excoriating the local Republican organization and admonishing listeners to forget parties and think like Americans: "When your water bill comes in it doesn't make any difference whether you are a Republican or a Democrat, you swear just the same, and when your gas bill and electric light bills come in, it isn't that you belong to one political party or the other, you swear — if you don't you ought to.... Why do we pay more for our electric lights than most any other city in the country? Why is a man who opposes the corporations' slightest move marked for slaughter? We want an honest citizens' government and that is the reason for calling this meeting."[42] The message was clear: A vote for local Republicans was a vote for big shots, many of whom had conflicts of interest. That was a rallying cry on which to build a campaign. With his national perspective, John O. had captured the mood of class warfare now overtaking America and adapted it to fit Bath.

Who should lead the campaign? "Cries of Patten! Patten! Patten! drowned out every sound." The cries were not for John O. but for his tough-minded relative in the corner of the room. Captain Charles rose amid cheering and spoke: "I have gone through the ordeal once and it liked to killed me. You see how many gray hairs I have now. But one thing this city will want according to my figures is a financier — and a good one too. Trying to pay bills with no money to do it is beyond my comprehension." Captain Patten hinted at a burgeoning fiscal crisis.[43] If elected, he would adopt a strict pay-as-you-go policy and build confidence by reducing the city debt.

A week later, meeting at the Columbian Opera House, their speeches interspersed with concert-band selections, the Citizens' party drew up a platform. By Bath standards, it was radical. One plank called for outlawing municipal appropriations insufficient to meet current expenses — a budgetary gimmick by which incumbents could keep the tax rate low and let future administrations clear up the debt. Another plank prohibited conflicts of interest by municipal officers. Another called for the city to take over the water and electric companies.

During the caucus hoopla, while accepting the nomination for mayor, Captain Patten told his supporters that he had been hoping for a quiet life but once more would respond to the public call. His chances, of course, were much better than in previous campaigns because the influential *Times* was on his side. The *Times* made its pro-Patten position quite clear, but liberal journalist John O. printed the gamut of opinions in the days before the election. This policy permitted a clever, aggressive attack by the opposition — enough to make even the most thick-skinned politician consider other lines of work.

One inquiring soul, for example, wrote to the *Times* to ask why, in the name of progressive democracy, young people were expected to vote for an old fogy like Patten. What of a progressive nature had his 1890-91 administration accomplished? Another challenged the captain's well-known readiness to pledge a few thousand dollars toward new businesses, some of which never got off the ground for lack of similar pledges. If he were truly interested in improving Bath's economy, the reader wondered, why didn't the captain provide sufficient up-front money to ensure a venture's successful beginning? Certainly he could afford it. "Our local papers seem very fond of calling him the 'bluff and honest old sea dog.' We must admit that he is often bluff and rough and gruff, but

I fail to see wherein he is any more honest than thousands of our fellow citizens, certainly not one whit more honest than [Republican nominee] John O. Shaw. Is it a special sign of honesty to have inherited a fortune, to live an idle life so far as any good to the community goes, to sit in the window of a corner bank reviling our more energetic and useful citizens?"[44]

Picture the old sea dog at the Lincoln Bank, looking out his office window, wondering if the quiet life he sought is just around the corner. Or picture John O. Patten, a man with political ambitions of his own, reading the buzz of political opinion in his office at the *Times* and perhaps wondering if his populist caucus speech produced a bad fit between issues and candidate.

On 6 March 1893, Charles E. Patten won the mayoralty election — by three votes. The Republicans took most wards. "This is as close an election as was ever held in Bath," the *Enterprise* noted on 8 March, "and leaves the Republicans with vain regrets that they did not make just a little greater effort. Although Captain Patten will be Mayor this year, the scheme of the Democrats for getting control is defeated...."[45]

That potentially combustible arrangement never came to be, for one more surprise awaited. Four days after the election, the incumbent city government held a special meeting and considered the budgets of various municipal agencies. Then, while the outraged Captain Patten and other citizens looked on, it authorized appropriations in excess of the year's tax collections, producing a forthcoming shortfall of $8,812 (almost $158,000 in 1995 terms). Where would the money come from? It would be borrowed. The next administration — Patten's — would have to cover the debt by collecting unpaid taxes from 1892. Patten's view was that he had been cynically torpedoed. Accordingly, he walked away angrily, handing in his resignation on the eve of taking office.

The unfriendly *Enterprise* chided Patten for "deserting the ship, as it were, just as she is about to sail" and declared itself out of patience with him. "It is a late hour for him to come to such a decision, and really it doesn't seem as if he were treating the people of Bath fairly in taking this course." It was anybody's guess what would happen next — aside from general municipal confusion.

What happened next was that Captain Patten embarked upon the quiet life. A month later, in another election, mayoralty candidate John Shaw defeated Captain John Kelley by 179 votes. Bath was once more in Republican hands. Patten probably was relieved at the developments that spared him a year's wrangling with the city council. There was another consolation in being out of office in 1894: disaster avoidance. In January of that year, a small downtown fire behind the Sagadahock House got out of control and, because of a water-works shutdown, incinerated the huge old hotel and several other businesses.

A few weeks after the big fire of '94, the Republicans won again. The city's new mayor was James W. Wakefield. In the end, Emperor William had possessed the stomach and stamina to wage Bath's annual battles of taxes, city debt, and effective leadership. But neither he nor anyone else would win them. A century later, Bath's city fathers will still be wrangling over the very same issues.

Although he has had enough of partisan politics, Captain Patten is not embittered by the experience. He upholds the family philanthropic tradition with numerous, confidential acts of personal charity, few of which gain public notice, and by a hefty donation to the Patten Free Library's book fund in 1896. In 1899, he helps arbitrate a dispute between the local trolley line and the city. All the while, he personally cares for his invalid wife "with all the ardor of a youthful lover."[46] Occasionally, the Pattens are seen strolling in public arm in arm, Charles carrying a camp stool so that Jessie can rest as needed. He is a regular sight in downtown banks and stores until, on 15 June 1903, at age sixty-nine, he suffers a fatal heart attack while walking home from his rounds.

Charles Patten's obituary praises his personal qualities but notes that "modesty was one of his fundamental traits of character and his objection to talking about himself was so strong that it is difficult to obtain particulars of his life."[47] His will bequeaths generous sums to members of Jessie's family and reserves most of its assets for her use.[48] There are, however, bequests totaling $75,000 (about $1.15 million in 1995 value) to various charitable organizations in Bath. The Old Ladies' and Old Couples' Homes, Central Church, the Patten Free Library, and the city's charitable fuel fund each receive $10,000; the rest goes to the Maine General Hospital, the Goodwill Home for Girls, the Goodwill Farm for Boys, and several other organizations. Patten's bequest "is believed to be the largest amount ever bequeathed to public institutions by any citizen of Bath."[49] And more is to come. In 1908, after the death of Jessie Patten, another $75,000 will be distributed to Charles's favorite charities.[50]

With the deaths of Charles Davenport in 1901 and Charles Patten in 1903, the Pattens' close-knit maritime clan is about used up. In the words of the *Times,* "Captain Patten was the last of his generation of the family and only one other survivor of the name remains a citizen of Bath, Capt Frank Patten, son of the late Capt Lincoln Patten, a cousin."[51]

Perhaps it was Frank's role as the last seagoing Patten that caused the childless Charles to take an interest in the young mariner. Perhaps it was the fact that, as a member of the Topsham Pattens, Frank did not enjoy the carriage-trade privilege to which the Bath branch was accustomed. In any case, the two were very close. When Frank needed a financial boost to buy a share of his latest command, *Kineo,* Charles Patten lent him the requisite money. A few weeks later, Charles died. In his will, the old sea dog had forgiven the loan.

Captain Frank Patten was in Galveston, loading the giant schooner *Kineo,* when the Sewall office informed him of Charles Patten's death. The news hit him very hard. "To say I was shocked," he wrote home, "is nothing to what I did feel. It seemed to me like losing a father. Among my mail there are several letters from him, and knowing his handwriting so well and then opening your letter and finding he had gone seemed like some impossible thing."[52] Frank's real father was Lincoln Patten, master of many vessels (including the *India,* discussed in chapter 5), who had died in 1900.

Frank Patten, described as "no bigger than a pint of cider but right on deck with the goods," had followed the usual family career pattern, going to sea as a boy and working his way to the quarterdeck in stages, teaching himself navigation while before the mast.[53] His first command was the bark *Niphon,* on which he had shipped as mate. When the *Niphon's* skipper became sick and died in Rio, Frank Patten assumed command, took the vessel around the Horn to San Francisco, and brought her back to New York.[54] By the time he was thirty-four, in 1889, he had been around the Horn twenty times. Like so many other members of the clan, he had a reputation for being warmhearted — at sea, he kept a pocketful of seed handy to feed exhausted birds that dropped onto his deck — but he was nobody's fool.

The last seagoing Patten was also the personification of changes that were taking place in American shipping. Too young to serve on Patten ships, he gained experience in various deepwater square-riggers, steamers, and coastwise schooners, acquiring an unlimited ticket for both sail and steam. Often employed by Arthur Sewall & Company, he participated in that firm's efforts to make sailing vessels competitive in the twentieth century. His wife, Charlotte (nicknamed Pat) was a capable navigator who sailed with him. Daughter Nellie May, born in 1897, was also aboard. The family's melodramatic experiences at sea earned them local celebrity and a measure of fame along the trade routes they sailed. Their most memorable exploits took place aboard Sewall vessels.

It is tempting to call the Sewall dynasty the successors to the Pattens, for that family, which started building ships on the Kennebec about the same time as George and John Patten, carried on the sail tradition in Bath, amassing a formidable fleet of locally built vessels by the end of the century. Many of these ships were built in the old G. F. & J. Patten yard. Unlike the Pattens, however, the Sewalls waged an aggressive campaign to refine sailing-ship technology. For decades, they succeeded, but that is another story.

After their launching in Bath, Sewall square-riggers seldom if ever returned to the Kennebec. They earned their keep by moving bulk freight over very long distances. Sewall captains kept in close touch with the home office via voluminous correspondence and frequent wire transmissions. Instructions telegraphed from Bath were sent in a code based upon a system of word substitutions, a common practice among shipping firms. Frank Patten's reports from far-flung ports indicate that he was the very model of a Sewall master: precise, uncomplaining, and thoroughly comfortable with his responsibilities.

In June 1899, Frank Patten took the huge, wooden *George Stetson* out of Portland, Oregon, loaded with lumber for Tientsin, China — a typical voyage for a Sewall ship. The *Stetson,* built for another Bath account in 1880, had been acquired later by Sewall & Company and was in first-rate condition. Nothing of note occurred on the voyage until 10 September, when the ship was off P'engchia Hsu, an island north of Taiwan. "I had just returned to the deck from working up the position of the ship," Patten later reported, "and was walking the poop when just before the bell was struck at 8 P.M., an alarm of fire was given by the Sail Maker (Frank Geddie).

"I rushed forward and found on getting on the forecastle head that all hands were there before me, and that the crew including officers were tearing ropes out of the fore hatch which had just been opened, and that dense clouds of black pitch smoke was pouring out of the hatch."[55]

The fire had broken out in a forward compartment that contained six tons of coal, "old junk, pitch Barrels and 1 Rosin Barrel that was stowed on the coal.... The flames and smoke poured up through this small hatch, driving us away. The fire was fought as hard as could be, men and officers doing all in their power to put it out but in the confined space...the smoke and flames kept driving us away time and again. In the mean time the fore hatch was pouring up smoke and fire and the hatch was attempted to be put on but it was impossible to get near the hatch."

Despite a bucket brigade, the flames engulfed the forward portion of the *Stetson*, so he stood toward distant land. Realizing the situation was hopeless, Patten had bread and water put in the ship's boats, told Pat to dress herself and Nellie May warmly, and gave the order to lower boats. There was only time to snatch a chronometer and a Winchester rifle. The three boats shaped a course for the island, about twenty-five miles distant, but adverse conditions intervened. As Pat later recalled, "For two days and nights we tossed in an open boat on the ocean, with nothing but hard bread and water to live on, and the sun boiling down on us. The baby slept most of the time, while I held the chart over her to shield her from the rays of the sun. My face, hands, and arms were burned by the sun to a solid mass of blisters. Before reaching land our fresh water supply got scarce. The sailors tried several times to steal a demijohn of water I had saved for the baby at a time when almost everyone in the boat was asleep from exhaustion. Once I defended it alone with my loaded rifle beside me. The crew was a bad lot and I was too frightened to sleep."[56]

When at last they reached shore, all parties were able to arrange passage to Naha, Okinawa, aboard a small Japanese steamer, using the ship's lifeboats as security. Before the steamer sailed, said Pat, "Every native on the island came off on the steamer to see us. An officer stood about ten feet from baby and me and tried to keep the mob away from me. They would come up and feel of my hair, as it hung down my back, for I had no hair pins. We are the only white people they have ever seen." Arriving at Naha, the Pattens found an interpreter, reported their situation, and were put up at the city's best hotel. "Some of our toughest sailors went to another hotel," Pat later reported, "where they stole each others' clothes and sold them for soki [sake].... Then they got drunk, smashed up things and drove the proprietor and everyone out of the hotel and took charge themselves. The native police did not dare to touch them. We stayed there four days while the governor made arrangements for us.... The captain sleeps with my rifle beside him, and I do not sleep at all.... When we left one sailor was so drunk they had to put a rope around him and hoist him on board."[57] The bedraggled *Stetson* contingent took a steamer to Nagasaki. According to Pat, "When we arrived at Nagasaki we looked like the emigrants who arrive at New York. Our clothes were all drabbled and dirty. My sleeves were stripped to my elbows and my arms were bandaged with two dirty handkerchiefs."[58]

From the moment the *Stetson* was abandoned, Frank Patten had been ruminating about what or who had caused the fire. As the lifeboats made their way to shore, he concluded that "the fire was not an accident." Conditions on board had been peaceful, the men well fed and not overworked. "The only man saving all his clothing," Patten remembered, "was the man that gave the alarm of fire." That man's furtive behavior in the boat further convinced the captain that he had an arsonist on his hands. Patten, who had been mate on the Sewall bark *Kenilworth,* remembered that the suspect had likewise served aboard that vessel "when she was afire on her passage from Hilo to N.Y., and Bos'n Doyle charged him with being a 'Jonah', and said 'I will never go shipmates with you again as every ship you go in has a fire aboard of her,' and...he said 'What are you going to do when you get with such G — D — Officers?'" In his report to the U.S. consul in Nagasaki, Patten stated his opinion that the ship had been deliberately, vindictively torched.

Patten expected to initiate proceedings against the suspect when all hands reached San Francisco, but a coded telegram from the Sewall office read, "Do not think it advisable to prosecute unless you can recover damages." He therefore paid off the *Stetson* crew before leaving Nagasaki and, with Pat and Nellie May, headed for home aboard an army transport from Nagasaki to San Francisco. Eventually, the Pattens reached Bath.

In 1901, Frank Patten took command of the four-masted coastwise schooner *May Neville,* built by Captain James Hawley. A number of dignitaries, including Charles E. Patten, attended the vessel's launching. The owner's daughter, Miss Ethel Hawley, christened the new ship with a bottle of sweetened water. As the *Times* pointed out, the *Neville* was imposing and elegant: "The cabin is well arranged and finished in a pretty combination of quartered oak, mahogany and sycamore and trimmings of black and gold. The apartments are commodious and have all the accommodations of an up-to-date dwelling on land. The vessel is fitted with all the latest appliances, has a Moulton windlass and hoisting engines, steam pumps, etc...."[59] As before, Patten's wife and daughter sailed with him to the Caribbean.

In 1902, Frank returned to Bath to help design and build a Sewall superschooner, *Kineo,* which represented a step forward in sail technology. Although Arthur Sewall & Company clung to sail technology, the firm was innovative within that constraint. In 1893, the company had commenced building square-riggers of steel, eventually completing nine. That know-how, plus the attractions of the coastwise coal trade, inspired the Sewalls to build the *Kineo.* In 1902, a high-tech schooner promised long-term profits and a way to keep sail competitive with steam vessels.

As every shipmaster and merchant knew, schooners, with relatively few fore-and-aft-rigged sails, could be managed by much smaller crews than square-rigged vessels. In addition, their insurance rates and maintenance were lower, their cargo capacity per ton higher, and they could sail closer to the wind than square-riggers. But their massive fore-and-aft sails made them far more clumsy and dangerous in adverse weather, which was why virtually all schooners were confined to coastwise trade. At the turn of the century, a new breed of immense, capacious, multimasted schooners were making profits for their owners by hauling Appalachian coal from Norfolk, Virginia, to coastwise ports in North America. In this trade, bigger was better, and the *Kineo* would be one of the biggest. Frank Patten, the *Kineo*'s designated first master, enthusiastically took shares in the new vessel, thanks to Charles Patten's timely loan.

On a bleak, drizzly afternoon in April 1903, the huge steel schooner, still mostly unrigged, slid down the ways at the Sewall yard as whistles blew and people cheered. As described in the *Times,* "Some bunting was displayed in spite of the rain, and the graceful slide and plunge of the beautiful ship made a charming sight.... A large delegation of prominent citizens from all sections of the State arrived on the noon train and were entertained with a delightful lunch at the home of the Hon. Harold M. Sewall on Washington street.... The craft possesses many novel features in construction..., all contributing to the safety[,] speed or comfort of the vessel or general economy in handling her. Among her principal features is an arrangement for carrying 1,242 tons of water ballast in bulk without having recourse to the double bottom system usually adopted in steamers for this purpose.

"The hoisting engines...are threefold in purpose; they are arranged for handling cargo, for handling the vessel's sails and for working the hand pumps by messenger chains.... The floor of the galley, engine room and pump room are covered with cement and handsomely tiled.... The Kineo will be ready for sea in the course of two or three weeks."[60] When her five steel masts were stepped, she was a stirring sight, measuring more than 274 feet in length and 45 feet in the beam. She was the first steel five-master built anywhere and the last vessel built by the Sewalls.

In 1903 and 1904, Frank Patten got the bugs out of the *Kineo* in coastwise voyages. Her labor-saving equipment passed muster and Patten was pleased to find that her small, fourteen-man crew could be cut back to twelve.[61] Then, in 1905, came a government contract to carry an oceanic cargo. Having won the Spanish-American War, the United States was now constructing naval bases in the Philippines. In 1904, Congress expanded the old Jones Act, which reserved coastwise shipping for American-flag vessels, to include the Philippines. Here was an incentive to make long sailing voyages free of foreign competition. The *Kineo*'s first long haul would be from Norfolk to Manila with coal for the U.S. Navy.

At the time of her launching, the *Kineo*'s publicity had said she was suitable for oceanic trade, suggesting that Sewall & Company intended to use her for more than coastwise voyages. In other words, she may have been conceived partly as a test vessel to replace square-riggers on long-haul routes. Even the latest steel ships and barks were becoming uneconomical to operate because of the large, skilled crews they required. Could a steel schooner, with several masts and power-assisted hoisting, overcome the rig's deepwater limitations? More to the point, could it cope with such unpleasant surprises as typhoons and Cape Horn weather? After consulting with the heads of successful schooner fleets, Sewall & Company decided the answer was yes. Certainly it was worth a try. If vessels such as the *Kineo* could do the work of the big square-riggers, it would give sail a new lease on life. In Frank Patten, the Sewalls had a versatile skipper with expertise in schooners, square-riggers, worldwide shipping routes, and adversity. He and his family were more than ready for the test.

Taking a coal schooner halfway around the world was big news, and wherever the *Kineo* went on her long voyage, she drew media attention. She sailed for Manila by way of the Cape of Good Hope and the Indian Ocean, a week behind the four-masted steel bark *Edward Sewall*, also bound for Manila. Patten was eager to show that the *Kineo* could beat square-riggers at their own game, and on her passage to Manila, she almost succeeded, proving nearly as fast on the long haul as the *Sewall*. In calm seas and trade winds, the *Kineo* was the match for any ship or bark. But in heavy seas, she became a monster, her huge sails flapping violently, rending canvas and breaking the jaws that held booms and gaffs to her masts. On a schooner, losing a gaff or boom jaw was much more serious than, say, losing a topgallant yard on a square-rigger. The *Kineo* was damaged repeatedly in such a fashion, indicating that she simply was not up to the long distances her owners wanted her to cover. During the month of April, Patten recorded, "I have been obliged to Lower sails to save them eight times. In nearly every case there was a moderate fair wind but the Westerly swell caused the sails to slat [flap] awfully."[62]

On 9 August 1905, after discharging her coal in Manila and undergoing repairs, the *Kineo* headed for Newcastle, New South Wales, to load another coal cargo, this time for Kahului, Maui, in the Hawaiian Islands. On this voyage, things did not go well. Eleven days out of Manila, the schooner was caught for four days in the legendary Pacific typhoon of 1905. Angry seas inflicted considerable loss of rigging and equipment and stove in the vessel's gasoline-powered launch. But she came through the typhoon, at least passing her endurance test.

Becalmed after the typhoon, the vessel made almost no progress toward her destination. Food ran short. After about a month, off Guam, the schooner signaled for fresh vegetables, but almost none were to be had right away, so Patten elected to sail on. The next stop was Goban Bay, Solomon Islands, where again there were no fresh vegetables. They all had been consumed, a local trader explained, by feasting islanders. Bedeviled by calm weather and again dismantled by rough weather, the *Kineo* tacked back and forth in the general direction of northeastern Australia. To make matters worse, the livestock aboard sickened and died. Worst of all, the crew came down with beriberi, a disease endemic to the region.

The effects of the disease on all hands made it impossible to shoot for Newcastle, so Patten made for Brisbane, arriving off Cape Moreton on 20 November 1905. Because of adverse winds, he had to anchor until a tow could be arranged into Brisbane. By the time towing delays and medical quarantine were overcome, one *Kineo* sailor died of beriberi. A Brisbane doctor inspected the vessel and concluded that "the sickness was caused by the water that had been used on board, which was not of good quality. It had been shipped at Manila." Everyone aboard was down with the disease except Nellie, whom the Brisbane

Daily Mail described as "a bright little girl of eight summers."[63] One seaman was in critical condition; "Mrs. Patten was also very bad but he thought she would soon get well
after getting ashore. Dr. Bancroft found the vessel in exceedingly clean condition, and
granted pratique [health clearance], but the crew, 14 all told, including the captain, his
wife and child, would have to go to the hospital and be attended to.... The *Kineo* is to be
docked here for cleaning and painting, as her hull is in a very dirty condition."[64] Her slow
progress had invited a massive infestation of barnacles and she also had suffered massive wear and tear since leaving Manila, causing Patten to question her viability as an
oceangoing freighter.

The *Kineo* at last made it to Newcastle, loaded coal, and proceeded to Maui, where
she discharged her cargo and took on sugar for Philadelphia. Her expected time to round
Cape Horn and reach the Delaware River was 130 days. By October 1906, the vessel was
a month and a half overdue and her whereabouts was anybody's guess. In Bath, people
considered the odds against her survival. A *Times* article pointed out that "the schooner
has not been spoken since she left Hawaii.... The fact that an unusually large number of
icebergs have been reported in the vicinity of Cape Horn, together with the long absence
of the vessel, is the principal source of anxiety. On the other hand, as the vessel is schooner
rigged, it is acknowledged that the time ordinarily made by square-riggers over the same
course is not a criterion.... Capt. Patten himself once made the passage in ninety-seven
days, which is remarkably quick time.... The Kineo is an unusually staunch vessel and it
is felt that stress of weather could scarcely do her any serious injury. Were she to strike
an iceberg, however, it would probably be her undoing. The calm belts in the tropics,
however, have frequently accounted for long voyages around the Horn..., and it is hoped
that something of this sort accounts for the failure of Capt. Patten to put in an earlier
appearance at Delaware Breakwater."[65]

The *Kineo* was still afloat, and the *Times* was partly correct about her poor passage.
She had in fact been unlucky in finding fair winds in the South Pacific. But in a fresh
breeze, her deck was washed by seas, making her difficult to manage and murder on sails
and rigging. Out of hoops by which the sails were made fast to the masts, the crew had
to improvise them from whatever scrap they could scrounge aboard. There were also
smashed boats, twisted davits, shattered topmasts, and a broken steam boiler that required
heavy work to be done by hand — all by the time she had reached the River Plate. There
was also the bizarre sight, off Cape Horn, of a 1,300-foot iceberg towering high above
and dangerously near the struggling schooner.[66] Patten was by now convinced that big
schooners had no business in the Cape Horn trade.[67] But he kept going.

Off the mouth of the Amazon, a passing steamer spotted a distant five-masted
schooner. That report made headlines in the United States because there could be only
one five-master in those waters: the long-lost *Kineo*. At last, 205 days from Maui, the
Kineo limped into Philadelphia. The schooner had completed a circumnavigation, and
her arrival made more headlines; but the Sewalls would not tempt fate by sending her
into deep water again.

In Philadelphia, the Pattens received hundreds of telegrams from well-wishers congratulating them on surviving the ordeal. And when Pat and Nellie ("THE KINEO HEROINES") arrived in Bath in December 1906, they supplied the local press with interesting tidbits about their long ordeal. Nellie, now nine, captivated the *Times* reporter with her precocious candor: "She is a little lady who does not hesitate to say what she means. When [during the *Kineo's* nightmare] the hatches were battened down and the entire crew were below decks, Nellie played with her pet collie undismayed by the fear on the men's faces. She was not afraid and told them so. She had a child's confidence in the ability of her father and never for an instant was in doubt of the result, a safe arrival in port...."[68]

Nellie had received parental schooling aboard ship, but her parents thought it was time she received some more structured education, so she and her mother stayed ashore while Frank Patten took the *Kineo* coastwise. According to family tradition, Nellie did not adjust well to the classroom. Eventually, she either spent summers aboard the *Kineo* or returned full-time with her mother to the schooner.

It need hardly be said that life aboard a five-masted coal schooner was not ideal for a willful girl in her early teens, especially when shadowed by protective parents. When Nellie was thirteen or fourteen, she and the *Kineo's* mate, Fred Ferrell, fell for each other. Ferrell was almost twenty-eight years older than Nellie and, despite a boisterous nature, a good friend of Captain Frank's, so it is no surprise that the romance was kept strictly secret, as was the couple's plan to marry. Meanwhile, Pat had given birth to a second child, Mary. For the sake of the frail baby's health, she left the *Kineo*; despite her objections, Nellie was put in school in Philadelphia. During a stopover in Port Arthur, Texas, however, Fred Ferrell left the schooner, traveled to Philadelphia, and married Nellie. This, too, was kept secret. A few months later, when the Pattens visited Nellie, she put her foot down and demanded that she be permitted to leave school. Allegedly, when her parents said no, she became hysterical and broke the news that she was Mrs. Fred Ferrell. There was more: Captain and Mrs. Frank Patten were about to become grandparents. Bowing to the fait accompli, the astonished Pattens took Nellie back aboard the *Kineo,* where they apparently satisfied themselves that the marriage would succeed.[69] It did.

Pattens and Ferrells sail together on the *Kineo* until 1912. That year, suffering from diabetes, Frank Patten retires from the sea. He turns the *Kineo* over to Ferrell, supposedly with this blessing: "You stole my daughter, so now, dammit, take my ship."[70] Then the last seafaring Patten goes ashore.

Fred and Nellie May Ferrell continue life aboard the *Kineo,* which Sewall & Company has chartered to the booming Texas Company. In 1916, the vessel is sold to that company, but Fred continues as her skipper. Renamed *Maryland* and equipped with auxiliary power, she has years of coastwise service left in her.

For their retirement, Frank and Charlotte Patten purchase a chicken farm in South Byfield, Massachusetts. That would seem a difficult change for an old sea dog to make, but Frank does not have long to cope with the challenge. In January 1913, just weeks after leaving Bath, he catches a severe cold and dies from complications at age fifty-eight. Noting his passing, the *Times* does not, as in previous Patten obituaries, mention that the illustrious family line of mariners has run out. This time, however, it has.

NOTES

1. Owen, p. 284.
2. Ibid., p. 286.
3. Emma O. Patten to Arthur Sewall, Bath, undated [probably 1882] (Sewall Family Papers, MMM).
4. Reed, p. 345.
5. John O. Patten to William D. Sewall, New York, 3 November 1890 (Sewall Papers, MMM).
6. *Bath Daily Times,* 1 May 1899.
7. *Bath Enterprise,* 2 January 1897.
8. *Bath Independent,* 4 September 1897.
9. *Bath Enterprise* (extra edition), 1 September 1897.
10. *Bath Daily Times,* 31 December 1896.
11. *Bath Enterprise* (extra edition), 1 September 1897.
12. Ibid., 30 August 1897.
13. Ibid., 1 September 1897.
14. *Bath Independent,* 4 September 1897.
15. *Bath Daily Times,* 29 August 1897.
16. Ibid., 1 May 1899.
17. Inventory of the estate of James F. Patten, 1883 (Probate Records, Sagadahoc County Court House, Bath, ME).
18. Reed, p. 342.
19. Owen, p. 251.
20. *Bath Daily Times,* 28 February 1884.
21. Ibid., 26 February 1886.
22. Ibid., 27 February 1886.
23. Ibid.
24. Ibid., 28 February 1887.
25. Owen, p. 256.
26. *Bath Enterprise,* 22 February 1890.
27. *Bath Daily Times,* 27 February 1890.
28. Quoted in full in *Bath Enterprise,* 12 March 1890.
29. *American Sentinel* (Bath), 6 March 1890.
30. *Bath Daily Times,* 26 February 1890.
31. Ibid., 3 March 1890.
32. Owen, p. 255.
33. *Bath Enterprise,* 31 December 1890.
34. Ibid., 17 January 1891.
35. Ibid., 7 February 1891.
36. *Bath Daily Times,* 24 February 1891.

37. *Bath Enterprise,* 28 February 1891.

38. Ibid.; *Bath Daily Times,* 3 March 1891.

39. *Bath Enterprise,* 4 March 1891.

40. Ibid., 24 February 1892.

41. Ibid., 9 March 1892.

42. *Bath Daily Times,* 17 February 1893.

43. Ibid.

44. Ibid., 27 February 1893.

45. *Bath Enterprise,* 8 March 1893.

46. *Bath Daily Times,* 15 June 1903.

47. Ibid.

48. Inventory of the estate of Charles E. Patten, 1903 (Probate Records, Sagadahoc County Court House, Bath, ME).

49. Ibid.; *Bath Daily Times,* 30 June 1903.

50. Ibid., 6 March 1908.

51. Ibid., 15 June 1903.

52. Frank W. Patten to Arthur Sewall & Company, Galveston, 14 July 1903 (Sewall Papers, MMM).

53. Mark Hennessy, *The Sewall Ships of Steel* (Augusta, ME: Kennebec Journal Press, 1937), p. 365.

54. *Bath Daily Times,* 20 January 1913.

55. Frank Patten to Arthur Sewall & Company, Nagasaki, 26 September 1899 (Sewall Papers, MMM). Patten's other quoted statements about the *George Stetson* are taken from this letter.

56. *Bath Daily Times,* 3 November 1899.

57. Ibid.

58. Ibid., 27 October 1899.

59. Ibid., 23 January 1901.

60. Ibid., 16 April 1903.

61. Frank Patten to Arthur Sewall & Company, Galveston, 16 July 1903 (Sewall Papers, MMM).

62. Hennessy, *Sewall Ships of Steel,* p. 368.

63. *Daily Mail* (Brisbane), 21 November 1905, quoted in *Bath Daily Times,* 8 January 1906.

64. Ibid.

65. *Bath Daily Times,* 22 October 1906.

66. Charlotte A. Beach, "Neptune's Daughter Nellie" (typescript [copy], n.d., collection of Reg Ferrell, Arlington, TX). This work, by Nellie May's daughter, is a collection of family stories about her illustrious mother.

67. Hennessy, *Sewall Ships of Steel,* pp. 371-72.

68. *Bath Daily Times,* 10 December 1906.

69. Beach, pp. 18-19.

70. Ibid., p. 20.

Afterword

In Bath, the Pattens' influence declined quickly and dramatically by the turn of the twentieth century. When Frank Patten retired to his chicken farm, the clan's pool of nautical talent was exhausted. So were the particular economic and technological conditions that the family had mastered. So too was the enormous maritime capital that Patten merchants and masters had generated. Most of that wealth had long since been reinvested or spent outside of Bath. Likewise, the wooden square-riggers that had earned the Pattens millions had also vanished — every one of them.

Of course, nothing lasts forever; but, almost a century later, physical evidence of the Pattens' maritime heyday is hard to find. If you travel along Front Street to the site of G.F. & J. Patten's shipyard (which was later the Sewall and Texas Company yards), all you will find is a steep, overgrown riverbank studded with stumpy, nondescript pilings. It takes some imagination to visualize the years of noisy construction and festive launchings that characterized that yard, even though the house George F. Patten built still overlooks the scene. Down the street, Captain John's onetime home, which overlooked the Patten wharf (and, later, the gas company), now presides over a barren, silent expanse of idle waterfront that last served as a storage lot for coal, salt, and scrap iron. During their lifetimes, the Patten brothers and their children had witnessed dramatic changes in Bath. Accordingly, were they to return, they could probably accommodate most of the last century's changes. But they surely would be astonished to find so much of the city's waterfront neglected and unused.

You will find another small physical reminder at the family burial plot, located in a corner of Maple Grove Cemetery: a few rows of solid, squat gravestones surrounding a tall granite obelisk memorializing George and Hannah Patten. There is nothing tumbledown about the site, but clearly, the graves are seldom visited. (Incidentally, and contrary to rumor, no one named Patten y Balderrama is interred with the Pattens of Bath.)

Then there are the family's assorted memorabilia. Virtually all Patten business records have vanished, but you'll find a few handsome ship portraits and a short stack of correspondence at the Maine Maritime Museum in Bath. Captain John's marble bust still resides at the Patten Free Library, although you must look in a dark stairwell to find it. In the library reading room, John Hilling's paintings of the South Church arson are on display.

And, if you ask nicely, you can still peruse William King's personal copy of _Spiritual Improvement_, or _The Suspicious Husband_, or _Eccentric Female Biography_ — all kept in a locked case with the rest of the governor's collection, courtesy of George and John Patten. Other family heirlooms have been scattered far and wide, now the property of descendants with names other than Patten.

In view of the family's onetime prominence, this meager assortment of artifacts would seem poignant, except for the fact that Patten values are alive and well in Bath. During their colorful lifetimes, and even more at the time of their posthumous bequests, Pattens were celebrated for their sense of civic responsibility and readiness to share their wealth with organizations they deemed meritorious. And for generations, the family unostentatiously provided personal assistance to countless worthy but needy individuals. By doing so, they generated a local philanthropic tradition that is one of the city's most distinctive assets.

When Galen Moses, for example, came forward to fund the construction of a city library, he was following up on the groundwork of the previous Patten generation. Other prosperous citizens (many named Patten) then came forward to make the institution a reality. It is no accident that the finished library bore the Patten name, or that, in succeeding decades, it would thrive on the private gifts of Bath citizens.

When Charles Davenport flourished under the tutelage of George and John Patten, he, like them, became a dedicated community benefactor. But Charles's son and heir, George Patten Davenport, outdid his father. Known around Bath as a pennypinching eccentric, George Davenport dressed in worn-out clothes, walked around town to save carfare, and even read discarded newspapers. However, at his death in 1927, he left $1.1 million (equal to $8.7 million in 1995 currency) in trust "for the benefit of needy children, especially those of Bath, Maine," and for educational, benevolent, and charitable institutions "especially those in Bath, Maine." At its inception, the Davenport Trust Fund was the largest charitable foundation in Maine. In more than one way, it was directly linked to the Patten social conscience. Prompted by such examples — and benefiting thereby — Bath citizens are to this day prodigiously generous in their private support of charitable organizations.

Some things last longer than others. The Pattens would be pleased.

Appendix A

Simplified Genealogical Charts and Selected Family Notes
by
Ralph Linwood Snow

The Patten family grew by leaps and bounds during its first century in America. The selected biographical sketches below contain names of 210 family members, representing approximately half of the Maine Pattens born prior to the twentieth century.

The data presented in this appendix: (a) track the maritime branches of the family; (b) focus on the Kennebec River region; (c) have some relevance to this work.

Twenty-seven shipmasters are identified, plus an additional eight mariners who died in foreign countries or at sea, probably while serving aboard ship. By family custom, young men went to sea to mature and to learn a trade. Not all reached command rank. Some perished at sea or in foreign ports. Others no doubt found the attractions of life ashore far more appealing than life at sea. It is therefore likely that many more Pattens went to sea than the thirty-five listed names, which represent 17 percent of the total. Patten females strengthened maritime connections by marrying seventeen shipmasters.

The following conventions are observed in the genealogical data:

- The first generation consists of the four brothers who came to New England in the first quarter of the eighteenth century.
- Roman numerals on the family tree represent generations.
- Generations in Family Notes are indicated by superscript numbers following names.
- All children's names marked by asterisks have a more detailed Family Note to be found under the sequence number to the left of their names.
- Abbreviations:

    > c.= child of
    > adptd. = adopted
    > bapt.= baptized
    > b.= born
    > m.= married
    > d.= died
    > div.= divorced
    > w/= with
    > @ = at

    State abbreviations follow current postal conventions.

PATTEN FAMILY TREE

Simplified

A. GENERATIONS I, II

Note: Numbers in parentheses refer to the Family Notes that follow.

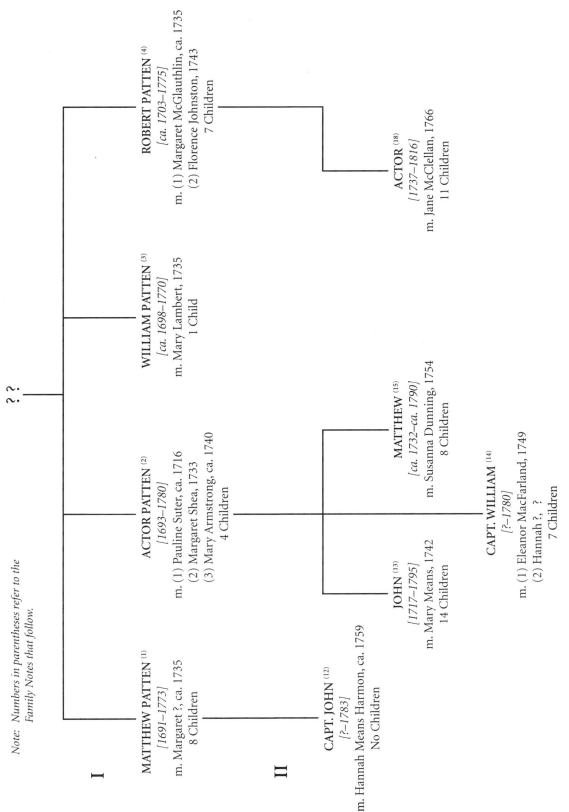

I

MATTHEW PATTEN [1]
[1691–1773]
m. Margaret ?, ca. 1735
8 Children

ACTOR PATTEN [2]
[1693–1780]
m. (1) Pauline Suter, ca. 1716
(2) Margaret Shea, 1733
(3) Mary Armstrong, ca. 1740
4 Children

WILLIAM PATTEN [3]
[ca. 1698–1770]
m. Mary Lambert, 1735
1 Child

ROBERT PATTEN [4]
[ca. 1703–1775]
m. (1) Margaret McGlauthlin, ca. 1735
(2) Florence Johnston, 1743
7 Children

? ?

II

CAPT. JOHN [12]
[?–1783]
m. Hannah Means Harmon, ca. 1759
No Children

JOHN [13]
[1717–1795]
m. Mary Means, 1742
14 Children

CAPT. WILLIAM [14]
[?–1780]
m. (1) Eleanor MacFarland, 1749
(2) Hannah ?, ?
7 Children

MATTHEW [15]
[ca. 1732–ca. 1790]
m. Susanna Dunning, 1754
8 Children

ACTOR [18]
[1737–1816]
m. Jane McClellan, 1766
11 Children

B. GENERATIONS III, IV

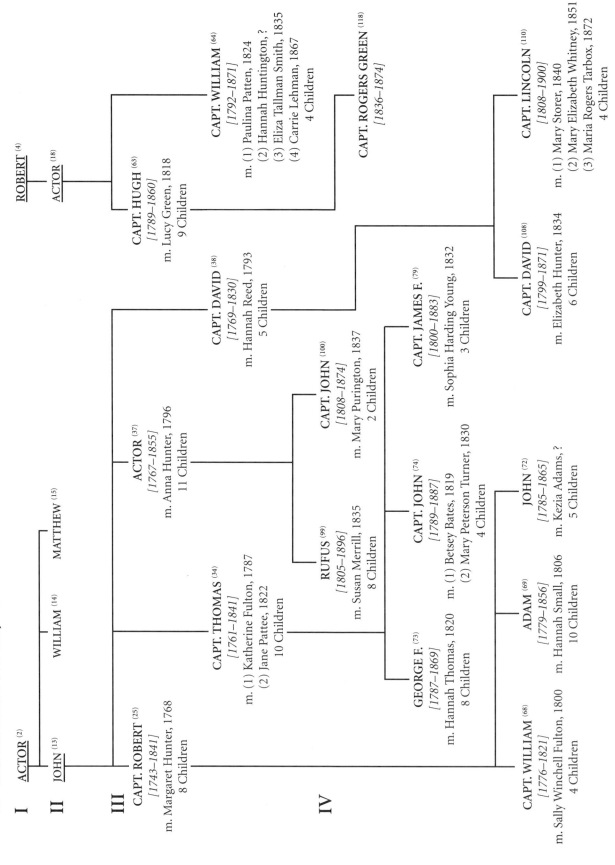

I   ACTOR [2]

II   JOHN [13]

ROBERT [4]

ACTOR [18]

III

CAPT. ROBERT [25]
[1743–1841]
m. Margaret Hunter, 1768
8 Children

WILLIAM [14]

MATTHEW [15]

CAPT. HUGH [63]
[1789–1860]
m. Lucy Green, 1818
9 Children

CAPT. WILLIAM [64]
[1792–1871]
m. (1) Paulina Patten, 1824
    (2) Hannah Huntington, ?
    (3) Eliza Tallman Smith, 1835
    (4) Carrie Lehman, 1867
4 Children

CAPT. ROGERS GREEN [118]
[1836–1874]

ACTOR [37]
[1767–1855]
m. Anna Hunter, 1796
11 Children

CAPT. DAVID [38]
[1769–1830]
m. Hannah Reed, 1793
5 Children

CAPT. LINCOLN [110]
[1808–1900]
m. (1) Mary Storer, 1840
    (2) Mary Elizabeth Whitney, 1851
    (3) Maria Rogers Tarbox, 1872
4 Children

CAPT. DAVID [108]
[1799–1871]
m. Elizabeth Hunter, 1834
6 Children

IV

CAPT. THOMAS [34]
[1761–1841]
m. (1) Katherine Fulton, 1787
    (2) Jane Pattee, 1822
10 Children

CAPT. JOHN [100]
[1808–1874]
m. Mary Purington, 1837
2 Children

CAPT. JAMES F. [79]
[1800–1883]
m. Sophia Harding Young, 1832
3 Children

RUFUS [99]
[1805–1896]
m. Susan Merrill, 1835
8 Children

CAPT. JOHN [74]
[1789–1887]
m. (1) Betsey Bates, 1819
    (2) Mary Peterson Turner, 1830
4 Children

JOHN [72]
[1785–1865]
m. Kezia Adams, ?
5 Children

GEORGE F. [73]
[1787–1869]
m. Hannah Thomas, 1820
8 Children

ADAM [69]
[1779–1856]
m. Hannah Small, 1806
10 Children

CAPT. WILLIAM [68]
[1776–1821]
m. Sally Winchell Fulton, 1800
4 Children

C. ALL DESCENDED
FROM JOHN[2], ACTOR[1]

III   CAPT. ROBERT

IV   CAPT. WILLIAM   ADAM   JOHN   CAPT. THOMAS   GEORGE F.   CAPT. JOHN   CAPT. JAMES F.   ACTOR   CAPT. DAVID

RUFUS   CAPT. JOHN   CAPT. DAVID   CAPT. LINCOLN

V

CAPT. ALFRED [124]
[?–1847]
m. Maria Ross, 1835
2 Children

CAPT. ROBERT [125]
[1812–1855]
m. Beulah F. Purington, 1837
3 Children

CAPT. HORATIO [135]
[1818–1884]
m. Alvicia Small, ?
1 Child

CAPT. BARDWELL [139]
[1821–1890]
m. Frances Meserve, 1851
4 Children

CAPT. JARVIS [141]
[1827–1888]
m. Charlotte Whitmore, 1854
8 Children

CATHERINE [143]
[1821–1875]
m. Wildes Walker, 1840
3 Children

JAMES T. [147]
[1830–1888]
m. Isabel Smith, 1855
4 Children

GEORGE M. [150]
[1836–1901]
m. Frederica Camp, 1859
4 Children

CAPT. THOMAS R. [151]
[1821–1847]
m. Caroline Cooper, 1844

CAPT. G.E.R. [152]
[1823–1882]
m. Emma Owen, 1859
2 Children

CAPT. CHARLES [155]
[1834–1903]
m. Jessie Jones, 1857
No Children

CAPT. ABEL M. [158]
[1836–1864]
m. ?

CAPT. JAMES M.W. [166]
[1839–1874]
m. Sarah Whittemore, 1867
2 or 3 Children

CAPT. OSCAR [160]
[1839–?]
m. Lillian Harding, 1890

FREDERICK H. [156]
[1838–1889]
m. Clara Kendrick, 1883
No Children

CAPT. DAVID A. [169]
[1839–1865]

CAPT. FRANK W. [176]
[1855–1913]
m. Charlotte Shaw, 1894
2 Children

NELLIE MAE [209]
[1897–1950]
m. Capt. Fred Ferrell, ca. 1912
3 Children

JOHN OWEN [207]
[1861–1899]
m. (1) Lucy Larrabee, 1886 (div. 1896)
(2) Irene Ann Roberts, 1897

VI

CAPT. ALFRED P. [179]
[1838–1877]
m. Ellen Pierce, 1865

Family Notes

1. MATTHEW PATTEN[1]

    c. ? and ?

    b. 1691, Dunboe, Londonderry, Ireland

    m. ?, Margaret ? (?-ca. 1735)

    d. 1773, @ Saco, ME

Children[2]:

    5) Jane, b. 1717; m. 1743 to John Gray; d. 1810

    6) John, b. 1721 @ Wells, d. young

    7) Elish, b. 1724 @ Wells , d. young

    8) Susanna, b. 1724, d. 1813 @ Biddeford, unmarried

    9) James, b. 1730, d. 1770, land speculator

    10) Lydia, b. ?, d. 1802, unmarried

    11) Robert, b. 6/21/1732, m. 5/17/84, Susanna Goodwin (1764-1841), d. 3/14/1819 @ Arundel

    *12) Capt. John

Remarks: (1) Emigrated to America before his younger brothers came in 1727; (2) settled permanently in Saco area.

2. ACTOR PATTEN[1]

    c. ? and ?

    b. 1693, Dunboe, Londonderry, Ireland

    m. (1) ca. 1716, Pauline Suter (?-?); (2) 5/19/1733, Margaret Shea (?-?); (3) ca. 1740, Mary Armstrong, "widow" (?-?)

    d. ca. 1780 @ Surry

Children[2]:

    *13) John

    *14) William

    *15) Matthew

    16) Mary: b. ?, m. 1753, John Rae

Remarks: (1) Emigrated to America ca. 1727 with two brothers and families, arriving in Boston; (2) removed to Falmouth, ME, in mid-1730s; (3) purchased 40 acres in Biddeford, moving there in 1738; (4) moved in 1755 to Yarmouth and thence to Surry with son Matthew, ca. 1768.

3. WILLIAM PATTEN[1]

    c. ? and ?

    b. between 1694 and 1702

    m. 11/22/1735, Mary Lambert @ Boston

    d. late August or early September 1770 @ Boston

Children[2]:

    17) Robert, b. ?, d. 1777; a sailor who did not "lead a decent and becoming life"; apparently was married twice but had no children.

4. ROBERT PATTEN[1]

    c. ? and ?

    b. ca. 1703 @ Dunboe, Londonderry, Ireland

    m. (1) Margaret McGlauthlin (?-ca. 1743); (2) 12/26/1743, Florence Johnston

    d. ca. late March 1775 @ Arundel

Children[2]:

    *18) Actor

    19) Margaret, m. Israel Cleaves

    20) Robert

    21) James

    22) John

    23) Mary, b. 1752, m. 1769, Wm. Wilson of Topsham, d. 1833

    24) Rachel, m. 1792, Capt. Wm. Smith

Remarks: (1) Settled on southwestern Maine coast.

12. CAPT. JOHN PATTEN[2]

    c. Matthew[1] and Margaret ?

    b. ?

    m. after 10/1759 to Hannah (Means) Harmon (?-1823), widow of Nathaniel Harmon of Scarborough

    d. 1783 in wreck of sloop *Judith* off Marshfield, MA

Children[3]: none

Remarks: Purchased land in Bowdoinham and Pownalborough in partnership with brother Robert.

13. JOHN PATTEN[2]

    c. Actor[1] and Pauline Suter

    b. 1717 in Ireland

    m. 6/19/1742, Mary Means (1721-1800)

    d. 4/7/1795 from injuries received in fall from horse

Children[3]:

*25) Robert

26) Sarah, b. 1745 @ Biddeford, m. 1764, Robert Fulton @ Topsham

27) Jane (Jean?), b. 1747, m. 1783, William Randall @ Topsham, d. 1833

28) Mary, b. 1749, m. Sam'l Jameson, d. 1795

29) Hannah, b. 1751, m. 1775, Capt. Thomas Harward @ Brunswick, d. 1848

30) Margaret, b. 1753, m. 1777, Capt. James Maxwell @ Topsham, d. 1831; mother of Noble Maxwell

31) John, b. 1754, captured by British 1779 while cutting hay on Sheepscot marshes with brother Wm. and brothers-in-law Robt. Fulton and Thomas Harward; subsequently escaped or released but died @ Topsham 1780

32) William, b. 1757, died in British prison [see above], ca. 1779-80

33) Dorcas, b. 1759, m. 1784, James Hunter, Jr. @ Topsham, d. 1813

*34) Thomas

35) Joseph, b. 1763, drowned in Merrymeeting Bay w/infant son in 1809

36) Matthew, b. 1765, d. 1775

*37) Actor

*38) David

Remarks: (1) In partnership w/brother William [14], brother-in-law Thomas Means, and Gowan Fulton purchased 661 acres at Cathance Point, Bowdoinham, in 1749; (2) expanded holdings substantially in subsequent years by an additional 800 acres; (3) blacksmith, farmer, militia lieutenant, selectman; also began to build vessels on the Cathance in partnership with John Fulton, Robert Hunter, and brother William.

14. WILLIAM PATTEN[2]

c. Actor[1] and Pauline Suter
b. ? in Ireland
m. (1) 1749, Eleanor MacFarland (?-1769?) @ Biddeford; (2) ?, Hannah ?
d. 1780

Children[3]

39) James, b. ca. 1750, served through most of Revolutionary War in Continental Army, died in West Indies ca. 1800

40) Matthew, b. ca. 1752, served in Continental Army 1777-81, d. ca. 1800

41) John, b. ?, d. ?

42) William, b. 1756, enlisted "for duration" in 1776 and served at least until 1781, d. after 1783

43) Robert, b. ?, d. ?

44) Charles, b. 1771, d. 1793 on passage from West Indies

45) Sarah, b. ?, d. ?

Remarks: (1) Moved to Bowdoinham w/brother John and acquired land at Cathance Point, as well as shares in a mill and other properties over the years; (2) principally engaged in the coasting trade and shipbuilding partnership w/John.

15. MATTHEW PATTEN[2]

c. Actor[1] and Pauline Suter
b. ca. 1732 @ Boston
m. 1754, Susanna Dunning (1736-1810) @ Biddeford
d. ca. 1790

Children[3]:

46) James, b. 1756 @ Saco; his great-grandson, Gilbert Patten, was author of Frank Merriwell series

47) Sarah, b. 175? @ N. Yarmouth

48) Jane, b. 175? @ N. Yarmouth, d. young

49) John, b. ca. 1763

50) Susanna, b. before 1767 @ N. Yarmouth

51) Mary, bapt. 1772 @ Ellsworth

52) Robert, bapt. 1772 @ Ellsworth

53) Jane, b. 1774, m. 1795, James MacFarland, d. 1832

Remarks: (1) Moved 1757 from Biddeford/Saco area to North Yarmouth w/father and stepmother; (2) ca. 1768, took up land at Township #6 (modern-day Surry), purchasing considerable land over the years (the Patten name is still attached to a number of locations in the area); (3) apparently traded by boat in this then-remote area of coast, which came under effective British control during the Revolution.

18. ACTOR PATTEN[2]

c. Robert Patten[1] and Margaret McGlauthlin
b. 1/2/1737, Ireland
m. 11/20/1766, Jane McClellan @ Falmouth
d. 7/25/1816 @ Topsham

Children[3]:

54) Robert, b. 1766, d. 1767

55) Elizabeth, m. Benj. Patterson of Saco

56) Actor, b. 3/5/1771, m. 12/7/1800, Anna Wilson, d. 4/27/1829 @ Topsham

57) Abigail, m. 8/26/1798, Wm. Tate, d. 1/4/1863

58) Robert, b. 1777, m. 6/30/1806, Phebe Ricker, d. 2/12/1867

59) Mary, m. 1/24/1803, Dr. Thomas Buckminster of Saco

60) Jane, m. 2/26/1807, Col. Jonathan Marston, d. 4/18/1871

61) Rebecca, m. 3/18/1813, Robert McClellan, d. 1/20/1861

62) Rachel, b. 7/8/1784, d. 4/4/1874

*63) Hugh

*64) William

Remarks: (1) Settled on land in Topsham purchased by father in 1761 on Androscoggin; (2) captain in McCobb's regiment during Revolution; (3) added 1,500 acres to his holdings post-Revolution.

25. CAPT. ROBERT PATTEN[3]

c. John[2] (Actor[1]) and Mary Means

b. 5/14/1743 @ Biddeford

m. 12/19/1768, Margaret Hunter (1747-1831) @ Topsham

d. 3/14/1841 @ Topsham

Children[4]:

65) Mary, b. 1768, m. 1787, Capt. Wm. Hunter

66) Jane, b. 1772, m. (1) 1799, Capt. James Peterson of Bath; (2) 1806, Capt. Abraham Butterfield

67) Susan, b. 1774, m. 1799, Capt. John Rogers, Jr.

*68) Capt. William

*69) Adam

70) Robert, b. 1780, d. 1801

71) Margaret, b. 1781, m. 1802 Francis Adams

*72) John

Remarks: (1) Farm at end of Cathance Neck known as Patten Point; (2) mariner and shipbuilder, commander of several vessels of the dozen or so he built at Patten Point shipyard; (3) Bowdoinham selectman for five years; (4) did well financially despite losing several vessels (sole owner of one) and losing two residences to fire; (5) introduced first chaise to Topsham.

34. CAPT. THOMAS PATTEN[3]

c. John[2] (Actor[1]) and Mary Means

b. 2/10/1761 @ Topsham

m. (1) 3/1/1787, Katherine Fulton (1766-1816); (2) 4/30/1822, widow Jane Pattee (1769-1860)

d. 5/20/1841 @ Topsham

Children[4]:

*73) George Ferguson

*74) Capt. John

75) Mary, b. 1792, d. 1792

76) Anne F., b. 1793, m. 1823, Rev. Adam Wilson of Wiscasset

77) Paulina, b. 1796, m. 1824, Capt. Wm. Patten (Actor[2], Robert[1]), d. 12/12/1826 @ Havana

78) Eliza, b. 1798, d. infancy

*79) Capt. James Fulton

80) Thomas, b. 1802, d. infancy

81) Statira, b. 1806, d. 1828

82) Thomas Means, b. 1810, d. 1816

Remarks: (1) Mariner; (2) at 22, commanded sloop *Industry;* (3) owner and sometime captain of schooner *Orange,* captured by French, claims of which were not settled until nearly a century later.

37. ACTOR PATTEN[3]

c. John[2] (Actor[1]) and Mary Means

b. 1/15/1767 @ Topsham

m. 2/4/1796, Anna Hunter (1772-1853)

d. 8/21/1855 @ Bowdoinham

Children[4]:

95) Peggy, b. 1796, m. 1822, Capt. John Fulton

96) Alexander Lithgow, b. 1799, d. 1824

97) Freeman Parker, b. 1810, m. (1) 1828, Mary Stone (?-1844); (2) 1845, Elizabeth Hildreth (1801-66)

98) Nancy, b. 1803, d. 1839

*99) Rufus

*100) Capt. John

101) Isaac R., b. 1810, d. 1849

102) Jane, b. 1810, m. 1836, Joseph Merrill of Topsham

103) Penelope, b. 1812, m. 1831, Loring Stinson Fisher

104) Louisa, b. 1815, m. 1841, Moses Riggs, d. 1877

105) Albert, b. 1818, d. 1820

Remarks: (1) Farmer living in Bowdoinham; (2) in 1806, owned brig *Mary,* captained by Benj. Snow.

38. CAPT. DAVID PATTEN[3]

c. John[2] (Actor[1]) and Pauline Suter Patten
b. 10/24/1769 at Topsham
m. 12/26/1793, Hannah Reed (1770-1828)
@ Topsham
d. 1/22/1830 @ Topsham

Children[4]:

106) Mary, b. 1794, m. 1818, Capt. George Rogers, d. 1821
107) Rachel, b. 1796, d. 1858
*108) Capt. David
109) Lucinda, 1801, m. 1823, Capt. George Rogers (widower of sister Mary), d. 1829
*110) Capt. Lincoln

63. CAPT. HUGH PATTEN[3]

c. Actor[2] (Robert[1]) and Jane McClellan
b. 7/29/1789 @ Topsham
m. 1/27/1818, Lucy Green @ Topsham
d. 2/18/1860

Children[4]:

111) Charles William, b. 11/29/1819, living in San Francisco in 1887
112) Abigail Augusta, b. 10/5/1820, m. 12/31/1846, Col. Thomas Oliver, d. before 1879
113) Adelia L., b. 3/18/1824, m. 2/22/1845, Rev. Asa Loring, lived in Iowa in 1879
114) Frances A., b. 7/5/1826, m. Capt. Andrew T. Percy, d. 1/23/1867
115) Sarah M., b. 6/25/1828, d. 8/14/1857
116) Elizabeth J., b. 11/10/1830, d. ?
117) James McKeen, b. 6/10/1833, d. 11/2/1844
*118) Capt. Rogers Green
119) Mary C.G., b. 5/28/1838, d. infancy

Remarks: (1) Lived in Topsham and Phippsburg; (2) service at sea outside the Kennebec region.

64. CAPT. WILLIAM PATTEN[3]

c. Actor[2] (Robert[1]) and Jane McClellan
b. 9/20/1792 @ Topsham
m. (1) 9/26/1824, Paulina Patten @ Topsham (1796-12/12/1826); (2) ?, Hannah Huntington (ca. 1800-1/1835); (3) 9/8/1835, Eliza Tallman Smith (1801-2/25/1863); (4)1867, Carrie Lehman (?-?) @ Philadelphia
d. 8/15/1871 @ Philadelphia

Children[4]:

120) Ann Mary, bapt. 7/6/1825 by Winter Street Church [?] minister, d. 7/13/1825
121) Hannah Pauline, b. 6/28/1836 @ Bath, m. (1) 3/14/1854, in London, Capt. Frederick T. Hatch [he died at sea 12/1854]; (2) 1/29/1857, John C. Darrah, @ Richmond, ME; (3) 9/17/1890, Capt. Henry L. Gregg, @ Delanco, NJ; d. 5/9/1904
122) Rachel Jane, b. 4/27/1838 @ Richmond, m. 1/29/1857, Capt. Joseph S. Elwell, d. Philadelphia 5/27/1932
123) Ann Maria Therese, b. 8/11/1840, m. 11/12/1868, Col. James Beatty Roney @ Philadelphia, d. 8/9/1910

Remarks: (1) First wife, Paulina, was George F. Patten's younger sister; (2) captained three George Patten vessels: *Statira* (1821-25), *George* (1825-26), and *Globe* (1831-41?); (3) struck out on own in 1841, building and managing a dozen vessels, some with Capt. Wm. Sturtevant after 1850; (4) lived in Bath until 1837, then moved to 1,000-acre farm given them by father-in-law Peleg Tallman; in 1846 moved into Richmond village; (5) failed during 1857 panic, in part because of *Pride of America,* an expensive, impractical clipper ship; (6) spent last years in Philadelphia.

68. CAPT. WILLIAM PATTEN[4]

c. Capt. Robert[3] (John[2], Actor[1]) and Mary Means
b. 2/16/1776
m. 2/6/1800, Sally Winchell Fulton (?-1868) @ Bath
d. 4/27/1821

Children[5]:

*124) Capt. Alfred
*125) Capt. Robert
126) William, b. ?, d. prior to 1837
127) Margaret, b.?, m. prior to 1837, Levi Young

Remarks: (1) Commanded father's sloop *Susannah* and brig *Comet;* (2) also listed as captain of Peleg Tallman's *Pride of America.*

69. ADAM PATTEN[4]

c. Capt. Robert[3] (John[2], Actor[1]) and Mary Means
b. 5/7/1779
m. 7/27/1806, Hannah Small (1779-1850)
d. 1/8 or 9/1856

Children[5]:

128) Gilbert, b. 1807, d. 1812
129) Henry, b. 1808, d. 1848
130) Mary L., b./d. 1810
131) Robert, b. 1811, d. 1812
132) Adelaide, b. 1813, d. 1814
133) Lucy Ann, b. 1815, m. 1856, Harvey Haley
134) Francis S., b.1817
*135) Capt. Horatio A.
136) John Wesley, b. 1820, m. 1848, Sarah Eliza Reed, d. 1888
137) Alexander, b. 1823, d. 1843 @ Liverpool

Remarks: (1) Farmer in Bowdoinham; kept tavern known as "The Bunch of Grapes."

72. JOHN PATTEN[4]

c. Capt. Robert[3] (John[2], Actor[1]) and Mary Means
b. 10/4/1785
m. ?, Kezia Adams (1786-1878)
d. 8/28/1865

Children[5]:

138) Robert Francis, b. 1819, m. Phebe Birdsall; lawyer in Abbeville, LA; d. 1867 (family in distress letter in Sagadahoc County probate court file for John[4] Patten's estate)
*139) Capt. Bardwell
140) William Sidney, b. 1824, d. 1845
*141) Capt. Jarvis
142) John Lyman, b. 1829, m. (1) 1862, Elizabeth Purrington; (2) 1874, Sarah Hall; d. 1897

Remarks: (1) Bowdoin, class of 1808 (A.M. in 1811), studied @ Andover Theological Seminary 1809-11, but did not enter ministry; (2) taught school in North Carolina before entering business in Charlestown, MA; (3) returned to Bowdoinham in 1824 to farm the family homestead and operate a store; (4) served in Maine legislature 1832, 1844-45.

73. GEORGE FERGUSON PATTEN[4]

c. Capt. Thomas[3] (John[2], Actor[1]) and Katherine Fulton
b. 9/18/1787 @ Bowdoinham
m. 2/5/1820, Hannah Thomas (1793-1862)
d. 9/29/1869 @ Bath

Children[5]:

*143) Catherine Fulton

144) George, b. 1823, d. 1831
145) Hannah Thomas, b. 12/29/1825, m. 10/1/1844, Jarvis Slade
146) Statira, b. 2/17/1828, m. 8/29/1860, John S. Elliott, d. 6/25/1893
*147) James Thomas
148) Paulina, b. 5/24/1832, m. 8/15/1855, Winthrop Tappan, d. 3/2/1916
149) Ann Augusta, b. 10/5/1834, m. 10/31/1854, Rev. Eliphalet Whittlesey
*150) George Maxwell

Remarks: (1) Learned shipbuilding in Topsham/Bowdoinham, principally at grandfather's Patten Point yard; (2) served as militia captain in War of 1812; (3) moved to Bath in 1820 and established shipyard, where he built ships through 1868; (4) served in Maine legislature (1838-39, 1864-65), as overseer at Bowdoin College (1842-69), and president of Patten Library Association (1847-57); (5) with brothers Capt. John and Capt. James, created one of largest fleets of merchant vessels in antebellum United States.

74. CAPT. JOHN PATTEN[4]

c. Capt. Thomas[3] (John[2], Actor[1]) and Katherine Fulton
b. 8/27/1789 @ Topsham
m. (1) 10/17/1819, Betsey Bates (1794-1826) @ Boston; (2) 3/26/1830, Mary R. (Peterson) Turner (1800-1862) @ Bath
d. 2/24/1887 @ Bath

Children[5]:

*151) Capt. Thomas Rogers
*152) Capt. Gilbert Elbridge Russell
153) Mary Paulina, b. 1/8/1831, d. 8/16/1836
154) John Levi, b. 10/23/1836, d. 12/22/1860

Remarks: (1) Went to sea early and, prior to War of 1812, was mate under Capt. Peterson, future father-in-law; (2) served wartime on British-flag vessels as well as an American privateer; (3) joined in partnership with George F. ca. 1822, occasionally taking vessels for one or two voyages; (4) active in community affairs, serving in Maine legislature and as mayor of Bath.

79. CAPT. JAMES FULTON PATTEN[4]

c. Capt. Thomas[3] (John[2], Actor[1]) and Katherine Fulton

b. 9/24/1800
m. 11/14/1832, Sophia Ann (Harding) Young
(1809-82)
d. 1/14/1883 @ Bath
Children[5]:
   *155) Capt. Charles Edward
   *156) Frederick Harding
   157) Emma Reed, b. 8/19/1843, d. 3/1/1876
Remarks: (1) Junior partner in the three-brother
Patten firm; (2) spent half his life at sea.

99. RUFUS PATTEN[4]

   c. Actor[3] (John[2], Actor[1]) and Anna Hunter
   b. 11/15/1805 @ Dresden
   m. 4/2/1835, Susan Merrill (?-1890)
   d. 10/15/1896
Children[5]:
   *158) Capt. Abel Merrill
   159) Octavius Harding, b. 2/3/1837 [sic],
   d. 10/1862 @ sea
   *160) Capt. Oscar
   161) Adelia Mary, b. 1/29/1842, m. 1/15/1873,
   Capt. George L. White
   162) Emma Mary, b. 1/29/1842
   163) Susan Mitchell, b. 5/14/1845, m. 11/6/1873,
   Jesse Franklin Snow
   164) Sarah Fulton, b. 8/22/1848, m. 10/3/1878,
   Humphrey Mallett
   165) Henry Wilmot, b. 9/24/1850, m. 11/27/1873,
   Fannie M. Quint
Remarks: (1) Carpenter and builder; Rufus and family
lived in several area towns, including Dresden,
Phippsburg, and Topsham.

100. CAPTAIN JOHN PATTEN[4]

   c. Actor[3] (John[2], Actor[1]) and Anna Hunter
   b. 1/27/1808
   m. 12/28/1837, Mary Purington (?-1874)
   d. 6/9/1874 @ Quincy, IL
Children[5]:
   *166) Capt. James Madison Winchell
   167) Nancy Louisa, b. 6/6/45, m. 9/1/1866, Col.
   William Andrew Schmidt of Chicago
Remarks: (1) Capt. John and Anna sailed together for
many years, she having made eleven transatlantic
round-trips; (2) retired to Illinois in 1867 to be near
their daughter.

108. CAPTAIN DAVID PATTEN[4]

   c. Capt. David[3] (John[2], Actor[1]) and Hannah Reed
   b. 2/10/1799
   m. 9/23/1834, Elizabeth L. Hunter (1815-82)
   @ Machiasport
   d. 1/23/1871 @ Bath
Children[5]:
   168) Mary Ellen, b. 6/5/1836, m. Rev. Roland B.
   Howard, d. 1871
   *169) Capt. David Albert
   170) Hannah Elizabeth, b. 5/6/1843, m. Charles H.
   Rogers
   171) Anna, b. 12/31/1844, d. 2/27/1864
   172) Jane L., b. 6/23/1848, d. 6/9/1853
   173) Horace Reed, b. 1854, d. 10/26/1876 @ San
   Francisco
Remarks: (1) First command was G.F. & J. Patten ship
New Orleans in 1830; (2) commanded several others
before striking out on own with brother Lincoln,
starting with *Tempest.*

110. CAPT. LINCOLN PATTEN[4]

   c. Capt. David[3] (John[2], Actor[1]) and Hannah Reed
   b. 12/12/1808
   m. (1) 11/30/1840, Mary Storer (1816-49), who
   died @ Le Havre; (2) 6/30/1851, Mary Elizabeth
   Whitney (1827-66); (3) 10/10/1872, Maria
   (Rogers) Tarbox
   d. 11/23/1900 @ Bath
Children[5]:
   174) Edward Lincoln, b. 4/10/1846, d. 1864
   @ Rangoon
   175) David Clement, b. 9/29/1847, d. 2/28/1865
   from fall @ Liverpool
   *176) Captain Frank Whitney
   177) Mary Storer, b. 7/24/1862, m. 10/14/1885,
   William Bevier Mussenden @ Bath
Remarks: (1) Commanded several vessels during long
sea career, including *Delaware, Tempest,* the first
Caspian, Roswell Sprague, India, and *Parker M.
Whitmore;* (2) joined brother David in firm of D. & L.
Patten, managing and owning three vessels in 1850s-
60s.

118. CAPT. ROGERS GREEN PATTEN[4]

   c. Hugh[3] (Actor[2], Robert[1]) and Lucy Green

b. 4/22/1836
m. no
d. 2/8/1874 @ Brunswick
Children[5]: none
Remarks: (1) At age 18, brought Houghton ship *Rochester* to London after death of captain and chief mate; (2) commanded *Clara Ann* of Bath @ 19; (3) master of Houghton vessels *Europa* and *Prussia;* (4) resided in Brunswick.

124. CAPT. ALFRED PATTEN[5]

c. Capt. William[4] (Robert[3], John[2], Actor[1]) and Sally (Winchell) Fulton
b. ?, probably between 1801 and 1810
m. 7/22/1835, Maria Ross @ Monson, MA
d. drowned 1/25/1847 @ New Orleans while in command of bark *Dudley*
Children[6]:
178) Cornelia Gray, b. 5/12/1836, m. Abner Godfrey
*179) Capt. Alfred P[urington?]
Remarks: (1) Bark *Dudley* owned by Wm. Purington of Bowdoinham, who became executor of Capt. Alfred's estate; (2) buried @ Magnolia Cemetery, Mobile, AL, in his daughter's plot.

125. CAPT. ROBERT PATTEN[5]

c. Capt. William[4] (Robert[3], John[2], Actor[1]) and Sally (Winchell) Fulton
b. 7/14/1812
m. 11/30/1837 Beulah Foster Purington @ Bowdoinham
d. 7/20/1855
Children[6]:
180) William Edward, b. 7/8/1839, d. infancy
181) Mary Maria, b. 9/1840, d. 8/26/1855
182) Robert Edwin, b. 7/28/1850, d. 6/27/1853 @ sea
Remarks: (1) Commanded *Cornelia* (1836), *Napoleon* and *Sheffield* (1838), *Lion* (1844), *Robert Patten* (1845), *Marathon* (1847), *Sea Nymph* (1851), *Civilian* (1855).

135. CAPT. HORATIO A. PATTEN[5]

c. Adam[4] (Robert[3], John[2], Actor[1]) and Hannah Small

b. 9/23/1818
m. ?, Alvicia Small (1821-79)
d. @ Brunswick, 2/26/1884
Children[6]:
183) Mary Emma Springer, adptd., b. 9/20/1850, d. 10/21/1882
Remarks: (1) Was managing owner and captain of the ship *Mary Emma,* built by Pennell @ Brunswick, 1864.

139. CAPT. BARDWELL PATTEN[5]

c. John[4] (Robert[3], John[2], Actor[1]) and Kezia Adams
b. 1/9/1821
m. 10/21/1851, Frances J. Meserve (1828-1908)
d. 6/28/1890
Children[6]:
184) Charlotte Keziah, b. 10/15/1852, d. 3/17/1858
185) Mary Caverly, b. 3/21/1858
186) Robert Everett, b. 3/4/1861, m. 10/2/1895, Helen (Sampson) Leavitt
187) Rev. Arthur Bardwell, b. 3/26/1864, m. 10/1/1896, Kate Howes Ryder
Remarks: (1) Sailed for his cousins for many years, concluding with bark *Penang;* (2) lived in the Robert Patten homestead; (3) considered to be a poet; (4) brother of Jarvis.

141. CAPT. JARVIS PATTEN[5]

c. John[4] (Robert[3], John[2], Actor[1]) and Kezia Adams
b. 6/13/1827
m. 10/1/1854, Charlotte E. Whitmore
d. 5/16/1888, Washington, DC
Children[6]:
188) Francis Jarvis, b. 11/21/1852, graduated West Point 1877, m. 10/29/1884, Hattie Bessey; active as an inventor, d. 1900
189) Hortense Charlotte, b. 6/3/1855, m. 3/13/1879, Lt. John Herbert Philbrick (classmate of Francis Jarvis)
190) Anna Baker, b. 1858
191) Lizzie Barker, b. 1860, d. 1862
192) Katherine Kezia, 3/15/1864
193) Gertrude Camilla, b. 1865, d. 1/28/1876
194) Goldwin Smith, b. 1871, became an actor and changed surname to Patton
195) Victoria Mansur, b. 1874, d. infancy
Remarks: (1) Possessed a classical education, com-

manded several square-riggers and a steamship that rounded Cape Horn for San Francisco; (2) after coming ashore, set up a maritime shipping brokerage in London and U.S.; (3) first U.S. commissioner of navigation, 1884; (4) co-authored *Port Charges and Requirements on Vessels in the Various Seaports of the World* and *The Telegraphic Code.*

143. CATHERINE FULTON PATTEN[5]

c. George F.[4] (Thomas[3], John[2], Actor[1]) and Hannah Thomas
b. 1/3/1821
m. 7/5/1840, Wildes P. Walker @ Bath, (div. 10/17/1854, NY Superior Court)
d. 5/5/1875 @ Ischia, Italy

Children[6]:

196) Katherine P. Walker, b. 5/1841, m. Edward M. Warden 4/18/1867; lived in Paris, two sons and two daughters survived her, the latter two being Baroness Leicester and Frau Col. Franz Hans von Wauttenberg, wife of Austrian military attache to Switzerland; d. 12/1917
197) Georgia Veazie Walker, b. 1843, d. Bonn, Germany, 1897
198) Caroline S. Walker, b. 1844

Note: no evidence that the Walker daughters had any contact with their father after the divorce
Remarks: (1) Said to be Capt. Noble Maxwell's heartthrob despite a 30-year age gap; (2) unhappy marriage to Wildes P. Walker ended in NYC, with judge denying Wildes Walker right to remarry during Catherine's lifetime (this ruling removed by Sagadahoc County Superior Court, Bath, 1868); (3) she returned to Maine with daughters and lived with father; (4) moved to Europe upon father's death.

147. JAMES THOMAS PATTEN[5]

c. George F.[4] (Thomas[3], John[2], Actor[1]) and Hannah Thomas
b. 7/4/1830
m. 1/27/1855, Isabel Smith @ Astoria, NY
d. 6/1/1888 @ Waynesville, NC

Children[6]:

199) Henry Smith, b. 11/25/1855, m. 10/4/1880, Hattie Bostwick
200) Frederick Winthrop, b. 12/8/1862, m.

11/7/1900, Jane Armstrong Cox
201) James Merrill, b. 7/6/1867, m. Edith Harrod
202) Edward Clarence

Remarks: (1) Proprietor and co-owner of spike factory lost to fire, also James T. Patten Co., importers and dealers in bar iron and steel; (2) active in local banking; (3) supervised building of bark *Ivanhoe* @ Boothbay Harbor, purchased by Pattens; (4) principal in Patten Car Works venture, suffered severe losses when it failed; (5) ended career as railway equipment representative in New York.

150. GEORGE MAXWELL PATTEN[5]

c. George F.[4] (Thomas[3], John[2], Actor[1]) and Hannah Thomas
b. 11/13/1836
m. 6/1859, Frederica Camp (ca. 1837-1908)
d. 4/10/1901 @ Bath

Children[6]:

203) Capt. George Herman (USA), b. 5/12/1860, attended USMA @ West Point, served in Spanish-American War, d. 11/2/1932
204) Hannah Thomas, b. 6/2/1862, m. 9/29/1898, Dr. Percy Roberts of divorce-case fame, d. 1912
205) Frederick Mortimer, b. 5/12/1864, d. ?
206) Katherine Fulton, b. 7/14/1876, d. 1/1/1895 in New Year's Eve RR crossing accident

Remarks: (1) Co-owned with brother the spike factory destroyed by fire in 1856 with $3,000 loss; (2) proprietor of brass foundry and built first boilers and steam engines for oceangoing ships in Bath *(Idaho* and *Montana);* sold foundry to Torrey in 1869; (3) joined cousin G.E.R. Patten and brother James to open Patten Car Works, which failed in 1877.

151. CAPT. THOMAS ROGERS PATTEN[5]

c. John[4] (Thomas[3], John[2], Actor[1]) and Betsey Bates
b. 5/3/1821 @ Boston
m. 9/29/1844, Caroline E. Cooper (?-11/22/1844) @ Pittston
d. 3/23/1847 @ Bath

Children[6]: none
Remarks: (1) Learned his trade under Noble Maxwell on the *Monmouth;* (2) first and only command was *Louisiana* in 1843-44; (3) was in New Orleans on *Florence* in December 1845 as passenger.

152. CAPT. GILBERT ELBRIDGE RUSSELL PATTEN[5]

c. John[4] (Thomas[3], John[2], Actor[1]) and Betsey Bates
b. 2/28/1823 @ Boston
m. 11/24/1859, Emma Maria Owen (4/4/1836-9/18/1924) @ Bath
d. 1/12/1882 @ Bath

Children[6]:
*207) John Owen
208) Clara M[aria?], b. 1/6/1864, m. 2/10/1887, Richard E. Goodwin of Boston @ Bath, d. 7/8/1898 @ Augusta (she had one daughter, Clara, who later married Kilbourne Maxwell Kendall)

Remarks: (1) Went to sea at 15, first command (*Halcyon*) at 22; (2) other ships included *Fawn, Falcon,* and *John Patten;* (3) subsequently partner with father until Gilbert's death in 1882; (4) partner in Patten Car Works.

155. CAPT. CHARLES EDWARD PATTEN[5]

c. Capt. James F.[4] (Thomas[3], John[2], Actor[1]) and Sophia Ann (Harding) Young
b. 1/12/1834 @ Bath
m. 1857, Jessie Jones (1833-1908), @ London
d. 6/15/1903 @ Bath

Children[6]: none

Remarks: (1) First went to sea on *Italy,* Capt. Reed, when 16; first command was *Britannia* at 22; (2) other commands included *Moravia* and the Houghtons' *Samaria;* (3) wife Jessie almost always accompanied him at sea; (4) after retiring, became active in local affairs and was twice elected mayor, refusing to serve after his second election; (5) left a large fortune after his wife's death to public and private agencies in Bath, his generosity perhaps exceeded only by that of George Patten Davenport.

156. FREDERICK HARDING PATTEN[5]

c. Capt. James F.[4] (Thomas[3], John[2], Actor[1]) and Sophia Ann (Harding) Young
b. 5/13/1838 @ Bath
m. 4/26/1883, Clara Kendrick (?-1912) @ Bath
d. 7/23/1889 @ Bath

Children[6]: none

Remarks: (1) Worked in shipping business in New York prior to father's death; (2) returned to Bath to assist in administering father's estate; (3) one of original founders of Bath Water Company.

158. CAPT. ABEL MERRILL PATTEN[5]

c. Rufus[4] (Actor[3], John[2], Actor[1]) and Susan Merrill
b. 9/19/1836
m. yes—date?, name?, d. 9/19/1864
d. 9/19/1864

Children[6]: none

Remarks: (1) Captain of Pittston-built ship *W.S. Lindsay* when wrecked in 1863; (2) master of new Southard-built bark *Tommie Hussey,* 1864; en route Scotland-Portland, *Hussey* was run down at night by unidentified ship, only one survivor.

160. CAPT. OSCAR PATTEN[5]

c. Rufus[4] (Actor[3], John[2], Actor[1]) and Susan Merrill
b. 4/3/1839
m. 11/13/1890, Lillian (Maxwell) Harding
d. ?

Children[6]: ?

Remarks: (1) Captained ship *India* 1878-79.

166. CAPT. JAMES MADISON WINCHELL PATTEN[5]

c. John[4] (Actor[3], John[2], Actor[1]) and Mary Purington
b. 1/17/1839 @ Bowdoinham
m. 1/15/1867, Sarah Gray Whittemore
d. 12/31/1874

Children[6]:
not identified, but he was described as an "affectionate and devoted husband and father"

Remarks: (1) Commanded *Assyria* 1868-71; (2) reportedly retired from seagoing career but was persuaded to deliver *Amity* to new owners in Antwerp in 1874; caught in a gale, *Amity* sank, only two survivors; (3) known as "the handsome Patten."

169. CAPT. DAVID ALBERT PATTEN[5]

c. Capt. David[4] (David[3], John[2], Actor[1]) and Elizabeth Hunter
b. 2/18/1839
m. no
d. 2/14/1865

Children[6]: none

Remarks: (1) Learned the trade aboard *Halcyon,*

Delaware, Caspian, and *New Orleans;* (2) commanded D. & L. Patten bark *Sarepta* (1864-65) before dying during voyage to India.

176. CAPT. FRANK WHITNEY PATTEN[5]

c. Lincoln[4] (David[3], John[2], Actor[1]) and Mary Elizabeth Whitney
b. 9/15/1855
m. 6/18/1894, Charlotte Shaw @ Portland
d. 1/19/1913 @ Newbury, MA.
Children[6]:
*209) Nellie Mae
210) Mary, b. 1910, d. 1989
Remarks: (1) Too young for Patten vessels, served years aboard square-riggers, schooners, and steamships; (2) vessels he served on include *W.F. Babcock, Hornbolt, Storm King, Kenilworth, E. Monto, Algiers, Olivette;* (3) commanded *Henry Villard, George Stetson, May V. Neville,* and *Kineo;* (3) completed legendary round-the-world voyage on 5-masted schooner *Kineo.*

179. CAPT. ALFRED P[URINGTON?] PATTEN[6]

c. Alfred[5] (William[4], Robert[3], John[2], Actor[1]) and Maria Ross
b. 11/11/1838 @ Bowdoinham
m. 10/18/1865, Ellen F. Pierce @ Old Town, ME (?-11/5/1871)
d. 5/27/1877
Children[7]: unknown
Remarks: (1) Commanded *Canada* (1868-69); (2) buried in Forest Hills Cemetery @ Old Town, with wife.

207. JOHN OWEN PATTEN[6]

c. Gilbert E.R.[5] (John[4], Thomas[3], John[2], Actor[1]) and Emma Owen
b. 4/20/1861
m. (1) 2/23/1886, Lucy W. Larrabee, div. 1896; (2) 1897, Irene Ann Roberts (Mrs. P.W. Roberts)
d. 4/29/1899 of tuberculosis in Arizona
Children[7]: none (second wife had twin daughters by previous marriage)
Remarks: (1) Attended Johns Hopkins University; (2) widely traveled, including voyage around Cape Horn on ship *Tacoma,* 1881; (3) reporter, later managing editor, of *Boston Post;* (4) owner-publisher of *Bath Daily Times;* (5) involved in much-publicized scandal with Mrs. P.W. Roberts, young wife of local doctor; led to divorce by first wife and eventual marriage to Mrs. Roberts.

209. NELLIE MAE PATTEN[6]

c. Frank Whitney[5] (Lincoln[4], David[3], John[2], Actor[1]) and Charlotte Shaw
b. 1897
m. Capt. Fred Ferrell, ca. 1912
d. 1950
Children[7]: all born aboard *Kineo/Maryland*
211) Capt. Frank Patten Ferrell, b. 1913, served as executive officer of USS *New Jersey* in WWII; post-war, port and trials captain for Sun Shipbuilding
212) Charlotte Agnes Ferrell, m. Herbert A. Beach
213) Fred Ferrell, Jr., b. 1917, m. Frances E. Massey, d. 1980
Remarks: (1) Completed epic, round-the-world voyage on *Kineo* by age 9; (2) placed in private school, in part to separate her from middle-aged chief mate Fred Ferrell, whom she secretly married at age 15; (3) with her husband and infant son, returned to *Kineo* under father's and, later, husband's command; (4) husband retained command until Texas Oil Co. sold vessel in mid-1940s.

Appendix B

PATTEN VESSELS
by
Ralph Linwood Snow

The following list includes vessels built by and/or for members of the Patten family along the banks of the Kennebec River, the Cathance River, and Merrymeeting Bay. It is probably not complete, and a few vessels may be included that are not properly credited to the Pattens. Captain Robert Patten[3] [John[2], Actor[1]], born in 1743, inherited the family estate on the Cathance River and Merrymeeting Bay. Here he built a dozen vessels ranging from 81 to 188 tons in the period 1783-1816. Six of his sons and grandsons became master mariners, and his daughters joined their lives with master mariners as well. It was at Captain Robert's shipyard that young nephew George F. Patten learned the shipwright's trade.

Beginning in 1820, George F., John, and James F. Patten created the largest Patten fleet and one of the largest antebellum merchant fleets in the United States. George moved his shipbuilding operations to Bath, which possessed a more complete infrastructure for a shipbuilder and budding merchant trader. The Patten partnership would stand the test of time. The "Anchor Line" had remarkably few outside investors beyond the shipmasters who commanded Patten vessels, a few relatives such as cousin Noble Maxwell, and the firm's dutiful clerk, Charles Davenport.

Technically, George F. and John broke up their partnership in 1860, each pursuing his own interests. George continued to build vessels at the old Patten shipyard for a few more years. John and his son Gilbert E.R. formed a new firm named John Patten & Son, building in a shipyard just south of the old King's Dock. Operational matters for George and John apparently were still managed by the ubiquitous Charles Davenport. Aside from two steamships, George and John did not invest in each other's vessels after 1860.

With the construction of the *Nimbus* in 1869, the Bath Pattens built their last ship, although John Patten & Son continued to have a few ships built in subsequent years by Goss & Sawyer.

Captain William Patten [Actor[2], Robert[1]], a second cousin once removed of George F., John, and James F. Patten, created the second-largest fleet of Patten-built/managed vessels. Although he was a third-generation Patten to George & Company's fourth-generation status, he was of an age with the three brothers, commanded three of their earlier vessels, and had married their sister Paulina. In 1837, he struck out on his own, no doubt assisted by his second wife's connections and substantial inherited fortune. Although associated with various partners over the next twenty years, it appears that he was the senior in most if not all of these partnerships. All but one of his thirteen vessels were built in Richmond, where he lived for a while on a 1,000-acre farm given his wife by father-in-law Peleg Tallman. After his business failed in 1857, William moved to Philadelphia.

Over a fifteen-year span, brothers David and Lincoln Patten had three ships built, which they apparently managed and, in some cases, commanded. George F. and John Patten owned shares in their first vessel, *Tempest*.

I. Patten Built/Owned Vessels: Pre-Revolution

1768
MERRYMEETING, Sloop
Builder: John Patten, ? Howard
Site: Topsham
Tonnage: 90
First Master: William Patten
Owners: John Patten, John Fulton, Adam Hunter

1770?
DEFIANCE, ?
Builder: John Patten
Site: Topsham
Owner: John Patten

1772?
INDUSTRY, Schooner
Builder: John Patten
Site: Topsham
First Master: James Maxwell
Owner: John Patten

II. Robert Patten Built/Owned Vessels: Post-Revolution to 1815

1783
INDUSTRY, Sloop
Builder: Robert Patten
Site: Topsham
Tonnage: 93
Size: 67'3"x21'6"x7'7"
First Master: Thomas Patten
Owners: John Patten, Robert Patten, Thomas Patten, James Fulton, Samuel Jameson

1785
FRIENDSHIP, Sloop
Builder: Robert Patten
Site: Topsham
Tonnage: 81
Size: 63'x20'x7'7"
First Master: Jonathan Williams
Other Master: Thomas Patten
Owner: James Fulton

1795
PEGGY, Schooner
Builder: Robert Patten
Site: Topsham
Tonnage: 119
Size: 72'x22'3"x8'8"
First Master: N. Purington
Other Master: John Rogers
Owner: Robert Patten

1796
ORANGE, Schooner
Builder: Robert Patten
Site: Topsham
Tonnage: 120
Size: 71'9"x22'8"x8'7.5"
First Master: Thomas Patten
Other Master: John Holman
Owner: Robert Patten
Disposition: Seized by French privateer *La Resolve* in October 1798 on voyage Barbados-Boston.
Remarks: Became one of the so-called French Spoliation Claims that were not settled for nearly a century.

1797
MINERVA, Brig
Builder: Robert Patten
Site: Topsham
Tonnage: 128
Size: 70'10"x22'8.5"x9'4.25"
First Master: John Fulton
Other Master: William Rogers
Owners: David Patten, John Patten, John Jameson

1799
SUSANNAH, Sloop
Builder: Robert Patten
Site: Topsham
Tonnage: 94
First Master: William Patten
Owner: Robert Patten

1800
LARK, Schooner
Builder: Robert Patten
Site: Topsham
Tonnage: 108

Size: 73'10"x21'4"x7'11"
First Master: Thomas Patten
Owner: Thomas Patten

TOPSHAM, Schooner
Builder: Robert Patten
Site: Topsham
Tonnage: 99
First Master: Robert Patten
Owner: Robert Patten

1802
MERCURY, Schooner
Builder: Robert Patten
Site: Topsham
Tonnage: 105
Size: 72'x22'1.5"x7'8.5"
First Master: John Rogers, Jr.
Other Master: John Preble
Owners: Robert Patten, Adam Patten

1804
VENUS, Schooner
Builder: Robert Patten
Site: Topsham
Tonnage: 106
Size: 71'10"x21'8.5"x7'11"
First Master: Robert Patten
Owner: Robert Patten

1805
LUCINDA, Sloop
Builder: Robert/David Patten
Site: Topsham
Tonnage: 81
Size: 66'x20'2.5"x7'1"
First Master: James Todd
Owner: David Patten

1811
COMET, Brig
Builder: Moses Merrill/R. Patten
Site: Topsham
Tonnage: 188
Size: 87'1"x24'8"x10'
First Master: William Patten
Owner: Robert Patten

III. Vessels built by George F. Patten, G.F. & J. Patten, G.F. Patten & Co., and John Patten & Son, 1816-69

A. ALPHABETICAL LISTING

Amity: 1858, Ship
Andes[1]: 1826, Ship
Andes[2]: 1832, Ship
Ann Maria: 1816, Brig
Ariel: 1852, Ship
Assyria: 1854, Ship
Brilliant: 1823, Brig
Britannia: 1853, Ship
Canada: 1859, Ship
Caspian[1]: 1834, Ship
Caspian[2]: 1855, Ship
Catherine: 1824, Ship
Ceres: 1833, Schooner
Champlain: 1851, Ship
Champion: 1828, Ship
Clara Brookman: 1853, Ship
Delaware: 1838, Ship
DeSoto: 1858, Ship
Falcon: 1849, Ship
Fawn[1]: 1846, Brig
Fawn[2]: 1860, Ship
Florence: 1840, Bark
George: 1825, Brig
George F. Patten: 1848, Ship
Globe: 1831, Ship
Halcyon: 1842, Ship
Hudson: 1862, Ship
Idaho: 1866, Steamship
India: 1869, Ship

Italia: 1863, Ship
Italy: 1846, Ship
Ivanhoe: 1859, Bark
James F. Patten: 1857, Ship
Japan: 1868, Ship
Jasper: 1821, Brig
John Patten: 1856, Ship
London: 1838, Ship
Louisiana: 1843, Ship
Maine: 1844, Ship
Majestic: 1829, Ship
Manchester: 1835, Ship
Marshfield: 1852, Ship
Mobile: 1851, Ship
Monmouth: 1840, Ship
Montana: 1865, Steamship
Moravia: 1863, Ship
New Orleans: 1830, Ship
Nimbus: 1869, Ship
Noble: 1822, Brig
Palestine: 1833, Ship
Parsee: 1864, Bark
Penang: 1864, Bark
Sabino: 1862, Ship
Sheffield: 1836, Ship
Statira: 1819, Brig
Transit: 1860, Ship
Trenton: 1840, Ship

B. CHRONOLOGICAL LISTING

1816
ANN MARIA, Brig
Builder: George F. Patten
Site: Topsham
Tonnage: 153
Size: 78'x22'4"x10'1"
First Master: John Patten
Other Masters: ?

Owners: G.F. & J. Patten, Thomas Patten

Disposition: Unknown.

Remarks: Named for G.F. Patten's oldest sister; at least five years in Caribbean trade.

1819

STATIRA, Brig

Builder: George F. Patten

Site: Topsham

Tonnage: 183

Size: 80'2"x23'4"x11'3.5"

First Master: John Patten

Other Masters: Charles Little, Wm. Patten, ? Timmons, John Barker, Rob't Bosworth

Owners: G.F., J., & J.F. Patten

Disposition: Sold in 1829.

Remarks: Named for G.F. Patten's youngest sister; Atlantic and Caribbean trades.

1821

JASPER, Brig

Builder: George F. Patten

Site: Bath

Tonnage: 223

Size: 84'6"x24'7.5"x12'4"

First Master: John Patten

Other Masters: ? Knight, John L. Rich, John Fisher, Edward Oliver

Owners: G.F. & J. Patten

Disposition: Sold to Gibbs interests 6/25/36 and converted to a whaler.

Remarks: Atlantic and Caribbean trades; reported condemned in New Zealand in 1853.

1822

NOBLE, Brig

Builder: George F. Patten

Site: Bath

Tonnage: 274

Size: 95'3"x25'6"x12'9"

First Master: Noble Maxwell

Other Masters: A.N. Littlefield, Geo. Mustard, R.P. Mann, Jos. Brown

Owners: G.F. Patten, Noble Maxwell, Samuel Winter

Disposition: Unknown.

Remarks: Named for cousin Noble Maxwell; Caribbean and transatlantic trades; rerigged as bark in 1838 and still under Patten flag in 1844.

1823

BRILLIANT, Brig

Builder: George F. Patten

Site: Bath

Tonnage: 243

Size: 90'3"x24'10"x12'5"

First Master: John Patten

Other Master: ? Handy

Owners: G.F., J., & J.F. Patten

Disposition: Unknown.

Remarks: West Indies trade.

1824

CATHERINE, Ship

Builder: George F. Patten

Site: Bath

Tonnage: 314

Size: 100'6"x26'6.5"x13'3.25"

First Master: John Patten

Other Masters: ? Lyon, Josiah Thatcher

Owners: G.F., J., & J.F. Patten

Disposition: Foundered 9/22/34 en route from Sydney, Nova Scotia, to Boston with coal.

Remarks: First full-rigged ship built by Pattens; named for George F. Patten's first-born child; engaged in transatlantic and coastwise trades.

1825

GEORGE, Brig

Builder: George F. Patten

Site: Bath

Tonnage: 251

Size: 93'3"x24'8"x12'4"

First Master: Wm. Patten

Other Master: J.F. Patten

Owners: George F. Patten, John Patten, Wm. Frost

Disposition: Unknown.

Remarks: Named for George F. Patten's first son, who died young; Gulf trade; disappeared from register after 2 or 3 years.

1826

ANDES[i], Ship

Builder: George F. Patten

Site: Bath

Tonnage: 364

Size: 110'x27'2"x13'7"

First Master: John Patten

Other Masters: J.S. Tompkins, S. Briggs, J. Patten
Owners: George F. Patten, John Patten, Ed. Kelleran
Disposition: Disappeared ca. 1831-32 from unknown causes.
Remarks: Listed as a coastwise packet ca. 1831.

1828
CHAMPION, Ship
Builder: Thomas M. Lewis
Site: Bath
Tonnage: 378
Size: 110'4"x27'8"x13'3"
First Master: Ed. Kelleran
Other Master: J.F. Patten
Owners: George F. Patten, John Patten, James F. Patten
Disposition: Wrecked 1837.
Remarks: Primarily in cotton trade.

1829
MAJESTIC, Ship
Builder: George F. Patten
Site: Bath
Tonnage: 390
Size: 114'3"x27'6"x13'9"
First Master: Noble Maxwell
Other Master: Geo. F. Mustard
Owners: George F. Patten, John Patten, Noble Maxwell
Disposition: Went ashore Boulogne-sur-Mer(?) 1/10/42, no survivors.
Remarks: Engaged in cotton trade w/England.

1830
NEW ORLEANS, Ship
Builder: Dennis Lines
Site: Bath
Tonnage: 389
Size: 116'9"x27'1.5"x13'6.75"
First Master: David Patten
Other Master: J. Patten
Owners: George F. Patten, John Patten, Wm. Richardson
Disposition: Went aground at mouth of Kennebec, 9/4/34; sold to Boston parties and salvaged.
Remarks: Cotton trade.

1831
GLOBE, Ship
Builder: Dennis Lines

Site: Bath
Tonnage: 419
Size: 121'4.5"x27'6.5"x13'6.25"
First Master: Wm. Patten
Other Masters: ?
Owners: George F. Patten, John Patten, Wm. Patten, Wm. Richardson
Disposition: Stranded in Bahamas 3/17/41 with cotton, bound New Orleans-Portsmouth (NH), total loss.

1832
ANDES[2], Ship
Builder: George F. Patten
Site: Bath
Tonnage: 444
Size: 125'x27'11"x13'11.5"
First Master: James F. Patten
Other Master: J. Patten
Owners: George F. Patten, John Patten, James F. Patten, Noble Maxwell
Disposition: Foundered 1837 on voyage from Turks Island to Bath w/salt.
Remarks: Cotton trade; chartered to Russell Line as a New York-New Orleans packet in 1834.

1833
CERES, Schooner
Builder: Dennis Lines
Site: Bath
Tonnage: 130
Size: 80'1.75"x23'0.5"x8'1"
First Master: Wm. Decker, Jr.
Other Masters: M. Skolfield, Jos. H. Tarbox, Robt. E. Soule
Owners: George F. Patten, John Patten, Noble Maxwell, Wm. Decker, Jr.
Disposition: Unknown, post-1844.
Remarks: Caribbean trade; carried lumber from Bath.

PALESTINE, Ship
Builder: George F. Patten
Site: Bath
Tonnage: 470
Size: 127'x28'6"x14'3"
First Master: A.L. Littlefield
Other Masters: J.H. Purington, O.R. Mumford, B.H.

Johnson, Henry E. Scott

Owners: George F. Patten, John Patten, Noble Maxwell, Augustus Littlefield

Disposition: Still in Patten fleet as late as 1848.

Remarks: General trade; N. Maxwell sold his share for $14,000 in 10/43.

1834

CASPIAN[i], Ship

Builder: John Larrabee

Site: Bath

Tonnage: 529

Size: 113'10"x29'8.5"x14'10.25"

First Master: David Patten

Other Masters: Lincoln Patten, O. Patten, Wm. Trufant, L.S. Wyman, Wm. Torrey, George Delano

Owners: George F. Patten, John Patten

Disposition: Stranded on Gingerbread Grounds en route Boston to New Orleans with ice in 1854.

Remarks: In cotton trade; extensively rebuilt in 1854 after being ashore in a gale; Capt. Delano died of yellow fever.

1835

MANCHESTER, Ship

Builder: John Larrabee

Site: Bath

Tonnage: 570

Size: 134'6"x30'6.5"x15'3.25"

First Master: J.F. Patten

Other Master: Robt. Bosworth

Owners: George F. Patten, John Patten

Disposition: Sold in 1846 to New York parties.

Remarks: Atlantic and coastwise packet carrying cotton and passengers.

1836

SHEFFIELD, Ship

Builder: G.F. & J. Patten

Site: Bath

Tonnage: 590

Size: 135'x31'0.5"x15'6.25"

First Master: Noble Maxwell

Other Masters: Robert K. Patten, John P. Smith

Owners: George F. Patten, John Patten, Noble Maxwell

Disposition: Apparently sold 1847-48; under British flag in 1864.

Remarks: General Atlantic trade.

1838

DELAWARE, Ship

Builder: G.F. & J. Patten

Site: Bath

Tonnage: 662

Size: 142'x32'x16'

First Master: David Patten

Other Masters: Lincoln Patten, Jarvis Patten, J.H. Tarbox

Owners: George F. Patten, John Patten, Noble Maxwell, Chas. Davenport, David Patten

Disposition: Unknown.

Remarks: General and cotton trades.

LONDON, Ship

Builder: G.F. & J. Patten

Site: Bath

Tonnage: 637

Size: 140'x31'7.5"x15'9.75"

First Master: James F. Patten

Other Masters: J.O. Baker, James Ross

Owners: George F. Patten, John Patten, James F. Patten, Noble Maxwell

Disposition: Unknown.

Remarks: Engaged in cotton and packet trades.

1840

FLORENCE, Bark

Builder: G.F. & J. Patten

Site: Bath

Tonnage: 349

Size: ?x?x?

First Master: Wm. Decker

Other Masters: S.T. Woodward, Timothy Mitchell, L.S. Wyman

Owners: George F. Patten, John Patten, Noble Maxwell, Wm. Decker, Jr.

Disposition: Sold to San Francisco parties ca. 1863.

Remarks: General trade; town of Florence in Oregon named for vessel after she foundered and nameboard washed up on local beach in November 1875.

MONMOUTH, Ship

Builder: G.F. & J. Patten

Site: Bath

Tonnage: 729

Size: ?x?x?

First Master: Noble Maxwell

Other Masters: James F. Patten, D.S. Ryan
Owners: George F. Patten, John Patten, James F. Patten, Noble Maxwell
Disposition: Sold to Liverpool owners in 1862.
Remarks: Largest vessel built in Bath at that time.

TRENTON, Ship
Builder: G.F. & J. Patten
Site: Bath
Tonnage: 668
Size: ?x?x?
First Master: Noble Maxwell
Other Masters: R.P. Manson, S.P. Emmons, J.S. Bennett
Owners: George F. Patten, John Patten, James F. Patten, Noble Maxwell
Disposition: Sold to British owners in 1860.
Remarks: Reportedly made a record passage from New York to New Orleans, 1842.

1842
HALCYON, Ship
Builder: John Larrabee
Site: Bath
Tonnage: 797
Size: 157'x33'3"x16'7.5"
First Master: David Patten
Other Masters: G.E.R. Patten, A.T. Wade
Owners: George F. Patten, John Patten, Chas. Davenport, David Patten
Disposition: Foundered in western Atlantic 6/11/51, en route Liverpool to New York; 300 passengers and crew rescued by two cotton freighters bound to Liverpool.
Remarks: Cotton trade to ports in England, France, and Italy.

1843
LOUISIANA, Ship
Builder: John Larrabee
Site: Bath
Tonnage: 747
Size: 149'x33'2"x16'7.5"
First Master: T.R. Patten
Other Masters: E.P. Stinson, Stephen E. Cole
Owners: G.F. & J. Patten

Disposition: Sold to NY parties in 1846; lost with two other packets during fierce gale in Irish Sea in 1856.
Remarks: Cotton and emigrant trades.

1844
MAINE, Ship
Builder: G.F. & J. Patten
Site: Bath
Tonnage: 749
Size: ?x?x?
First Master: Abner T. Wade
Other Masters: Augustus N. Littlefield, Wm. Freeman, Jr.
Owners: George F. Patten, John Patten, A.N. Littlefield
Disposition: Struck Pond Island ledge at mouth of Kennebec on 11/19/53, fell over on beam ends at low tide; little was salvaged.
Remarks: Cotton and emigrant trades.

1846
FAWN, Brig
Builder: John Larrabee
Site: Bath
Tonnage: 170
Size: 90'x23'8"x9'
First Master: Wm. Duncan
Other Masters: J.H. Tarbox, G.E.R. Patten
Owners: George F. Patten, John Patten, John Larrabee, Hosea Hildreth, Matthew Patten, J.H. Tarbox
Disposition: Sold in California after eventful trip to San Francisco during Gold Rush.
Remarks: Last brig built by Pattens.

ITALY, Ship
Builder: John Larrabee
Site: Bath
Tonnage: 749
Size: 149'8"x33'2"x16'2"
First Master: John O. Baker
Owners: George F. Patten, John Patten, J.O. Baker
Disposition: Found abandoned at sea by bark *Henrietta* 2/13/53, but had appearance of having been ashore with rudder, running gear, sails, and anchors missing; after salvaging some bales of cotton, *Henrietta* went on; *Italy* had, indeed, been ashore, and all hands were rescued and gear salvaged before she floated off.

1848
GEORGE F. PATTEN, Ship
Builder: G.F. & J. Patten
Site: Bath
Tonnage: 778
Size: 152'2"x33'5.5"x16'8.75"
First Master: E.P. Stinson
Other Master: Timothy G. Mitchell
Owners: George F. Patten, John Patten, James F.
Patten, Chas. Davenport, E.P. Stinson
Disposition: Sold to Arendal, Norway, interests in
1866; renamed *Claus Heftze*
Remarks: General transatlantic freighting until Civil
War; then entered Pacific trade.

1849
FALCON, Ship
Builder: G.F. & J. Patten
Site: Bath
Tonnage: 813
Size: 157'6"x33'6.5"x16'9.25"
First Master: John P. Smith
Other Masters: G.E.R. Patten, Abner T. Wade, Jarvis
Patten
Owners: George F. Patten, John Patten, James F. Patten
Disposition: Went ashore Cape Breton Island 5/24/57,
total loss.
Remarks: Cotton trade.

1851
CHAMPLAIN, Ship
Builder: G.F. & J. Patten
Site: Bath
Tonnage: 513
Size: 131'4"x29'3.25"x14'7.625"
First Master: Seth Woodward
Other Master: L.S. Wyman
Owners: George F. Patten, John Patten, James F.
Patten, S. Woodward
Disposition: Destroyed by fire in 1859 at Buenos Aires.
Remarks: Coastwise packet service and transatlantic
trade.

MOBILE, Ship
Builder: John Larrabee
Site: Bath
Tonnage: 961

Size: 172'8"x34'8"x17'4"
First Master: Jos. H. Tarbox
Owners: George F. Patten, John Patten, James F.
Patten, J.H. Tarbox
Disposition: Navigation error by 2nd mate caused her
to strike Arklow Bank on Irish coast in 1852; of 60
passengers and 23 crew, only 9 were rescued, not
including Capt. Tarbox.
Remarks: Primarily cotton trade.

1852
ARIEL, Ship
Builder: Johnson Rideout
Site: Bath
Tonnage: 1,330
Size: 191'6"x38'9"x19'4.5"
First Master: J.Q.A. Reed
Other Masters: Frank Delano, Henry W. Green
Owners: George F. Patten, John Patten, James F.
Patten, Johnson Rideout
Disposition: Seized by Confederate authorities at New
Orleans in 1861; burned by them in 1862 when U.S.
Navy moved to recapture New Orleans.
Remarks: G.F. & J. Patten's first thousand-tonner;
cotton and packet trade.

MARSHFIELD, Ship
Builder: John Larrabee
Site: Bath
Tonnage: 999
Size: 177'x34'10.5"x17'5.25"
First Master: J.H. Torrey
Owners: George F. Patten, John Patten, G.E.R. Patten,
J.H. Torrey
Disposition: Sold foreign 3/28/63, renamed *Jeanne
Meyer.*
Remarks: Cotton trade until Civil War, then shifted to
carrying wheat and flour.

1853
BRITANNIA, Ship
Builder: G.F. & J. Patten
Site: Bath
Tonnage: 1,091
Size: 181'6"x36'x18'
First Master: Wm. Torrey
Other Masters: Charles E. Patten, T. Smith, G.A. Webb

Owners: George F. Patten, John Patten, James F. Patten, G.E.R. Patten, Wm. Torrey
Disposition: Sold in 1869.
Remarks: C.E. Patten, son of James F., enjoyed his first command on this vessel when he was 22.

CLARA BROOKMAN, Ship
Builder: G.F. & J. Patten
Site: Bath
Tonnage: 1,071
Size: 184'6"x35'3.38"x17'7.8"
First Master: Aaron G. Higgins
Owners: George F. Patten, John Patten, Aaron G. Higgins
Disposition: Ashore and total loss at Squam Inlet, NJ, 7/27/57; cargo valued at $140,000.

1854
ASSYRIA, Ship
Builder: John Patten
Site: Bath
Tonnage: 1,364
Size: 196'6"x38'8"x19'4"
First Master: Abner T. Wade
Other Masters: John P. Delano, J.M.W. Patten
Owners: George F. Patten, John Patten, James F. Patten, John Levi Patten, Abner T. Wade
Disposition: Sold to British owners in 1871; lost in 1872 between Quebec and Plymouth, England.
Remarks: Largest vessel built by Pattens.

1855
CASPIAN[2], Ship
Builder: John Larrabee
Site: Bath
Tonnage: 925
Size: 171'x34'2"x17'1"
First Master: Wm. H. Trufant
Owners: George F. Patten, John Patten, James F. Patten, Chas. Davenport, J. Larrabee
Disposition: Lost on first transatlantic voyage from New Orleans to Europe with cotton in 1855; hit reef on Cuban coast during gale; Capt. Trufant washed overboard and drowned.
Remarks: Named for first *Caspian* and command given to the longtime master of the namesake, Capt. William Trufant.

1856
JOHN PATTEN, Ship
Builder: G.F. & J. Patten
Site: Bath
Tonnage: 960
Size: 174'x34'6"x17'3"
First Master: G.E.R. Patten
Other Masters: S.T. Woodward, Jarvis Patten, S.P. Emmons, E.W. Hill
Owners: George F. Patten, John Patten, James F. Patten, G.E.R. Patten, George M. Patten, Jarvis Patten
Disposition: Sold 1873 and rerigged as bark; hailed from Liverpool as late as 1881.

1857
JAMES F. PATTEN, Ship
Builder: John Patten
Site: Bath
Tonnage: 974
Size: 176'2"x34'6"x17'3"
First Master: S.T. Woodward
Other Master: N.E. Percy
Owners: George F. Patten, John Patten, G.E.R. Patten, J.L. Patten, George M. Patten, Seth Woodward, Chas. Davenport
Disposition: In Patten service as late as 1868.
Remarks: Like other Patten vessels, she engaged in general tramping following outbreak of Civil War.

1858
AMITY, Ship
Builder: G.F. & J. Patten
Site: Bath
Tonnage: 799
Size: 160'6"x32'10"x16'5"
First Master: Abner T. Wade
Other Masters: J.R. Stinson, L.P. Merrill, N. Baker, ? Drummond, James M.W. Patten
Owners: George F. Patten, John Patten, James F. Patten, G.E.R. Patten, J.L. Patten, George M. Patten
Disposition: Sold in 1874 subject to delivery to Antwerp; sprang a leak and foundered in North Atlantic; two crewmen rescued by Norwegian bark.
Remarks: Named as a protest against vitriolic sectional politics of period; always owned and managed by Pattens; made at least one voyage to India; rerigged as bark in 1872 after being dismasted.

DESOTO, Ship
Builder: John Patten
Site: Bath
Tonnage: 800
Size: 158'x33'2"x?
First Master: S.B. Reed
Other Master: Bardwell Patten
Owners: George F. Patten, John Patten, James F. Patten, J.L. Patten, S.B. Reed
Disposition: Sold to British owners and renamed *Leamington* in 1863; went missing on voyage from Pensacola for Liverpool in 1883.
Remarks: Packet, guano, and transatlantic trades.

1859

CANADA, Ship
Builder: John Larrabee
Site: Bath
Tonnage: 996
Size: 179'x34'7"x?
First Master: Llewellyn S. Wyman
Other Masters: Alfred Patten, Robert Doane
Owners: George F. Patten, John Patten, James F. Patten, G.E.R. Patten, J.L. Patten, George M. Patten, L.S. Wyman
Disposition: Sold ca. 1872, still active in 1880.
Remarks: Her flags were made by the ladies of the Richmond Congregational Church.

IVANHOE, Bark
Builder: James T. Patten
Site: Boothbay
Tonnage: 432
Size: 120'x28'2.5"x?
First Master: S.P. Emmons (1859-64)
Owners: James T., George F., and John Patten
Disposition: ?
Remarks: Purchased on the ways, partially built, in Boothbay; traded at New Orleans, Cuba, Brazil, and in the Mediterranean.

1860

FAWN[2], Ship
Builder: John Patten & Son
Site: Bath
Tonnage: 874
Size: 169'6"x33'4"x?
First Master: Robert P. Manson

Owners: John Patten, G.E.R. Patten, John Levi Patten, James F. Patten, Chas. Davenport
Disposition: Sold to NY owners during 1863; remained in service until dropped from registry in 1902.
Remarks: First vessel built by John Patten & Son in their North End shipyard.

TRANSIT, Ship
Builder: George F. Patten
Site: Bath
Tonnage: 934
Size: 176'x33'9"x?
First Master: Jarvis Patten
Other Masters: Wm. E. Whittemore, J.W. Drinkwater, N.E. Percy
Owners: George F. Patten, James F. Patten, Jarvis Patten, James T. Patten, George M. Patten
Disposition: Sold in 1878 to New York interests.

1862

HUDSON, Ship
Builder: John Patten & Son
Site: Bath
Tonnage: 999
Size: 180'8"x34'5.5"x17'2.75"
First Master: J.P. Potter
Other Master: S.B. Reed
Owners: John Patten & Son, Chas. Davenport
Disposition: Active as late as 1876.
Remarks: First vessel built in Bath with wire standing rigging; became a true tramp freighter during Civil War, leaving New York 12/62 and not returning to U.S. waters until 3/66; sailed to Europe, India, Persian Gulf, East Indies, and Australia.

SABINO, Ship
Builder: George F. Patten
Site: Bath
Tonnage: 1,039
Size: 185'x34'8"x17'4"
First Master: S.T. Woodward
Other Masters: T.G. Mitchell, Alfred Paine
Owners: George F. Patten, James F. Patten, S.T. Woodward
Disposition: Sold ca. 1875-76; under Norwegian flag by 1882.
Remarks: General trade, with frequent passages to Indian subcontinent.

1863
ITALIA, Ship
Builder: George F. Patten
Site: Bath
Tonnage: 1,019
Size: 183'5"x34'6"x17'3"
First Master: Jarvis Patten
Other Master: P.D. Whitmore
Owners: George F. Patten, James F. Patten, Jarvis Patten
Disposition: Sold to Whitmore at Bath ca. 1870-71; lost 7/10/71.
Remarks: General trade.

MORAVIA, Ship
Builder: John Patten & Son
Site: Bath
Tonnage: 1,045
Size: 186'10"x34'7"x17'4"
First Master: Charles E. Patten
Other Master: C.C. Morse
Owners: John Patten, G.E.R. Patten, Charles E. Patten, James F. Patten, Chas. Davenport
Disposition: In 1875, lost rudder; cargo of rails shifted and ship foundered on beam ends; passengers and crew rescued.
Remarks: General trade.

1864
PARSEE, Bark
Builder: John Patten & Son
Site: Bath
Tonnage: 559
Size: 137'10"x29'9"x14'10"
First Master: J.O. Baker
Other Master: G.W. Soule
Owners: John Patten, G.E.R. Patten, Chas. Davenport, J.O. Baker, Fred H. Patten
Disposition: Sold to J.O. Baker Co., NY, ca. 1869.
Remarks: Name of this vessel and her sister reflect growing importance of East Indies trade in 1860s.

PENANG, Bark
Builder: John Patten & Son
Site: Bath
Tonnage: 584
Size: 142'6"x29'10"x14'11"
First Master: Bardwell Patten

Other Master: ? White
Owners: John Patten, G.E.R. Patten, Chas. Davenport, Bardwell Patten, Fred H. Patten
Disposition: Sold ca. 1879.

1865
MONTANA, Steamship
Builder: G.F. & J. Patten
Site: Bath
Tonnage: 1,004
Size: 196'9"x30'8"x16'6"
First Master: John R. Kelley
Owners: George F. Patten, Chas. Davenport, John Patten, G.E.R. Patten, George M. Patten, J.S. Elliott, J.R. Kelley
Disposition: Sold to Ben Holiday in 1866; burned in Gulf of California 12/14/76.
Remarks: Largest steam vessel yet built in Bath; sailed from New York to San Francisco via Cape Horn 8/12/65; screw steamer with direct-acting single expansion, 44x36 engine, and 18x13 boiler generating 45 psi, all built by George M. Patten's foundry.

1866
IDAHO, Steamship
Builder: G.F. & J. Patten
Site: Bath
Tonnage: 1,077
Size: 198.1'x31.2'x16.9'
First Master: Jarvis Patten
Owners: George F. Patten, John Patten, James F. Patten, George M. Patten, James T. Patten, Jarvis Patten, G.E.R. Patten, Jarvis Slade
Disposition: Sold to California, Oregon & Mexico Steamship Company in 1867; wrecked in 1889 in Strait of Juan de Fuca
Remarks: The largest steamship built in Bath until 1881; sent around Cape Horn to San Francisco; operated San Francisco to Hawaii, then shifted Pacific Northwest; same machinery as *Montana*.

1868
JAPAN, Ship
Builder: George F. Patten
Site: Bath
Tonnage: 1,252
Size: 188.3'x38.2'x24.0'
First Master: S.P. Emmons

Owners: George F. Patten, James F. Patten
Disposition: Burned off Cape Horn with load of coal in August 1870.
Remarks: Last ship built by George F. Patten.

1869
INDIA, Ship
Builder: John Patten & Son
Site: Bath
Tonnage: 1,295
Size: 192.1'x36.5'x23.95'
First Master: Lincoln Patten
Other Masters: Oscar Patten, Alfred Patten, J.L. Rich, R.C. Clapp
Owners: John Patten & Son
Disposition: Still operating under John Patten in 1887.
Remarks: Long career in tramping trades.

NIMBUS, Ship
Builder: John Patten & Son
Site: Bath
Tonnage: 1,303
Size: 192.2'x37.1'x23.9'
First Master: John R. Kelley
Other Master: Reginald Leonard
Owners: J. Patten & Son, Chas. Davenport, J.R. Kelley, Francis Kelley
Disposition: Struck heavily on Columbia River Bar while being towed to sea with cargo of grain; later discovered to be rapidly filling and was abandoned 12/29/77.
Remarks: Last Patten-built vessel.

IV. William Patten & Associates

1841
RICHMOND, Ship
Builder: William Patten
Site: Richmond
Tonnage: 475
Size: 127'1"x28'8"x14'4"
First Master: G.F. Mustard
Owner: Wm. Patten

1845
GLOBE, Bark
Builder: William Patten
Site: Richmond

Tonnage: 367
Size: 114'x26'6"x13'3"
First Master: Charles Theobald
Owner: William Patten
Remarks: Named in honor of Capt. William Patten's former G.F. & J. Patten command.

1847
MEDALLION, Ship
Builder: William Patten
Site: Richmond
Tonnage: 548
Size: 136'3"x29'8"x14'10"
First Master: F. Houdlette
Owner: William Patten

ZENO, Brig
Builder: William Patten
Site: Richmond
Tonnage: 222
First Master: S.B. Dinsmore
Owner: William Patten

1848
WILLIAM PATTEN, Ship
Builder: William Patten
Site: Richmond
Tonnage: 608
Size: 140'8"x30'9"x15'4"
First Master: William Decker
Owners: William Patten, William Decker

1849
SCOTLAND, Bark
Builder: William Patten
Site: Richmond
Tonnage: 348
Size: 115'8"x25'8"x12'10"
First Master: A.T. Percy
Owner: William Patten

1850
GLENBURN, Bark
Builder: William Patten
Site: Richmond
Tonnage: 456
Size: 127'7"x27'11"x14'
First Master: H.Q. Sampson
Owner: William Patten

1851
MATANZAS, Bark
Builder: William Patten
Site: Richmond
Tonnage: 428
Size: 124'x27'6"x13'9"
First Master: David Stearns
Owner: William Patten
Remarks: Completed a Boston-Honolulu-Calcutta-Boston circumnavigation, 1853.

1852
HYDRA, Ship
Builder: William Patten
Site: Richmond
Tonnage: 499
Size: 134'6"x28'5"x14'2"
First Master: James Lunt
Owner: William Patten

PEERLESS, Ship
Builder: William Patten
Site: Richmond
Tonnage: 633
Size: 145'x30'10"x15'5"
First Master: Davis Blanchard
Owners: William Patten, William H. Sturtevant

1853
PRIDE OF AMERICA, Ship
Builder: Patten & Sturtevant
Site: Richmond
Tonnage: 1,826
Size: 226'x41'7"x29'9"
First Master: Jefferson Hathorn
Owners: William Patten, William H. Sturtevant
Remarks: One of a handful of extreme clippers built in Maine, and a major factor in the failure of William Patten's fortunes.

1854
THERESA, Ship
Builder: William Patten
Site: Richmond
Tonnage: 900
Size: 163'2"x34'8"x?
First Master: James Lunt
Owner: William Patten

Remarks: Named for Capt. William Patten's youngest daughter.

1856
LAMMERGEIER, Ship
Builder: Thomas Spear, Jr.
Site: Richmond
Tonnage: 1,000
Size: 170'2"x35'9"x?
First Master: William Patten
Owner: William Patten

MINNEHAHA, Schooner
Builder: Patten & Sturtevant
Site: Bowdoinham
Tonnage: 38
Size: 45'10"x15'5"x6'5"
First Master: M. Skolfield
Owner: G.W. Kimball

V. D. & L. Patten

1849
TEMPEST, Ship
Builder: David Patten
Site: Brunswick
Tonnage: 862
Size: 164'8"x33'8"x16'10"
First Master: Lincoln Patten
Other Masters: Edw. P. Stinson, ? Whitney
Owners: D. & L. Patten, Wm. Bradstreet, Moses Riggs, G.F. & J. Patten.
Disposition: Sold in London in 1862, hailing port Gibraltar in 1874.

1858
NATIONAL, Ship
Builder: G.C. Trufant
Site: Bath
Tonnage: 999
Size: 176'x35'x?
First Master: Ozias Long
Other Master: ? Small
Owners: D. & L. Patten, Ozias Long, J.R. Tibbetts, Alpheus Boyd, Wm. Doren, Wm. Melcher, E.P. Mallett, Wm. Bradstreet, Harvey Preble
Disposition: Sold foreign during Civil War; converted to storage hulk at Lyttelton, New Zealand, 1883; broken up 1923.

Remarks: Sistership of Trufant & Drummond's
   Roanoke.

1864
SAREPTA, Bark
Builder: John Harward
Site: Bowdoinham
Tonnage: 359
Size: 119'9"x29'1"x11'6"
First Master: David A. Patten
Other Masters: ? Oliver, ? Hardy
Owners: D. & L. Patten, Alpheus Boyd, John Harward
Disposition: Struck rocks on Boston-Aspinwall voyage,
   7/8/69, became waterlogged; salvaged part of cargo,
   sails, stores.

VI. Patten Miscellany

1806
MARY, Brig
Builder: Sam'l Sylvester
Site: Topsham
Tonnage: 167
Size: 85'4"x23'4"x9'6"
First Master: Benjamin Snow
Owner: Actor Patten, Jr.

1816
MARGARET, Schooner
Builder: Francis Small
Site: Topsham
Tonnage: 120
Size: 78'2"x22'8"x7'10"
First Master: William Patten
Owners: Wm. Patten, Robert Patten, Sally Patten
Remarks: This William Patten (1776-1821) was the
   son of Robert, the shipbuilder of Patten Point. Sally
   was his wife.

1818
CHERUB, Schooner
Builder: Sam'l Potter
Site: Bath
Tonnage: 131
Size: 74'x21'7"x9'6"
First Master: Jeremiah Patten
Owners: Wm. S. Pattee (Patten?), Jeremiah Patten,
   Sam'l Pattee (Patten?), Wm. Donnell

1823
LINCOLN, Ship
Builder: Hugh Patten
Site: Topsham
Tonnage: 230
Size: 85'x24'4"x12'10"
First Master: John Fulton
Owner: John Smith

1825
THOMAS, Brig
Builder: John Patten
Site: Bowdoinham
Tonnage: 160
Size: 83'x24'5"x9'1"
First Master: Joshua Purington
Owners: John Patten, George Jewett, Joshua
   Purington, Daniel Marshall
Remarks: This John Patten is the son of Robert, ship-
   builder of Patten Point and the father of Capts.
   Bardwell and Jarvis.

1826
PARAGON, Brig
Builder: John Patten
Site: Topsham
Tonnage: 147
Size: 82'2"x23'1"x8'10"
First Master: Ezekiel Purington
Owners: John Patten, E. Purington, Robert Patten,
   Benjamin Rideout, ? Kingsbury, Frederick Adam,
   David Stinson.
Remarks: The builder of this vessel returned to
   Bowdoinham in 1824 after living for a time in the
   South and at Charlestown, MA. Two of the co-own-
   ers came from Charlestown, a third was John's
   father.

1837
ARGUS, Brig
Builder: Thos. Harward
Site: Bath
Tonnage: 164
Size: 88'8"x23'11"x8'9"
First Master: John Webb, Jr.
Owners: J. Webb, Jr., Thos. Harward, Ed. Hodgkins,
   Wm. Patten.

Remarks: Capt. Wm. Patten [64] is sometimes credited with building this brig.

1851
SEA NYMPH, Ship
Builder: Robert Patten
Site: Bowdoinham
Tonnage: 732
Size: 150'x32'8"x16'4"
First Master: Robert Patten
Owner: Robert Patten
Disposition: Abandoned dismasted and leaking in mid-Atlantic 3/15/54.

1852
PAULINE, Ship
Builder: Arnold/Patten
Site: Bath
Tonnage: 476
Size: 136'x27'6"x13'9"
First Master: Oliver Colburn
Owners: Augustus Arnold, James T. Patten, G.T. Donnell, O. Colburn, S. Colburn.
Remarks: James T., eldest son of George F., was for a while a partner in the Arnold/Patten Company.

1868
MIST, Steam Yacht
Builder: George M. Patten
Site: Bath
Tonnage: 6
Size: 41'x7'x3'3"
First Master: ?
Owner: George M. Patten
Remarks: Built at George F. Patten's shipyard and equipped with machinery from George M.'s foundry, this steam yacht was sold to Greenville on Moosehead Lake in 1871.

1871
TWILIGHT, Steam Yacht
Builder: George M. Patten
Site: Bath
Tonnage: 15
Size: 54'x9'x4'
First Master: ?
Owner: George M. Patten
Remarks: Hull built by Harrington, machinery built at shop of Charles Staples in Portland, finished by George M. Patten at the old shipyard.

1875
ASTORIA, Ship
Builder: Goss & Sawyer
Site: Bath
Tonnage: 1,395
Size: 202'x40'x24'
First Master: John R. Kelley
Other Masters: John G. Potter, M.P. Andersen
Owners: John Patten & Son, C. Davenport, C.A. Davenport, Francis & J.R. Kelley.
Disposition: Sold foreign ca. 1887, abandoned 20 miles off Charleston, 8/23/93; derelict picked up, towed into port, and condemned.
Remarks: First of three ships John Patten & Son had built by Goss & Sawyer after G.E.R. Patten's health began to fail.

1876
ALAMEDA, Ship
Builder: Goss & Sawyer
Site: Bath
Tonnage: 1,474
Size: 211.3'x40'x24.1'
First Master: Henry R. Otis
Other Masters: James N. Nickels, Omar Chapman
Owners: John Patten & Son, C. Davenport & Co., J.R. Kelley, H.R. Otis, Chas. E. Moody
Disposition: Used as store hulk at Dunedin, New Zealand, 1895-1920s.
Remarks: Cape Horn grain trade; John Owen Patten, grandson of Capt. John, still owned in the ship with his sister in 1890. Reportedly sold then to San Francisco owners, later sold foreign.

1877
FLORENCE, Ship
Builder: Goss & Sawyer
Site: Bath
Tonnage: 1,684
Size: 223.1'x41'x26'
First Master: John R. Kelley
Other Master: Reginald Leonard
Owners: Chas. Davenport, J.R. Kelley, John Patten & Son
Disposition: Sold to West Coast owners in 1898 and dis-

appeared without a trace on passage from Tacoma
to Honolulu in 1902.

Remarks: Carried grain from West Coast to Europe
and coal from England to West Coast; named for
Capt. Kelley's daughter.

1881

TACOMA, Ship

Builder: Goss & Sawyer

Site: Bath

Tonnage: 1,739

Size: 222.2'x41'x17.7'

First Master: John R. Kelley

Other Masters: W.P. Sheldon, W.W. Stailing, B.G.
Godfrey

Owners: John Patten & Son, Charles Davenport,
George Davenport, John Owen Patten, J.R. Kelley,
H.R. Otis, C.E. Moody, E.F. Sawyer

Disposition: Crushed in ice pack 4/19/1918 while
owned by Alaska Packers.

Remarks: On her maiden voyage around Cape Horn,
John Owen Patten went as passenger. Between 1881
and 1897, made eleven New York-San Francisco
passages and two to Orient. Sold to San Francisco
owners in 1898 and subsequently to Alaska Packers.

Sources

Act Incorporating the Kennebec and Portland Railroad Company, Approved April 1836, with Additional Acts Approved April 9, 1841, and March 31, 1845. Augusta, ME: Severance and Dore, 1845.

Alexander, William T. *Harpswell on Casco Bay: Its Early History and Shipbuilding.* Portland, ME: The Print Shop, Inc., n.d.

American Sentinel (Bath), 1854-62.

Applebee, Robert, Collection of Bath Customs District Records. Penobscot Marine Museum, Searsport, ME.

Bailey, Thomas A. *A Diplomatic History of the American People.* 5th ed. New York: Appleton-Century-Crofts, 1955.

Baker, William Avery. *A Maritime History of Bath, Maine and the Kennebec River Region.* 2 vols. Bath, ME: Marine Research Society of Bath, 1973.

Banks, Ronald F. *Maine Becomes a State: The Movement to Separate Maine from Massachusetts, 1785-1820.* Somersworth, NH: New Hampshire Publishing Company; and Portland, ME: Maine Historical Society, 1973.

Bath, Brunswick and Richmond Directory. Bath, ME: John O. Shaw, 1870.

Bath Daily Times, 1862-1913, 1935, 1949.

Bath Independent, 1897.

Beach, Charlotte A. "Neptune's Daughter Nellie," Reginald Ferrell Collection, Arlington, TX. Typescript (photocopy), n.d.

Blunt, Joseph. *The Shipmaster's Assistant, and Commercial Digest.* 9th ed. New York: E. & G.W. Blunt, 1857.

Brewington, Dorothy E.R. *Marine Paintings and Drawings in Mystic Seaport Museum.* Mystic, CT: Mystic Seaport Museum, 1982.

Brewington, M.V., and Dorothy Brewington, eds. *Marine Paintings and Drawings in the Peabody Museum.* Rev. ed. Salem, MA: Peabody Museum of Salem, 1981.

Briggs, Ruth. "Ship Ventures of Old Bath." Maine Maritime Museum, Bath, ME. Typescript (photocopy), 1987.

Burden, Charles E., comp. Patten Genealogical Records. Maine Maritime Museum, Bath, ME.

———, comp. Records of Patten Mariners and Vessels. Maine Maritime Museum, Bath, ME.

Caniff, Milton. *Terry Lee, Flight Officer, U.S.A.* Racine, WI: Whitman Publishing Co., 1944.

Captains' File. Maine Maritime Museum, Bath, ME.

Clarke, Francis G. *The Seaman's Manual; containing a Variety of Matters Useful to the Navigator: Among which are Directions for Keeping Accounts.... The Law of Marine Insurance, etc.* Portland, ME: Shirley, Hyde & Co., Publishers, 1830.

Cleaveland, Nehemiah, and Alpheus Spring Packard. *History of Bowdoin College. With Biographical Sketches of Its Graduates from 1806 to 1879, Inclusive.* Boston: James Ripley Osgood & Company, 1882.

Cochran, Thomas C. *The Age of Enterprise: A Social History of Industrial America.* Rev. ed. New York and Evanston: Harper & Row, 1961.

Cutler, Carl C. *Queens of the Western Ocean: The Story of America's Mail and Passenger Sailing Lines.* Annapolis, MD: United States Naval Institute, 1961.

Davis, Walter Goodwin. *The Ancestors of James Patten, 1747?-1817, of Arundel (Kennebunkport), Maine.* Portland, ME: Southworth-Anthoensen Press, 1941.

[Decker, Wilbur F.]. "Notable Career of Noble Maxwell whose Wealth Reached Seven Figures." *Bath Independent,* 7, 14, 21 November 1935.

Densmore, David C. *The Halo: An Autobiography.* Boston: Voice of Angels Publishing House, 1876.

Donovan, Liza. "The History of 1016 Washington Street and its Owners." Maine Maritime Museum, Bath, ME. Typescript (photocopy), n.d.

Fairburn, William Armstrong. *Merchant Sail.* Ed. by Ethel M. Ritchie. 6 vols. Center Lovell, ME: Fairburn Marine Educational Foundation, 1954-55.

Genealogical Files. Bath Historical Society, Bath, ME.

Hennessy, Mark. "Bath's Grandest — the Sagadahock House." 1951. Reprinted in *The Times of Bath, ME,* October 1993, pp. 1-4.

———, comp. Historical Files on Bath Ships and Shipping. Maine Maritime Museum, Bath, ME.

———, *The Sewall Ships of Steel.* Augusta, ME: Kennebec Journal Press, 1937.

Hunter, Theodore, and Jarvis Patten. *Port Charges and Requirements on Vessels in the Various Ports of the World.* Rev. ed. New York: John Wiley & Sons, 1884.

Hutchins, John G.B. *The American Maritime Industries and Public Policy, 1789-1914: An Economic History.* New York: Russell & Russell, 1969.

Johnson, Ron. *The Best of Maine Railroads.* Portland, ME: Portland Litho, 1985.

Judd, Richard W., et al., eds. *Maine: The Pine Tree State from Prehistory to the Present.* Orono, ME: University of Maine Press, 1995.

Lemont, Levi P. *1400 Historical Dates of the Town and City of Bath, and Town of Georgetown, from 1604 to 1874.* Bath, ME: By the Author, 1874.

Lipman, Jean, et al. *Young America: A Folk-Art History.* New York: Hudson Hills Press and the Museum of American Folk Art, 1986.

List of Stockholders, with Amount of Stock Held by Each Jan. 1, 1854, in the Banks of Maine. Augusta, ME: William T. Johnson, 1854.

Lloyd's Register of Shipping. Published annually in single or multiple volumes. London: Lloyd's Register of Shipping, 1849-95.

Logbook of ship *Florence* of Bath, 1857. G.W. Blunt White Library, Mystic Seaport Museum, Mystic, CT.

MacGregor, David R. *Fast Sailing Ships: Their Design and Construction, 1775-1875.* 1973. Reprint, Annapolis, MD: Naval Institute Press, 1988.

———. *Merchant Sailing Ships, 1815-1850: Supremacy of Sail.* Annapolis, MD: Naval Institute Press, 1984.

———. *Merchant Sailing Ships, 1850-1875: Heyday of Sail.* Annapolis, MD: Naval Institute Press, 1984.

Martin, Kenneth R. *Nautical Folk Art.* Museum Catalogue. Bath, ME: Maine Maritime Museum, 1994.

———. *Whalemen and Whaleships of Maine.* Brunswick, ME: Harpswell Press, 1975.

———, and Ralph Linwood Snow. *Maine Odyssey: Good Times and Hard Times in Bath, 1936-1986.* Bath, ME: Patten Free Library, 1988.

Maxwell, Noble, Papers. Maine Maritime Museum, Bath, ME.

Morris, James. *Our Maritime Heritage: Maritime Developments and Their Impact on American Life.* Washington, DC: University Press of America, 1979.

North, Douglass C. *The Economic Growth of the United States, 1790-1860.* 1961. Reprint, New York: W.W. Norton, 1966.

Owen, Henry Wilson. *The Edward Clarence Plummer History of Bath, Maine.* 1936. Reprint, Bath, ME: Bath Area Bicentennial Committee, 1976.

Patten, Captain Charles E. Diary and Account Book, 1887-89. Charles E. Burden Collection, Bath, ME.

Patten Free Library, 1889-1940. Bath, ME: Patten Free Library, [1940].

Patten Papers. Maine Maritime Museum, Bath, ME.

Photograph File. Maine Maritime Museum, Bath, ME.

Record of American and Foreign Shipping. Published annually. New York: American Bureau of Shipping, 1869-90.

Records of the Bureau of Customs (Record Group 36). National Archives and Records Administration, Washington, DC.

Records of the Bureau of Marine Inspection and Navigation (Record Group 41). National Archives and Records Administration, Washington, DC.

Records of the Sagadahoc County Probate Court. Sagadahoc County Court House, Bath, ME.

Records of the Sagadahoc County Superior Judicial Court. Maine State Archives, Augusta, ME.

Reed, Parker McCobb. *History of Bath and Environs, Sagadahoc County, Maine, 1607-1894.* Portland, ME: Lakeside Press, 1894.

Report of the Directors to the Stockholders of the Maine Central Railroad Company. Published annually. Bangor, ME: Samuel S. Smith, 1863-67.

Report of the Directors to the Stockholders of the Maine Central Railroad Company, including Operations of the Portland and Kennebec... and Farmington Railroads...1872. Augusta, ME: Homan and Badger, 1872.

Reynolds, Erminie S., and Kenneth R. Martin. *"A Singleness of Purpose": The Skolfields and Their Ships.* Bath, ME: Maine Maritime Museum, 1987.

Rowe, William Hutchinson. *The Maritime History of Maine: Three Centuries of Shipbuilding and Seafaring.* 1948. Reprint, Gardiner, ME: Harpswell Press, 1989.

Sewall Family Papers. Maine Maritime Museum, Bath, ME.

Smith, Marion Jaques. *General William King: Merchant, Shipbuilder, and Maine's First Governor.* Camden, ME: Down East Books, 1980.

Smith, Walter B., and Arthur H. Cole. *Fluctuations in American Business, 1790-1860.* Harvard Economic Studies, vol. L. Cambridge, MA: Harvard University Press, 1935.

Snow, Ralph Linwood. *Bath Iron Works: The First Hundred Years.* Bath, ME: Maine Maritime Museum, 1987.

Starbuck, Alexander. *History of the American Whale Fishery.* 1878. Reprint, Secaucus, NJ: Castle Books, 1989.

Stinson, Edward P. Papers, 1828-69. Collection 95. G.W. Blunt White Library, Mystic Seaport Museum, Mystic, CT.

[Stinson, Edward P.]. "Uncle Ned" Correspondence. Collection VFM 801. G.W. Blunt White Library, Mystic Seaport Museum, Mystic, CT.

Sutherland, John H., ed. "The Journal of Captain Abner Turner Wade, Transcribed with a Commentary by A. Edward Conover." Charles E. Burden Collection, Bath, ME. Typescript (photocopy), 1991.

Taylor, George Rogers. *The Transportation Revolution, 1765-1815.* The Economic History of the United States, vol. IV. New York: Holt, Rinehart and Winston, 1951.

Torrey, William. Notarial Records. Maine Maritime Museum, Bath, ME.

Vital Records. City of Bath, ME.

Vital Records. Town of Bowdoinham, ME.

Vital Records. Town of Topsham, ME.

Wade, Capt. Abner. Account Book for Ship *Halcyon* of Bath, 1846-51, and ship *Falcon* of Bath, 1852-54. Collection of Charles E. Burden, Bath, ME.

Walker, Wildes, v. *Catherine P. Walker.* Town of Topsham Court Records, Topsham, ME, document SJC-SCSJC.

The Weekly Mirror (Bath), 1853-55.

Wheeler, George Augustus, and Henry Warren Wheeler. *History of Brunswick, Topsham, and Harpswell, Maine, including the Ancient Territory Known as Pejepscot.* 1878. Reprint, Somersworth, NH: New Hampshire Publishing Company, 1974.

Wood, Dennis. Abstracts of Whaling Voyages from the United States, 1831-73. Free Public Library, New Bedford, MA.

Index

ABOUT THE AUTHORS

A former history professor and museum director, **Kenneth R. Martin** holds an undergraduate degree from Dickinson College and M.A. and Ph.D. degrees from the University of Pennsylvania. He is the author, coauthor, and editor of more than fifteen books on maritime history and business topics. He collaborated with Lin Snow on two previous Patten Free Library publications: *Maine Odyssey: Good Times and Hard Times in Bath* and *"I Am Now a Soldier!": The Civil War Diaries of Lorenzo Vanderhoef.* His previous works for the Maine Maritime Museum include *Whalemen and Whaleships of Maine, Lobstering and the Maine Coast* (with Nathan Lipfert), and *"A Singleness of Purpose": The Skolfields and Their Ships* (with Erminie Reynolds). Martin lives in Woolwich, Maine, on the east bank of the Kennebec River, where he indulges his interests in jazz, nautical antiques, and folk art.

Formerly director of the San Diego Maritime Museum and Maine Maritime Museum, **Ralph Linwood Snow** is a professional maritime historian who lives in Woolwich, Maine, with his wife, Christie, and three dogs of varying decrepitude. A veteran of the Korean War, he holds an M.A. from Wesleyan University and a B.A. from the University of Massachusetts. During his early career, he taught history and served as an administrator in public and private secondary schools; he also was a historian with the National Park Service. Snow has authored and coauthored several books and articles — two with Ken Martin — including the award-winning *Bath Iron Works: The First Hundred Years,* published in 1987. He enjoys classical and folk music, reading maritime and military history, and puttering around the house.

J. H. Kimball

R. B. Barron

J. H. K

Patten Car setting up Shop
machine shop
Works
Construction Shop
Store Ho
Office
Lumber Store Ho
Iron Store House

M. Koy   A. H. Witt

Capt. W. Bither
Jno Sprague

S. D. Bailey

21   26   25

5   4   3

D. Shaw

H. Lanes

FITTS   ST.

W. F. Moses

J. W. Bailon   J. Norris

B. Gannet

John W. Magoun

Jas Robins

Capt. A. P. Boyd

R. H. Byrum

W. E. Whitmore

Jas Rogers

HIGH

NORTH

B. C. S. Bailey
54

E. nton

A's Est.

Smith

Dickson   Mrs. Bigelow   N. Coombs   Musserblen   D. O'Fare

G. C. Greenlief   Wm Hogan   Fogg   Capt. Delano   J. Vaughn   Dunton   A. F. Campbell

Jas Dunton

ST.

Dr Payne

John H. Lowell

A

Oliver   R. Harris   W. Sprague Hawthorne   J. E. Haley

J. E. H.   Page   D. F. Coomb

Leonard   J. E. Haley

R

Coombs   J. Smith

H. M. Dorey   Chas Clapp Jr

A. Page   G. A. Prebble

Goss   Mrs E Manson

F. Adams   S. J. Watson

G. C. Goss   F. Reed

J. C. Magoun   I. Orr

Episcopal Ch

Hatch Est

GREEN

H. arrington   Draper

Albert Hathorn   P. Villiamy

Delano   Mrs Gushing   G. S. Preble   S. W. Cushing   Capt. Thompson   Coombs   M. E. Gannet   J. Oliver

P. Stacy   F. Preble   H. W. Fields

Capt Mc Lellan   Jno Clark

Capt. H. Anderson   J. H. Harlow   J. C. Jameson   Mrs Larrabee

Edwin Reed

B. C. Bailey

G. M. Gardner   C. Bragg   Capt Douglass   J. M. Fraser   D. Hurd   Burke   S. P. Snipe

ST.

Chas Macgur   T. Ault   Mrs Durham   Rev. B. Hubbell   Howland

Dr Payne

Jno B. Swanton   Swedenborgian Church

Dr Payne

S. D. Bailey

Circus Ground

E. Randall   High School   Z. H.

ST.